Globalisation, Lifelong Learning and the Learning Society

Lifelong Learning and the Learning Society, Volume 2

In this the second volume of his trilogy *Lifelong Learning and the Learning Society*, Professor Jarvis expertly examines, from a sociological perspective, how lifelong learning and the learning society have become social phenomena globally. He argues that the driving forces of globalisation are radically changing lifelong learning. *Globalisation, Lifelong Learning and the Learning Society: Sociological Perspectives* shows that adult education/learning only gained mainstream status because of these global changes and as learning became more work oriented.

This indispensable companion critically assesses the learning that is required and provided within a learning society and provides a detailed sociological analysis of the emerging role of lifelong learning with examples from around the globe.

Divided into three clear parts the book:

- looks at the development of the knowledge economy
- provides a critique of lifelong learning and the learning society
- focuses on the changing nature of research in the learning society.

While totally stand-alone this book provides detailed sociological analysis of lifelong learning that helps to underpin the other two books in this series. This second volume of the trilogy will help the reader understand the social context within which our learning occurs by examining learning not only within the life-world but also within the much wider global context.

All three books will be essential reading for students in education, HRD and teaching and learning generally, in addition to academics and informed practitioners.

Peter Jarvis is an internationally renowned expert in the field of adult learning and continuing education. He is Professor of Continuing Education at the University of Surrey, UK, and honorary Adjunct Professor in Adult Education at the University of Georgia, USA.

Globalisation, Lifelong Learning and the Learning Society

Sociological perspectives

Lifelong Learning and the Learning Society, Volume 2

Peter Jarvis

Routledge
Taylor & Francis Group

LONDON AND NEW YORK

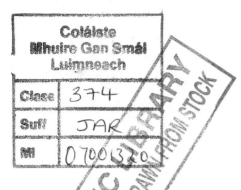
First published 2007
by Routledge
2 Park Square, Milton Park, Abingdon, Oxon OX14 4RN

Simultaneously published in the USA and Canada
by Routledge
270 Madison Ave, New York, NY 10016

Routledge is an imprint of the Taylor & Francis Group,
an informa business

© 2007 Peter Jarvis

Typeset in Goudy by RefineCatch Ltd, Bungay, Suffolk
Printed and bound in Great Britain by
Antony Rowe Ltd, Chippenham, Wiltshire

British Library Cataloguing in Publication Data
A catalogue record for this book is available from the British Library

Library of Congress Cataloging-in-Publication Data
Jarvis, Peter, 1937–
Globalisation, lifelong learning & the learning society :
sociological perspectives / Peter Jarvis.
p. cm.—(Lifelong learning and the learning society ; v. 2)
Includes bibliographical references and index.
1. Continuing education—Social aspects. 2. Education and
globalization. 3. Educational sociology. I. Title. II. Title:
Globalisation, lifelong learning, and the learning society.
LC5225.S64J373 2007
374—dc22
2006027003

ISBN10: 0–415–35542–7 (hbk)
ISBN10: 0–415–35543–5 (pbk)
ISBN10: 0–203–96440–3 (ebk)

ISBN13: 978–0–415–35542–1 (hbk)
ISBN13: 978–0–415–35543–8 (pbk)
ISBN13: 978–0–203–96440–8 (ebk)

Contents

Figures and tables

The author

Peter Jarvis is Professor of Continuing Education at the University of Surrey and adjunct Professor of Adult Education at the University of Georgia in the United States. In addition, he has been awarded a University Professorship *cum laudis* at the University of Pécs in Hungary. He holds the following degrees: B.D. (University of London); B.A. (Econ) (University of Sheffield); M.Soc.Sc. (University of Birmingham); Ph.D. (University of Aston); D.Litt. (University of Surrey). He has also been awarded an honorary doctorate by the University of Helsinki. He is a Fellow of the Royal Society of Arts. Among the honours that he has received are: the Cyril O. Houle World Award for Literature in Adult Education, the American Association of Adult and Continuing Education; a fellowship of the Japan Society for the Promotion of Science (University of Tokyo) to research into the education of adults; induction in the International Hall of Fame of Adult and Continuing Education in the USA; and the Comenius Award of the International ESVA Foundation. He was the Hon. President of the British Association of International and Comparative Education in 1999–2000 and he is an honorary life member of a number of associations of adult education in different parts of the world. Over the past twenty years he has been visiting professor in a number of universities in the United States, Canada and Europe and guest professor in a number of others. He is a frequent speaker at conferences around the world.

Peter Jarvis has authored many books: *Adult Education in a Small Centre: A Case Study*, University of Surrey, Dept. of Educational Studies (1982); *Professional Education*, Croom Helm (1983); *Adult and Continuing Education: Theory and Practice*, Croom Helm (1983) – now in its third edition as *Adult Education and Lifelong Learning: Theory and Practice*, RoutledgeFalmer (2004); *The Sociology of Adult and Continuing Education*, Croom Helm (1985); *Sociological Perspectives on Lifelong Education and Lifelong Learning*, University of Georgia, Dept. of Adult Education (1986); *Adult Learning in the Social Context*, Croom Helm (1987); *International Dictionary of Adult and Continuing Education*, Routledge (1990); *Paradoxes of Learning*, Jossey-Bass (1992); *Adult Education and the State*, Routledge (1993); *Ethics and the Education of Adults in Later Modern Society*, NIACE (1997); *The Practitioner Researcher*, Jossey-Bass (1999); *Learning in Later Life*, Kogan Page (2001); *Universities and Corporate Universities: The Lifelong Learning Industry and Global Society*, Kogan Page (2001).

He has co-authored the following: *The Teacher Practitioner in Nursing, Midwifery and Health Visiting*, Croom Helm (1985) – published as second edition *The Teacher Practitioner and Mentor in Nursing, Midwifery, Health Visiting and the Social Services*, Thorne (1997); *The Human Resource Development Handbook*, Kogan Page (1998); *The Theory and Practice of Learning*, Kogan Page (1998) – second edition (2003).

He has also edited *Twentieth Century Thinkers in Adult Education*, Croom Helm (1987) – second edition *Twentieth Century Thinkers in Adult and Continuing Education*, Kogan Page (2001); *Britain: Policy and Practice in Continuing Education*, Jossey Bass (1988); *Perspectives in Adult Education and Training in Europe*, NIACE (1992); *The Age of Learning*, Kogan Page (2000); *Theory and Practice of Teaching in a Learning Society*, Kogan Page (2001); *Adult and Continuing Education: Major Themes since the Enlightenment* (5 vols) with Colin Griffin, Routledge (2003); *From Adult Education to Lifelong Learning*, RoutledgeFalmer (forthcoming).

He has also co-edited: *Training Adult Educators in Western Europe*, Routledge (1991); *Adult Education: Evolution and Achievements in a Developing Field of Study*, Jossey Bass (1991); *Adult Education and Theological Interpretations*, Krieger (1993); *Developments in the Education of Adults in Europe*, Peter Lang (1994); *International Perspectives on Lifelong Learning*, Kogan Page (1998); *Human Learning: a holistic approach*, Routledge (forthcoming); *Living, Learning and Working*, Palgrave (forthcoming).

His books and papers have been translated into about twenty languages.

He is also founding editor of *The International Journal of Lifelong Education*, Chair of the Board of Editors of *Comparative Education* and he serves on a number of other editorial boards in Europe, Asia and the USA.

Preface and acknowledgements

In the first volume of this trilogy (Jarvis 2006) we examined a wide variety of theories of human learning from the perspective of the relatively comprehensive theory that I have developed over two decades of studying human learning. The theory of learning is related to human living itself rather than just to what is learned: it is both experiential and existential. The perspective adopted was primarily philosophical and psychological although it was accepted throughout that individuals live in society and that their learning is not unaffected by the social pressures that are experienced. Learning itself was defined as *the combination of processes whereby the whole person – body (genetic, physical and biological) and mind (knowledge, skills, attitudes, values, emotions, beliefs and senses) – experiences a social situation, the perceived content of which is then transformed cognitively, emotively or practically (or through any combination) and integrated into the person's individual biography resulting in a changed (or more experienced) person.*

This volume starts from the same philosophical perspective but concentrates on a more sociological perspective to learning, with references to the political and economic, and reflects a much earlier piece of writing that I undertook (Jarvis 1985) when I examined adult and continuing education from a sociological perspective. The sociology of lifelong learning has not been well developed in recent years and some interpretations of learning in the social context omit quite crucial considerations. One of the intentions of this book is to develop a critical approach to lifelong learning from a sociological perspective.

It is not the purpose in this volume to constantly refer back to the first volume although the opening chapters summarise my approach to learning and to lifelong learning. Thereafter, I intend to construct an argument from a sociological perspective whilst holding the same view about learning. Since education and learning have been politicised to a great extent in the past decade, this volume will also make reference to political theory and, in this sense, it also builds on the ideas contained in an edited collection *Human Learning: A Holistic Perspective* (Jarvis and Parker 2005) in which authors from a number of different academic disciplines address the topic of human learning. Throughout my academic career I have argued that in order to begin to understand human learning it is necessary to adopt a multidisciplinary perspective and this belief also underlies this trilogy on lifelong learning and the learning society. This volume, therefore, starts with the theory of learning discussed previously and immediately develops it in a socio-economic direction, recognising that in order to understand the social context within which our learning occurs we need to look at learning not only within the life-world but also within the much wider global context. Thereafter we will address the learning society, learning organisation, and so on. In the final volume of this trilogy, I want to reach *Beyond the Learning Society*, although this title might change a little over the next year. Chapter 12 and the Appendix point in the direction of my thinking for Volume 3.

I have been working on this subject for two decades now and have published many books and papers about it. In a sense, this book gathers together much of my understanding. Over that period and around the world, I have given many lectures and classes on this topic and those who have listened to the lectures and others have been unstinting in giving me feedback. In addition, many colleagues who have heard my lectures and read my papers have also been generous in their criticism of my work. Naturally, they have all enriched my thinking and I am enormously grateful to them. Many other colleagues have helped me but I want to mention one in particular, Dr Pauline Jeffree, who has encouraged me to work both by her friendship and her example. I am also immensely grateful to Philip Mudd of Routledge who encouraged me to write the trilogy and trusted me to complete it. I am now two-thirds of the way along the route, and I hope that I am beginning to repay that trust.

Naturally, what I have written is my responsibility and nobody else's. I have written it in the profound hope that it might help others who want to know a little more and unpick some of the rhetoric about lifelong learning: this includes students and teachers, course designers and educational managers, and also policy makers. All that I can hope is that in some ways it may prove useful to those who do me the honour of reading my work.

About the time I started this work I had a little health scare and writing this work has been extremely beneficial to me. However, one person above all has supported and encouraged me, has always been there when I needed her, and without whom this book would never have seen the light of day, and that is my wife Maureen: it is to her that I dedicate this trilogy in love and gratitude.

Peter Jarvis
Thatcham
June 2006

Chapter 1

Lifelong learning in the social context

As we explained in the Preface, the first volume of this trilogy focused primarily on philosophical and psychological approaches to learning although the social context was always recognised, so that in order to explore the sociology of lifelong learning it is necessary to revisit the previous argument and locate the individual learner in the social context (see also Jarvis 1985). Consequently, the first section of this chapter returns to the theory of learning adopted in Volume 1 and explains how a sociological perspective may be used to interpret the same material. Thereafter, the chapter will look at the social processes of learning and in the third section will examine the nature of social power and the way in which it impinges upon human learning. The chapter highlights the tension between social conformity and individualism and in so doing it will look back to the brief discussion on authenticity and autonomy that occurred in Volume 1 within the framework of learning theory. It concludes with a brief discussion of how specific sociological theories presuppose certain types of learning.

Theory of lifelong learning

Following the definition of learning, referred to in the Preface, we defined lifelong learning as *the combination of processes throughout a lifetime whereby the whole person – body (genetic, physical and biological) and mind (knowledge, skills, attitudes, values, emotions, beliefs and senses) – experiences social situations, the perceived content of which is then transformed cognitively, emotively or practically (or through any combination) and integrated into the individual person's biography resulting in a continually changing (or more experienced) person.*

Basically, this is the same definition as that for human learning but just slightly adapted to recognise the lifelong nature of learning. Indeed, it was argued that learning is possible wherever conscious living occurs, but that there is a real possibility that learning actually occurs beyond the bounds of consciousness – I have focused on pre-conscious learning from the time that I first wrote about learning (Jarvis 1987). An omission in Volume 1 was Marx's use of the idea of false consciousness and its relationship to learning – to which I will allude in the final chapter. However, it is important to note that we are born in relationship and that we live the whole of our lives within a social context; the only time when most of us sever all relationships is at the point of death. Consequently, no theory of learning can legitimately omit the life-world or the wider social world within which we live since learning is a process of transforming the experiences that we have and these always occur when the individual interacts with the wider society. However, experience itself begins with body sensations, e.g. sound, sight, smell, and so on. Indeed, we transform these sensations and learn to make them meaningful to ourselves and this is the first stage in human learning. We are more aware of it in childhood learning because many of the sensations are new and we have not learned their meaning, but in adulthood we have learned sounds, tastes, etc. and so we utilise the meaning as the basis for either our future learning, or for our taken-for-grantedness, in our daily living. For example, I know the meaning of a word (a sound) and so I am less aware of the sound and more aware of the meaning, and so on. I depicted this process in Figure 1.1.

Significantly, we live a great deal of our lives in situations we have learned to take for granted (box 1), that is we assume that the world as we know it does not change a great deal from one experience to another similar one (Schutz and Luckmann 1974), although such an assumption is a little more contentious in this rapidly changing world – but we will argue below that not all knowledge changes that rapidly. Over a period of time, we actually develop categories and classifications that allow this taken-for-grantedness to occur. Falzon (1998: 38) puts this neatly:

Encountering the world . . . necessarily involves a process of ordering

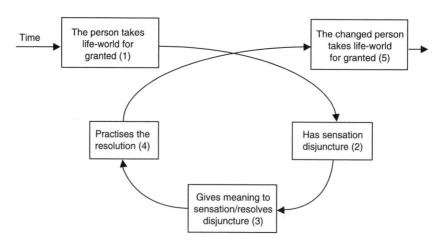

Figure 1.1 The transformation of sensations: initial and non-reflective learning.

the world in terms of our categories, organising it and classifying it, actively bringing it under control in some way. We always bring some framework to bear on the world in our dealings with it. Without this organising activity, we would be unable to make any sense of the world at all.

But we recognise that very young children may not always be in a position to make such assumptions; they are in a more continuous state of learning from novel situations.[1] Traditionally, however, adult educators have claimed that children learn differently from adults, but I am maintaining here that the processes of learning from novel situations is the same throughout the whole of life, but children have more new experiences than do adults and hence there appears to be some difference in their learning processes. In novel situations throughout life, we all have new sensations and then we cannot take the world for granted; we enter a state of disjuncture – the situation when our biography and the meaning that we give to our experience of a social situation are not in harmony – and immediately we raise questions: What do I do now? What does that mean? What is that smell? What is that sound? and so on. Now there are at least two aspects to this questioning process: I cannot give a meaning to the sensation that I have, and I do not know the meaning that those around me give it. Often they coincide and the answers that we get coincide, but it does not mean that the response to the second point necessarily answers the first! If it did, then there would be no room for disagreement, we would live in a totalitarian environment and learning would merely be a matter of remembering. The fact that they often coincide illustrates how culture is transmitted relatively from generation to generation.[2]

Significantly, disjuncture occurs in both of these ways, either because we cannot give meaning or because we do not know the meaning that others around us give. It can also occur in any aspect of our person – knowledge, skills, sense, emotions, beliefs, and so on. It can occur as:

- a slight gap between our biography and our perception of the situation to which we can respond by slight adjustments in our daily living which we hardly notice since it occurs within the flow of time;
- a larger gap that demands considerable learning;
- in a meeting between persons for it takes time for the stranger to be received and a relationship, or harmony, to be established;
- wonder at the beauty of the cosmos, pleasure and so forth at that experience. In some of these situations, it is impossible to incorporate our learning from them into our biography and our taken-for-granted. These are what we might call 'magic moments' for which we look forward and hope to repeat in some way or other.

Naturally disjuncture can occur in different dimensions of the whole person simultaneously or separately. Disjuncture, then, is a varied and complex experience but it is from within the disjunctural that we have experiences which start our learning processes. There is a sense in which learning occurs whenever harmony between our biography (past experiences) and our experience of the 'now' needs to be established, or re-established. Many of these disjunctural situations may not be articulated in the form of a question but there is a sense of unknowing or unease (box 2). However, unknowing is also a social phenomenon since one person's knowledge is another's ignorance, and so on. Through a variety of ways we give meaning to the sensation and our disjuncture is resolved. An answer (not necessarily a correct one, even if there is one) to our questions may be given by a significant other in childhood, by a teacher, incidentally in the course of everyday living, or through self-directed learning, and so on (box 3). The answers are social constructs and so we begin to internalise the social world through learning. Once we have acquired an answer to our implied question, however, we have to practise it in order to commit it to memory (box 4). The more opportunities we have to practise the answer to our initial question the better we will retain it in our memory.[3] Since we do this in our social world we get feedback, which confirms that we have got a socially acceptable resolution or else we have to start the process again, or be different. A socially acceptable answer may be called correct, but we have to be aware of the problem of language – conformity is not always 'correctness' and our whole understanding is social. Here we see 'trial and error' learning as we seek to learn the socially accepted answer. In addition, we have to recognise that those in power can define what is regarded as socially acceptable and we are only in a position to reject this answer the more confident we are of our own position. As we become more familiar with our socially acceptable resolution and memorise it we are in a position to take our world for granted again (box 5), provided that the social world has not changed in some way or other. Most importantly, however, as we change and others change as they learn, the social world is always changing and so our taken-for-grantedness in box 5 is always of a slightly different situation. The same water does not flow under the same bridge twice and so even our taken-for-grantedness is relative.

The significance of this process is that once we have given meaning to the sensation and committed a meaning to our memories then the significance of the sensation itself recedes in future experiences as the socially acceptable answer (meaning) dominates the process, and when disjuncture then occurs it is because we cannot understand the meaning, we do not know the meaning of the word, and so on. It is in learning it that we incorporate culture into ourselves; this we do in most, if not all, of our learning experiences. In this sense, we carry social meaning within ourselves – whatever social reality is it is incorporated in us through our learning from the time of our birth. Indeed, this also reflects the thinking of Bourdieu (1992: 127) when he describes habitus as a 'social made body' and he goes on in the same page to suggest that: 'Social reality exists, so to speak, twice, in things and in minds, in fields and in habitus, outside and inside of agents.' This is something that Epictetus first realised two thousand years ago (see Arendt, Book 2, 1977: 78) when he regarded the internal image as something 'deprived of its reality'. There is a sense, however, in which we might, unknowingly, be imprisoned behind the bars of our own minds,[4] although it could be argued that by an exercise of will we can break out of this, provided we know that we are imprisoned!

However, culture is not a monolithic phenomenon, and so we are exposed to a number of different interpretations of 'reality' in the great majority of circumstances, although there have been societies, especially primitive ones, in which only one interpretation is understood or accepted: these are totalitarian societies – or organisations – and they always seek to reproduce themselves – we will return to this later in the book.

Human learning, then, is more than just transforming the bodily sensations into meaning; it is the process of transforming the whole of our experience through thought, action and emotion and thereby transforming ourselves as we continue to build perceptions of external reality into our biography. I depicted this process in Figure 1.2. In this diagram I have tried to capture the continuous nature of learning by pointing to the second cycle. However, this diagram must always be understood in relation to Figure 1.1, since it is only by combining them that we can begin to understand anything of the complexity of human learning.[5] Box 1 has become a much more significant part of this attempt to understand human learning than even it was in the first volume of this trilogy. People are located in their life-worlds and in contemporary society the life-world changes so rapidly that Bauman (2003, 2005a) has typified it as liquid – that is it is never static, always changing. (We will explore the reasons for this rapid change in later chapters). Consequently, the rapidly changing life-world is frequently inducing a state of disjuncture, often just a slight one to which we adjust but sometimes it is a greater one which requires considerable learning. This rapidly changing world has, therefore, produced a situation where individuals are compelled to learn all the time in order to find their place in society. Lifelong learning is now endemic! Bauman (2005a: 1) opens his book *Liquid Life* in the following manner: 'Conditions of action and strategies designed to respond to them age quickly and become obsolete before the actors have a chance to learn them properly.'

Consequently, we live in a state where we are conscious of change all the time and this means that, unless we disengage from social living, we are constantly having potential learning experiences. Having had an experience (box 2), which occurs as a result of disjuncture, we can reject it, think about it, respond to it emotionally or do something about it – or any combination of the three (boxes 3–5). As a result we become changed persons (box 6) but, as we see, learning is itself a complex process. Once the person is changed, it

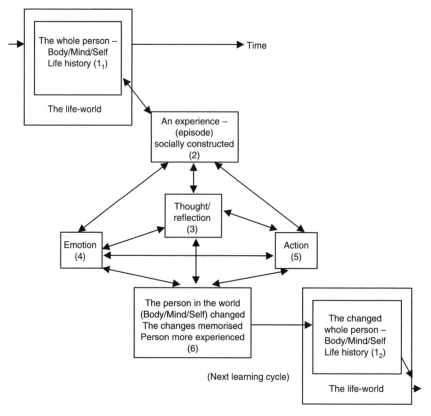

Figure 1.2 The transformation of the person through learning.

is self-evident that the next social situation into which the individual enters is changed – not only changed because the person has changed but changed because the other has also been undergoing learning experiences and has been changed as a result. We can conclude, therefore, that learning involves three transformations: the sensation, the person and then the social situation.

However, as life progresses the developing individuals become more stable and less likely to change radically in certain circumstances. In other words, individuals gain a sense of self and self-identity and they can become actors in the situation as well as recipients. Consequently, a tension might then develop between the social interpretations given to a certain situation and those given by individuals themselves; people are not necessarily so malleable as to mirror the social situation perfectly although, as a result of our early socialisation, we do reflect a great deal of our primary culture and are, in certain ways, emotionally committed to it. We can see, therefore, that there is a potential tension between ourselves, as individuals, and the social situation within which we live; when we can take the social reality for granted, it shows that we 'fit in' – that is, we conform. But when we feel a sense of unease, it may be because we are in a disjunctural situation or else we have no desire to conform to the expectations placed upon us. Both of these situations are potential learning situations. Feeling unease, or awkwardness, may be embarrassing because it suggests a sense of ignorance, but it may also be a matter of conscience[6] – we feel that we have to stand out for what we believe. Paradoxically, we can experience conscience problems when we conform because we have caved in to external pressures, or when we fail to do so because we have stood out for our beliefs, depending on our beliefs and values. Being true to ourselves or our values and beliefs demands confidence and courage amongst other things and so we are not always conformists and learning is sometimes innovative and creative – it is also self-initiated on occasions.

From this initial analysis, we can see that issues of autonomy and authenticity are raised from the outset of any theory of human learning in the social context. For instance, we may feel that when we choose to act in a certain way as a result of an experience or when social pressures are put on us to act in this manner, we are still free to act in another way even if we do not so. We might claim that while we chose to conform to the demands of a given situation, we knew that it was possible to act in another way and that we were capable of doing so. Consequently, we feel free to be autonomous individuals – but the extent to which we are is another question.

Nevertheless, we might feel that we have to be true to ourselves, and therefore we have to reject the demands of a given experience in order to be the selves that we have learned to be. Indeed, Nietzsche (Cooper 1983) has argued that to accept passively what we are told is to be inauthentic, whereas to be authentic we have to be true to ourselves at whatever cost, even if it means non-conformity. It also means that we do not accept passively what Nietzsche has taught us! In both of these situations, we can see the issue of power and we will return to this in the final section of this chapter, but before we do so, it is necessary to examine ways in which we learn to be social individuals and this constitutes the next section.

The social processes of learning

The process that we have described here might be depicted by Figure 1.3. In this diagram, the arc represents the all-encompassing culture into which we are born.[7] In primitive society it was possible to describe this as a single culture, but now this all-encompassing culture is what might also be described as multi-cultural. Culture is a problematic concept and merely by describing it as all-encompassing does not obviate the problem since it is not even the same phenomenon for all people in the same area – young people still grow up in the UK, for instance, with their ethnic cultures, even though

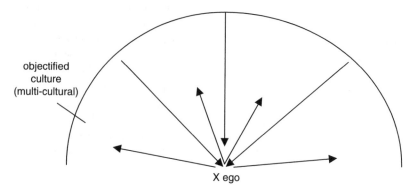

objectified
culture
(multi-cultural)

X ego

Figure 1.3 Socialisation – the internalisation of culture.

they also acquire a sense of 'Britishness' and others a sense of being a
Muslim, and so on. We all have our own life-worlds. Culture is also a difficult term to define, since it has many accepted meanings. Even so, at the risk
of simplifying the concept, we will define it as the totality of knowledge,
beliefs, values, attitudes and norms and mores of a social grouping, so that
we can see that learning is inextricably intertwined with culture and learning
is always a social and cultural phenomenon. Indeed, culture is all that is
learned by every individual. Each group and sub-group has its own distinctive culture and individuals may be members of many social groups and,
therefore, reflect a number of recognisably different cultures in their actions,
attitudes, beliefs, and so on.

Ego represents a single person (child, in the first instance) who is the
recipient of social pressures and of the responses to its disjunctural questions
and who internalises both the questions and the answers. While this process
might appear to be unidirectional, it is clearly not long before children start
to externalise and so they begin to live in a potential tension situation with
those who are their significant others, and the two sets of arrows depict the
processes of internalisation and externalisation. Through their initial learning, children are socialised into their social world, they internalise (learn) that
world so that social reality is now built into their biography, although very
rarely to such an extent that they just become mirrors of that reality although
the blurred reflections can usually be recognised.

It was Mead (Strauss 1964) who described this process in terms of
ego's interaction with the significant others within the children's life-world
who carry that social reality within themselves and manifest it in their
interaction with others, so that these arrows reflect inter-personal relations
that occur within the life-world. Indeed, there are at least three forms of
relationship within the life-world that need to be considered, and these relate
to the present and the future. In the present, there are two ways in which

people act with the external world – through immediate relationships with other individuals in the 'now' (I–Thou) and through an awareness of phenomena (past memories, things, events, and so on – I–It) (Buber 1959). There is also a relationship with the internalised world (Me) which might be described as I–Me; this might also be seen as the reflective process – this is the process in which we 'talk to ourselves' as we carry on an internal conversation about the ongoing events, as we stop and reflect, and so on. In a sense, it is the process of thinking itself. Even so, there is also an envisaged relationship with the world, which occurs when individuals think about the future while they are still in the present; they have desires, intentions, the will to act, and so on. In a similar manner, we can think about the past, or about an idea – we can contemplate, muse, and so on, and thus relate to ourselves and even rewrite our own biography in our own minds. This reflecting upon our past results in our own awareness of our life history and educational biography (Dominice 2000). These may be depicted as in Figure 1.4.

The double arrows represent a two-way relationship and the unbroken ones indicate that there is harmony between my biography and my experience of the situation: I am able to cope with the latter without forethought, as Schutz and Luckmann (1974: 7) write:

> I trust that the world as it has been known by me up until now will continue further and that consequently the stock of knowledge obtained from my fellow-men and formed from my own experiences will continue to preserve its fundamental validity. . . . From this assumption follows the further one: that I can repeat my past successful acts. So long as the structure of the world can be taken as constant, as long as my previous experience is valid, my ability to act upon the world in this and that manner remains in principle preserved.

This relationship is an interpersonal one so that when we are in agreement with those with whom we interact there is a sense of harmony between us and between the individuals and their culture. We are in harmony with our knowledge of the world in which we are acting, but also with the emotions that we share – when we know that we can repeat our past successful acts, we feel 'at ease' with ourselves in the world. This sense of being in harmony means that fundamental both to the learning process and to life itself there is an 'in-built' conservatism since we usually do seek to re-establish harmony rather than create situations where individuals are not at ease with their world.

Person to person	I ↔ Thou
Person to phenomenon (thing/event)	I → It
Person to self	I ↔ Me
Person to a future phenomenon	I → Envisaged Thou or It

Figure 1.4 The person-in-the-world.

But there are times when this harmony does not occur and we then experience disjuncture. Significantly, we can see that once we discuss the whole person, disjuncture can occur in any aspect of our person – knowledge, skills, sense, emotions, beliefs, and so on.

Naturally disjuncture can occur in different dimensions of the whole person simultaneously or separately. Disjuncture, as we have noted above, is a varied and complex experience but it is from within the disjunctural that we have experiences which start our learning processes. There is a sense in which learning occurs whenever harmony between our biography and our experience of the 'now' needs to be established, or re-established.

There is a sense in which the I ↔ Me relationship also occurs to some degree in the other three although it might also be an end in itself. It is the process of reflecting. At the same time, it is at the heart of desire, like and dislike, and other emotions that result in planning, thinking and, maybe, action. It is here, in the memories of previous experiences, I interact with myself and learn and grow.

As we grow and develop our own sense of identity another major issue enters into this relationship and that is how we wish to present ourselves to others (Goffman 1959, 1968, 1971). Goffman highlights the fact that we present ourselves in different ways according to how we want others to perceive us or how we anticipate the other expects us to perform. He also shows how others respond to individuals, especially those with perceived stigmas. In the former, we control our role performance but in the latter the other initially controls the interaction, although this can change depending on the confidence and the courage of the stigmatised person. Consequently, we can see that we learn from our socially constructed experiences – even experiences of the others with whom we interact and this brings to the fore the way that power and control operate in any interactive learning situation.

Additionally, during these processes there is an almost hidden element – time. Being-in-the-world automatically implies existence in time as well as space, and that it is impossible to step outside of either. Time is a contentious phenomenon – it is something that knows no boundaries and in which there is always emergence of newness – a sense of becoming. We are always becoming, but learning is an element in our being – it is always a present process but it always signifies becoming. Time is, in a sense, external to us and is a flow of ever-changing reality which Bergson (1998 [1911], 1999 [1965], 2004 [1912]; Lacey 1989) called *durée*. However, we are not always conscious of its passing and when, suddenly, we become aware of it, we often use such

Person to person	I ←//→ Thou
Person to phenomenon (thing/event)	I –//→ It
Person to self	I ←//→ Me
Person to a future phenomenon	I –//→ Envisaged Thou or It

Figure 1.5 The person experiencing the world.

expressions as 'How time flies'. Nevertheless, there are instances when we are thinking about the future and we have the opposite experience of time: 'Isn't time dragging?' When time drags we become very aware of the world in which we live, and this is important to our understanding of our own experience. When time flies, our biography may be in harmony with our situation and we may not consciously learn. We may also be acting with the flow (Csikszentmihalyi 1990). While we are acting in the world, we are not aware of the world beyond our actions, although our body continues to age through the ravages of time. However, frequently we are confronted with novel situations in this rapidly changing world, so that we cannot remain in harmony with the world and it is almost as if time stops and we experience the present situation – the 'now' (Oakeshott 1933).

It is this moment, when flow is interrupted, that I have called disjuncture. Disjuncture occurs when our biographical repertoire is no longer sufficient to cope automatically with our situation, so that our unthinking harmony with our world is disturbed and we feel unease. We have a tension with our environment. We become very conscious of our situation in the world – what Habermas refers to as a relevant segment of our life-world (Habermas 1987: 122). Indeed, we either problematise it or have it problematised for us.

This awareness is not only a segment of our life-world upon which we focus, it is also an episode in time; it is an experience. We need to distinguish this meaning of the word 'experience' from that of total experience or life-history, and we do so here by calling it *an experience* – an episodic experience (Figure 1.2, box 3). Episodes are not a fixed moment in time although many of them are short and immediate. This is the elusive present. Now we think, feel, and maybe do something about the outside world. We are aware of our world and have a sense of consciousness about it. The interaction between 'I' and 'the world', however, is itself a multifaceted phenomenon. For instance, our experience of the world varies in intensity, in formality and in mode. It can, amongst others, be spoken, written or non-verbal communication; formal, non-formal or informal; emotionally sensitive or cold; oral or silent; visual; tactile; virtual; something we like or approve or vice versa, and so on. The sensations we have of the world are what are also transformed. It is about the whole person.

But experiences also happen when we are in space, or place. In familiar places we are less likely to experience disjuncture but in new spaces disjuncture is much more possible. Yet one other phenomenon that has occurred in recent times has been the realignment of space and time, so that we can create virtual experiences from which we can also learn.

It is at the intersection of us and our world that we have experiences and are presented with the opportunities to learn. Nevertheless, the world is also changing rapidly; our life in the world continues but through frequent changes continuity has become instability and frequently, if not constantly, disjuncture. We are constantly exposed to learning opportunities but our learning always occurs throughout our lives within a social context. Indeed, we always carry within us the culture that we have learned and our learning and our taken-for-grantedness is always grounded in that internalised culture. However, the social world is not one in which power is equally distributed so that the horizontal arrows may not actually reflect social reality.

Human learning within power relationships

Realistically, most of our relationships are asymmetrical and in any relationship the actor has the ability to affect the other in some way or another: children, for instance, in relationship with their significant other are implicitly aware that the significant other knows more, is older, and so on; in school, children are aware of the authority of the teacher and the rules of the institution; in work, adults are aware that there are certain rules and regulations that have to be obeyed and that people with whom they work are often in a superior/inferior managerial position to themselves and have more or less power and influence in the organisation than they do, and so on. Consequently we can turn those arrows in Figures 1.4 and 1.5 around by ninety degrees and picture a vertical rather than a horizontal relationship. As a normal part of social living people often exercise power or influence over others, sometimes unconsciously, and so the interpersonal learning process must be seen from within this framework, that is, we learn to do what we are told (perhaps). However, learning does not always just occur at the behest of the other, nor do all our relationships occur in power situations. In addition, what the other teaches is not necessarily learned, memorised and practised without further thought, emotion or interpretation, and so on. Consequently, relationship is a complex phenomenon within which there is negotiation between the actors, in which power plays an important role, so that it is important at the outset of this book to explore its nature.

Power is not a simple unidirectional process of coercion or influence, as we have already seen: it also involves the way that we present ourselves in the interaction and what we expect from the other. In this sense interaction is always a negotiation, albeit often an unequal one, although our interpretation of the situation is our own and always influenced by our past. We can see, therefore, that power does not demand a determinist position, even though the playing fields are not flat – we are always involved in a potential dialogue. The social interaction need not even be a conflict or a competitive one – it can also involve co-operation. Power exists within these social interactions and it is people who exercise power or who respond to the signs of power according to our understanding of ourselves in the social context. We learn about power from the way we play our social role and the way that others seek to influence our understanding and our behaviour. Holloway (2002a, 2002b – cited in McLaren 2005: 64) makes a nice distinction here that captures some of this discussion when he distinguished between 'power to do' which is the ability to act and 'power over' which is the negation of doing. While 'power over' might probably be construed in a negative sense, the good teacher (and good manager) should also use this power to facilitate the doing or even to enhance it, consequently the use of 'power over' must in some way relate to motive and role within the social structure. But, as we will see below, this formulation is not sufficient to explain the operation of power in the contemporary world.

The situation is more complex than this, as we shall see later in the book, since there are intermediary power players in many situations and they act upon individuals in different ways and in different directions; for the moment we will suggest that these intermediate power players act between the substructure of the globe and the individual at regional and local levels. We will return to this discussion subsequently.

For Foucault, knowledge and truth are produced out of the power struggles between different fields of knowledge, different organisations, and so forth, although we have argued that not all knowledge emerges in this manner. This might, but need not, take us a little further than Marx's dictum in *The German Ideology* that the 'ideas of the ruling class are, in every age, the ruling ideas' (cited from Bottomore and Rubel 1963: 93) since Foucault does not locate power within classes but within people and their activities, but people occupy specific positions in society and some are in a more significant position to exercise power than are others. Indeed, their power position might not always depend on wealth or social class, but within the social networks within which we all function, as Weber (1948) showed.

Foucault introduces us to his ideas about governmentality, which might also be understood from our previous discussion. If we recall the idea that social reality is reconstructed within each of us, as we discussed above, then we have built within ourselves the mechanisms of control, through which we accept our place within the whole and act accordingly. This certainly accounts for our conformity to the prevailing situation, and some scholars regard education as a way of ensuring that this conformity is managed (Edwards and Usher 1994: 2). This power is exercised through interpersonal relationships or through the cultural practices and laws that demand some form of conformity to dominant ideas. That is, that we sometimes learn, memorise and practise what we are told. But we can think creatively, critically and so on, and reject or innovate on what we experience or what we are expected to learn; exercising the will to act in a non-conformist manner might produce punishment so that it demands courage and conviction. Power or acquiescence to power resides in the individual and is exercised within relationships. In this interpretation of power we can see Foucault's (1979: 27) treatment of power as 'a network of relations within our life-world, but it is one that is constantly in tension, in activity', which produces its own disjunctural situations through which learning occurs.

Foucault argues that it is through power that the subject is constituted, but this might appear to be something of an overstatement. At the same time it is true that the subject is constituted within the power relationship. He (1987: 11) goes on to claim that 'the subject constitutes himself in an active fashion, by the practices of the self'. These practices are 'not something the individual invents for himself' but 'patterns that he finds in culture and which are proposed, suggested and imposed on him by his culture, his society and his social group' (cited from Lukes 2005: 96–7). As we take our world for granted so our expectations of these networks of relationship become routinised and ultimately ritualised within our culture and, therefore, within ourselves. With the idea of the subject being constituted through this process, Foucault may actually be explaining the process of socialisation, which we will deal with in greater detail below, and if this is the case, what Foucault is claiming offers very little to the above analysis of learning to become a person through the processes of living in relationships in society. What he has explained is that power is contained within relationships and that it operates within each of us because we have constructed a social reality within each of us. However, Foucault does not explain the dimensions of power itself in the way that Lukes (2005) has done. Indeed, Lukes's (2005: 97) conclusion of Foucault's analysis of power follows from the above quotation:

> But with this answer the ultra-radicalism of Foucault's view of power dissolves. For it amounts to restating some elementary sociological commonplaces. Individuals are socialized: they are oriented to roles and practices that are culturally and socially given: they internalize these and may experience them as freely chosen; their freedom may, as Durkheim liked to say, be the fruit of regulation – the outcome of discipline and controls.

While Lukes may be a little too harsh on Foucault, it is clear that his analysis of the dimensions of power is very important to the way in which society functions. Indeed, the symbols of that power become built into our culture and into all levels of society as well, which are then legitimated in law or in metaphysical claims. Organisations also exist which reinforce this power network and, as Althusser (1972) argued and Edwards and Usher (1994) suggest, education is a way of ensuring conformity, for instance, schools become state ideological apparatuses or socialising agencies. Foucault claims that in the network of relations individuals can never escape from the exercise of power, the panopticon, but we need to step outside of ourselves and understand the way that society is operating beyond us, and what Althusser is showing is that power is reinforced through organisational support. But in the interactive relationship we both exercise power and are recipients of it – we can be both subject and agency, but from our earliest days we have been subjects and we have, to a considerable degree, learned to accept what we are told and so Foucault reiterates the issue of domination in relationship. But, as we have already pointed out, we can resist these social forces provided we have the will power, the confidence in our selves and the courage of our convictions, and so on. In the cases where we do exercise that freedom, we have to be prepared to accept the punishment for failure to conform that those in power in society demand.

Consequently, we might ask if Lukes has anything that aids our understanding of the power relationships within which we learn. Lukes (2005: 29) has proposed a three-dimensional view of power which critiques the behavioural emphasis on power evident in other theorists. Basically he recognises that in earlier social conditions the operation of power occurred in different ways, so that in the first instance it was direct and behavioural, then theorists qualified their understanding as society became more complex and the theories caught up with the social structures and finally in his analysis, the third dimension focuses upon four points:

- decision-making and control over the political agenda;
- issues and potential issues;
- observable (overt or covert), and latent conflict;
- subjective and real interests.

Taking these four points, together with the other two dimensions, it is clear that the ability to make decisions and enforce their outcome is an exercise in power, but in our study of learning we may not want to say that power is only exercised through controlling the political agenda – it might also be through the way that the learning materials are delivered or by the design of the educational syllabus/curriculum (agenda), and so on. Consequently, it is control over the social and cultural agenda, as well. Issues and potential issues refers to those areas where decisions are, or may not, be made – such as the resources of power and authority. Conflict, or potential conflict, can be resolved through coercion, force, manipulation, influence, persuasion, and so on. Lukes maintains that interests are themselves a product of the system through which we learn what we would like, and so on. Consequently, we can see the power of advertising which moulds our desires but which is also socially reproductive without being over-deterministic. We are all influenced to a considerable extent by the intrinsic power in both the media and in interpersonal relationships, even to the extent of constructing our own interests. Lukes (2005: 109) regards power as not something direct but much more insidious – it is the ability to secure a compliance of the people to be dominated. He goes on to argue that the control of techniques can result in adaptive preferences being controlled even to the extent that people 'accept their lot' in society. Indeed, there is a sense in which symbolic violence (Bourdieu and Passeron 1977) is always operative. Finally, Lukes (2005: 150) makes the point that:

> Power's third dimension is always focused on particular domains of experience and is never, except in fictional dystopias, more than partially effective. It would be simplistic to suppose that 'willing' and 'unwilling' compliance to domination are mutually exclusive.

Indeed, we can always resist power if we are alert to its exercise, if we are so concerned about our own psychological and bodily drives and desires, if we are prepared to face the consequences, and so on. But for the most part we are aware of the potential tension between ourselves and the wider world and we are prepared to accept both the overt exercise of domination and its more covert exercise. Power, therefore, is not a matter of determinism – in this sense it is under-deterministic. Consequently, we can see how Bourdieu's assertion that there are two social realities – one internal and the other external – has significance in this discussion. In addition, we can see that it is through the exercise of power and the willing acquiescence to conform that generates both cultural and social reproduction. But what does this tell us about the interests/values/beliefs that we have learned are non-conformist, radical and even rebellious? What does it tell us about the self itself? While much about the self is reflexive, we are more than our experiences and we can become actors in the social situation – this is a point to which we will return later in this book. But we can also see that it is not possible to construct a realistic understanding of learning without reference to the social context. Indeed, it is possible to argue that specific sociological theories of society almost demand certain approaches to learning, as we will show in the final section of this chapter.

Sociological theories and learning

It will be clear that the theoretical framework underlying this study might be seen as neo-Marxian, but this is coupled by a value system that finds its origins in the humanistic beliefs of the prophetic and social gospel concerns of Judeo-Christendom. It is recognised that other sociological perspectives would have perhaps produced a different analysis of lifelong learning and the learning society. Indeed, different sociological perspectives might even define learning itself differently, and they would certainly see the functions of learning in different ways. It must be emphasised that this discussion on the functions of learning relate to human learning rather than the form of lifelong learning, which we will discuss later in the study. In this section we will explore some of the major sociological theories and show how each implies the need for a dominant theory of learning but none allows for a complete theory of human learning, apart from symbolic interactionism, although even this has a number of weaknesses as far as our discussion is concerned.

From the outset it can be seen that the understanding of human learning discussed throughout this trilogy presupposes a symbolic interactionist approach to sociological theory, but not only interactionist. This approach has its roots in the work of George Herbert Mead (Strauss 1964), as did my very first book on adult learning (Jarvis 1987). Symbolic interactionism relies both on interaction with others (I ↔ Thou) and with ourselves (I ↔ Me). Society is seen as a fluid state which is held together by interactionist gestures and language which reflect the meanings that the individual actors give to their experiences and this allows for the individual to respond in either an innovative or established way. Goffman (1959, 1968, 1971) demonstrated that we actually use our perceptions of ourselves to project to others the images by which we want to be recognised – in childhood our social identity was ascribed to us but in adulthood we actually seek to construct it. Consequently, a wide variety of theories of learning find their place within this theoretical perspective since the self is dependent on the social but the social is dependent upon the individual. Clearly, one of the major weaknesses of symbolic interactionism is its omission of the power relationship which we have discussed in the previous section of this chapter and which forms a fundamental dimension to this discussion. However, the interpersonal relationship is not always coercive, often times it can be negotiated and often it is co-operative, which again reflects the fluidity of this theoretical perspective. One of the other dimensions which is missing from this theory is that of emotion, although its very flexibility allows us to incorporate emotions into both the meaning and the interaction.

A very similar approach to this is phenomenology which focuses upon the meaning that the actors give to their experiences of everyday life and the life-world. Consequently, we can see that Figure 1.2 is phenomenological and that it is built into our understanding of human learning per se. In one sense, symbolic interactionism is an action theory; action theories are all based on the meaning that actors give to their experience of the social situation. In contemporary society, meaning has given way to rational choice – reflecting Max Weber's classical studies of rationality. Yet for Weber, rationality has a number of dimensions: instrumental, value, traditional and affective. Rational choice theory has restricted rationality to one element of the whole, and, as we saw in our theory of learning, the other forms of rationality are also very prevalent. Consequently, this would appear to be an incomplete understanding of human action, in precisely the same way, as we argued in Volume 1, as are other theories of learning. In addition, there is little reference to the social structures, so that it is a one-sided theory of social action. Archer (2000:

55–85) also rightly criticises this theory since, in its very modern form, rationality tends to be based on instrumentalism, especially that of an economic form. She shows how personal commitment and other forms of caring and emotion are omitted from these considerations and so the theory is not based upon an adequate model of the human being. Even so, those who adopt it must necessarily adopt a theory of learning that assumes a degree of freedom and reflective thought which we discussed in the previous volume as being one aspect of an overall theory of learning.

One other approach that emphasises the agent is grounded theory which is really a method of interpreting data rather than a theory of action itself. It starts from the data and imposes meaning inductively on data that have no intrinsic meaning. In a sense, it presupposes human beings as reflective thinkers who seek to make meaning of sense experience and data about the world, so that it demands rational reflective theories of learning. Consequently, learning might be viewed as giving meaning to sense data in the way that we have discussed in Figures 1.1 and 1.2.

By contrast, there are two theories that begin from a diametrically opposed perspective – functionalism and systems theory – both of which are structural. The former is associated with the work of Durkheim (1915, 1964 [1933]) while the latter is related to the work of Talcott Parsons (1951). Durkheim argued that society is like an organism, albeit one which is gradually evolving as its structures are loosened due to the increasing division of labour. Individuals are products of these social structures and so they were compelled to learn how to fit into these structures and, as such, the dominant forms of learning implied are non-reflective and behavioural. Indeed, it might also be argued that learning produced individuals who fitted into society's structures and this was the function of learning. Clearly, the model of society was incomplete and so are the theories of learning associated with it, such as information processing and behaviourism. Nevertheless, a similar approach is to be found within bureaucratic organisational theory – a point to which we will return. In a similar manner, systems theory had four functional imperatives – adaptation, goal attainment, integration and pattern maintenance. Like functionalism, this theory presupposed the social structures and learning is a matter of adaptation so that the patterns of society should be maintained. Parsons (1951: 207–26) illustrates his argument with the socialisation of a child and the internalisation of the social values. Consequently, the theory presupposed the same approaches to learning as the functionalist model just discussed. The outcome of this approach is perhaps best depicted by the idea of the over-socialised view of the human being (Wrong 1963). Even so, we can see how scholars like Bourdieu (1973) built upon this in recognising that there is a considerable degree of social and cultural reproduction and this is also implicit in Figure 1.3. Significantly, however, the arrows in this figure indicate that this is not a unidirectional relationship. In the same manner, social constructivism argues that all explanations must stem from society rather than the individual and therefore it also assumes that learning begins with culture and social language so that it demands a similar theory of learning to that of structuralism and functionalism.

Marxist thought also presupposed that the dominant ideas would be learned uncritically by the mass of people, who developed a false class consciousness, and so the same approach to learning is implicit in it, although the morality of the Marxist position is that it assumes that the inequality in society is unacceptable. In Marxist thought it is the power of the elite that controls the cultural content and it is their ideologies and preferences that are transmitted through culture to the proletariat. The power that the elite exercise is not always overt and this led Gramsci to discuss this covert power which he called hegemony (Joll 1977). A similar perspective is to be found in the work of Nietszche (Cooper 1983) who regarded inauthenticity to be found in individuals who passively accept what they are told – that is, who learn non-reflectively. For Marx, however, the learning is not just a matter of accepting the knowledge, values and beliefs transmitted through the culture – it is a matter of responding to it and doing something about it. In this sense, it is revolutionary – demanding practice as well as cognition. Within education, perhaps the most well-known exponent of this position is Paulo Freire, who typified liberation theology since he was also a Christian.

Acceptance of the Marxist position led to critical theory which places less emphasis on the social structures and more on individuals who are capable of being critical of these social processes. Critical theory emerged from the Frankfurt School, and combined a Marxist critique with both a Freudian understanding of the unconscious and a Weberian approach to rationality. Critical theory presupposes that individuals are free to think critically and, consequently, the learning theories associated with it are more reflective and individual. The most well-known contemporary thinker from this school is Habermas. Clearly, when individuals are critical of the power elite of society conflict rather than harmony results, so that the same approaches to learning are to be discovered amongst conflict theorists.

A similar approach to society is contained in ethnomethodology, which also reflected a structural approach in as much as people were able to take the order of everyday life for granted. This social order is socially produced and that people generally learn and fit into the structures. Hence the approach to learning tends to be non-reflective in the first instance but immediately the order is destroyed individuals are able to think critically and reflectively in order to restore order. In this sense, the idea of disjuncture can be seen as quite central to ethnomethodological thinking since by all forms of reflective learning society's structures can be re-established.

In this brief section we have examined some of the major sociological theories that endeavour to explain contemporary society, in which we can clearly see how different theories of learning can be located within them.

Conclusion

In this chapter we have explored a fundamental aspect of learning – that we always learn in a social context and that the learning processes are themselves affected by the relationships within which we function. These relationships are affected by power so that we tend to mirror the culture(s) of our life-world. Nevertheless, our learning is not predetermined since learning is more than thinking but even our thinking is more than memorisation – we think critically, creatively, and so on. We learn through our emotions and through our actions. Human beings are social actors and our understanding of learning must be social as well as psychological. It is, therefore, necessary to pursue sociological perspectives on learning a little further in the next chapter.

Chapter 2

Human learning within a structural context

While the first volume of this work concentrated on philosophical and psychological perspectives on human learning, its third chapter looked specifically at the sociological implications of learning, examining culture, socialisation, indoctrination, brainwashing, time and space. It is necessary to revisit that chapter briefly here in order to continue to lay the foundations for future analysis. Consequently, we will take two sections from that chapter as the opening section of this chapter; thereafter, the focus will be on learning and agency and structure and, finally, relate learning to the major sociological theories.

Learning in the social context[1]

In this section we will examine the nature of the life-world, society and culture.

The nature of the life-world

Williamson (1998: 23) makes two very valid points about studying life-worlds:

- People live their lives in and through others, so that their understanding of themselves is inter-subjective;
- People strive to live meaningful lives.

Habermas (1981: 119) regards societies as both systems and life-worlds with the latter relating to social groups, whereas Schutz and Luckmann (1974: 3) start with individuals and suggest that the 'everyday life-world is the region of reality in which man [sic] can engage himself and which he can change while he operates in it by means of his animate organism'. Nevertheless, they highlight the point that we do not have perfect freedom in our life-world since there are a variety of obstacles and many other people inhibiting our spontaneity; we only have a relative degree of autonomy.

It is within this context of everyday life that we have experiences in which learning occurs.

But our learning is often unintended and frequently unnoticed, since we are often so familiar with our life-world that we take it for granted, live within the flow of time and just adapt our behaviour – almost unthinkingly – to changing circumstances. Each adaptation means that we also gradually alter our knowledge of the situation, although we are not always aware of it. This can be seen if we ask people to describe their learning experiences, as I did in my research, and they found it tremendously difficult to describe precisely how, or even when, they learned unless they described formal learning in which they had a teacher. In addition, it can account for the discrepancy between the espoused theories of action and the theories-in-use that Argyris and Schön (1974) discovered in their study of theories of action. Only when there are sudden changes or novel situations are people stopped in their tracks, as it were, because they do not know automatically what to do or how to respond to a question and so on. This is disjuncture; it is one that teachers try to create in formal educational settings – the teachable moment.

The life-world, however, is contained within the wider society and consequently it is not independent of the social forces generated by globalisation.[2] This means that the global pressures of the advanced capitalist world and information technology permeate the life-world so that individuals grow up and develop, learning to take for granted the culture generated by global capitalist forces. Our learning about the wider world is often unintended and pre-conscious but this occurs because these forces have colonised our life-world. Our life world also impinges upon other people's life-worlds. Not only is the life-world contained within a wider society, there is a total mixture of institutions and groupings within it, such as the family, formal and non-formal institutions such as school and work and informal meeting opportunities during leisure and so on. Each contains its own sub-culture and normally we adjust our behaviour automatically to fit into the organisations and groups with which we are familiar. It is for this reason that both incidental and pre-conscious learning are important forms of learning, although they are less frequently studied than some other types, but social organisation is dependent on them. At the same time, when we join new groups we have to go through a more conscious learning process during which we actually learn the sub-culture so that we can fit into that new group, whether it be a work group or a leisure one. The learning processes might not be very different but the settings in which we learn are: herein lies one of the linguistic problems with some terminology about learning. We are apt to talk about formal learning or non-formal learning and so on, but what we should actually be talking about is learning in formal situations, in non-formal situations, etc. The linguistic shorthand is misleading! Different people may react to and learn in a variety of ways in similar situations.

However, our life-worlds are not only about culture and our positions within the different sub-cultural groups, but they are also about time and space. For instance, the process of joining new organisations and learning their sub-culture takes time – social time and body time. But even more, each new learning experience occurs in time and so it is never a static phenomenon – change is endemic. It is, therefore, necessary to recognise the significance of time when we look at learning in social situations; it is even more important when we recognise that there is a sense in which disjunctural situations are ones when we become aware of time and its passing, so that at the heart of the experiences from which we learn are episodes of time.

As there is process through time, space is another major dimension of the life-world. Not only is the life-world for most people situated locally although, as Gouldner (1957–8) highlighted many years ago, there are a few – more now than there were then – whose life-world is cosmopolitan. Our life-world has also been expanded through globalisation and especially the exposure we all have to the information media, so that we become aware of ourselves within, say, Europe or America, our own country or state, our region, and so on. These all contribute to our multiple identities. But space is not only geo-graphical, we all live in social space, at the centre of some institutions and at the periphery of others, and during socialisation we move from the one towards the other. Where we are situated also affects the experiences we have from which we learn.

Society

Margaret Thatcher famously proclaimed that 'There is no such thing as society', but that was an overstatement. Society still exists although, in most instances, societies do not have total sovereignty nor do they have a single culture. They exist within a complex network of political and economic power relations which we will explore further in the next chapter. In addi-tion, they are multi-cultural. But the territory of the United Kingdom is still ruled over, in part, by a national government – although some of its power has been ceded to Brussels and the United States has assumed other aspects of that power – and there is still a sense of belonging to a country, so that we can claim 'I am British' or 'I am Danish', and so on. Consequently, there is still a phenomenon that we can call British society, or French society, etc. We do still vote for a government and it does exercise certain political and economic power, e.g. power over health and welfare, education and media, ecology, taxation, military force and law enforcement, and so on. Whilst no longer a sovereign state, it is by no means a powerless non-entity. However, it is now an intermediate source of power rather that the ultimate source but, as such, it should not be neglected in any discussions of power.

At a more local level we find local government exercising a limited amount of power, although there have been deliberate attempts to create more local power bases and increase the level of democracy in societies like the United Kingdom. Naturally, the power exercised at this level is limited and local and often tension exists between local and national governments. In their different ways each of these levels can influence the level and amount of lifelong learning offered within a specific vicinity. In the same way, there are many local areas that endeavour to retain their own sense of identity, their own traditions, and so on. Indeed, it could be argued that as the world becomes more of a global village, so local areas are rediscovering what makes them distinctive; they are seeking to retain their own language/dialect, their own customs and traditions, and so on. In a sense, they are seeking to retain their own cultures and in the remainder of this section we will explore culture and relate it to identity and experience, which is at the heart of learning.

Culture

Culture is a word with a multitude of different meanings but from an anthropological perspective culture may be contrasted with nature. Gehlen (1988: 29) writes:

> In order to survive, he [humankind] must master and recreate nature, and for this reason man must *experience* the world. He acts because he is unspecialized and deprived of a natural environment to which he is adapted. The epitome of nature restructured to serve his needs is called *culture* and the culture world is the human world. . . . Culture, therefore, is 'second nature' – man's restructured nature.
>
> (italics in original)

But unlike the animals, humans have minimal instincts and so they have to learn this second nature and pass it on from generation to generation, so that children's education is often seen as transmitting the most worthwhile knowledge from one generation to the succeeding one. In this sense, education is 'from above' since the dominant forces in the older generation decide what should be included in the curriculum – one way of viewing curriculum is that it is a selection from culture and so is the learning content in contemporary teaching and learning modules. Culture is all the knowledge, skills, attitudes, beliefs, values and emotions that we, as human beings, have added to our biological base. It is a social phenomenon; it is what we as a society, or a people, share and which enables us to live as society. In order for humanity to survive, it is necessary that we should learn our culture. Learning, then, becomes necessary for the survival of societies and in the process we, as human beings, learn to be. This learning occurs, as we have already pointed out, through personal interaction (I–Thou) with significant others (Mead: see Strauss 1964) in the first instance, and then within the wider life-world.

However, it is clear that globalisation and rapid social change have affected the nature of society and that our life-world is now multi-cultural. We all live in multi-cultural life-worlds which are gradually reflecting our locality. Consequently, we learn a diversity of interpretations of reality from the outset, especially through the mass media. This might well result in some persons not acquiring the same sense of security, sense of community membership and self-identity as people did in previous generations which, in turn, has given rise to identity-crisis, what Giddens (1991) refers to as 'existential anxiety'.

But the learning is not just embedded in the present, it is always future-oriented in order that humankind should master the world and survive:

> The acts through which man meets the challenge of survival should always be considered from two angles: They are productive acts of overcoming the deficiencies and obtaining relief, on the one hand, and they are completely new means for conducting life drawn from within man himself.
>
> (Gehlen 1988: 28–9)

These actions are communicative and manipulative. But for Gehlen, the common root of knowledge and action lies at the heart of the human response to the world or, in other words, experiential and situated learning, as opposed to the instinctive behaviour of animals. Instinctive behaviour is repetitious and reproductive, as indeed is patterned behaviour in social living, but in the latter we know that we could have done things differently. Learning, then, is a social necessity and through it human beings learn to be and to become.

Experiential learning begins with response to our life-world and it is within this that our learning takes place and we will briefly examine a number of learning processes that occur within the life-world, including socialisation and role-making, developing self and identity, and acquiring language, knowledge and meaning. In a real sense these are all interrelated and any separation here is for heuristic purposes only – we will deal with them in the following subsections: primary socialisation, secondary socialisation, brainwashing and indoctrination.

Primary socialisation

Culture is an ambiguous concept that functions both externally and internally. When we are born into the world we have no cultural awareness, although we have learned a number of phenomena pre-consciously in the womb. At birth then, culture is external to us but internal to our significant others and through interaction with them we internalise (learn, often non-reflectively and unintentionally in the first instance) it. Once they have shared and we have learned the relevant knowledge, values, beliefs, etc. the culture becomes our own subjective reality and as such helps determine the

way that we perceive and experience the world, and consequently we learn in it and from it. This is the process of socialisation which Berger and Luckmann (1966: 150) subdivide thus:

> Primary socialization is the first socialization an individual undergoes in childhood, through which he [sic] becomes a member of society. Secondary socialization is any subsequent process which inducts an already socialized individual into new sectors of the objective world of his society.

Crucial to this process is learning the language of the people since it is through language that meaning, knowledge and so on, are conveyed (see Figure 1.1). Language is at the heart of the greater part of our conscious learning and it will always reflect the culture of our life-world, as many childhood educators have demonstrated. Language, as such, is arbitrary and symbolic; no word, thing or event has intrinsic meaning, and it only assumes meaning when meaning is given to it, which occurs through narrative that unites the disparate episodic events in our lives. Consequently young children grow up to learn the meaning of words which they attach to experiences and to the phenomena in the world that they experience, but the process is more complex than this. Let us assume that my young grandson is looking at the computer on which I am writing this chapter but he does not know that it is a computer, nor does he yet know the word 'computer', although he can see the object/instrument that I am using. In fact the computer has no meaning for him. As he looks at it, the sensations on his retina are transmitted to his brain and so he is aware of the image of the computer and he still has to learn the word. At a later time he will learn to associate the word 'computer', a sound which is transmitted to his brain as sensations generated by the sounds he has heard, with this technological instrument. Eventually the visual and the sound sensations are linked in his mind and the object becomes a computer. He can then take the meaning of the word for granted – he has learned it non-reflectively, and it is almost as if there is no longer a separation between the word and the instrument. Even this non-reflective learning process is complex, associational and takes time before it becomes a subjective reality. Once he has accomplished it, he can shortcut the sound and just accept the meaning. We do this all the time. Naturally, in other languages the word denoting 'computer' may be very different. But once learned the word 'computer' has two realities – an objective reality and a subjective one. This is true of all the language that we learn in early childhood and without that language we would find it almost impossible to give meaning to phenomena in our life-world. But the language is not totally removed from the reality – discourse is grounded in reality. Once we have language, it helps to organise our experience and give it meaning. But the meaning we give anything is a social construction since it reflects the culture that we have learned from others during our primary socialisation and our experience of reality itself. Traditionally, as Mead demonstrated, this socialisation was affected by interaction with significant others, but in more recent times the media, especially television, have also become very significant and they assume a more dominant role in the lives of most people, especially the young.

However, once we have language, we can express ourselves, share our thoughts and become functioning members of our social group. We can also expand the breadth of our thinking, develop our own meanings of things and interpretations of events within our own purview, and we can become creative and innovative. This ability to think independently gives a second strand to our individuality – the first coming from our biological and genetic inheritance – so that we can see how our conception of our selves, as persons, is enabled by the development of language and meaning. With it, we develop self-confidence and this is another unintended and incidental facet of our learning. As we develop this sense of individuality, self-identity and selfhood, so we have a growing store of memories upon which we can assess new experiences and new learning and so we can engage in negotiation of meanings and interpretations with others within our life-world. In other words, we can develop our critical and creative faculties and these are relatively independent of our biological base. Consequently, the ability to learn reflectively develops with our growing ability to use language and, perhaps, our preferences for the way that we learn are also developed at this time.

Clearly some learning styles are culturally based, as recent research into Chinese learning styles has shown. Lee Wing On (1996: 35–6) cites Zhu Xi:

> Generally speaking, in reading, we must first become intimately familiar with the text so that its words seem to come from our own mouths. We should then continue to reflect on it so that its ideas seem to come from our own minds. Only then can there be real understanding. Still, once our intimate reading of it and careful reflection on it have led to a clear understanding of it, we must continue to question. Then there might be additional progress. If we cease questioning, there'll be no additional progress.

There is a cultural tradition here going back to the thoughts of Confucius himself: that memorising, understanding and reflecting should precede questioning, which is different from the Western tradition where questioning comes more rapidly in the order of things.[3] At the same time we must recognise that Confucian thinkers located learning within the context of teaching and so learners were expected to respect the master, learn his words, understand them and then to question. In the West, we have been influenced by the more 'natural', romantic and liberal connotations stemming from Rousseau's *Emile*. Learning, then, assumes a cultural form and we acquire some, but maybe not all, of our approaches to learning this way. The success of Chinese learners illustrates that this approach needs to be understood more thoroughly in the West (see also Jarvis 2006). In becoming aware that we are Western or from a Confucian heritage country, our self-identities are also expanded for not only do we have a sense of self, we can locate that self within a wider context, e.g. Western or Chinese, and so on. Western cultural beliefs and practices have also been learned in the same way and, as Keddie (1980) showed many years ago, Western individualism is learned in a similar socialisation process and reinforced by traditional education classes. In a similar manner we can see that authoritarian and democratic cultures will affect both the manner in which we learn and, perhaps, also the relationship between our learning and our behaviour.

In precisely the same way as we are affected by our ethnic cultures, so we are affected by the manner in which each culture treats gender. Whilst we are born with sexual differences, Parker (2005) points out that culture plays a larger role in learning our gender differences than do our genes. Consequently, we learn to be boys and girls and women and men. There are many studies which demonstrate the way masculine and feminine behaviour is acquired in different cultural and sub-cultural settings and Belenky *et al.* (1986) illustrate just how significant is this process to the creation of women's sense of self. These gender differences may also affect the way we experience phenomena (Crawford 2005).

In addition, we are socialised into our socio-economic class position in society, acquiring the language, sense of self and identity, and sub-culture relevant to our position in our social milieu. The fact that Western society is structurally now much more open means that it is possible to move to different socio-class positions as we develop. The same phenomenon is, naturally, not true for either our ethnicity or our gender. In all of these situations, however, the significance of our early socialisation in the development of our own lifelong learning should never be underestimated.

Culture, then, is far from value free. Whilst we can look at the processes of human learning and recognise what actually happens, it does not mean that we need to accept the values that are contained within the cultural practices. All cultures incorporate values and, therefore, the ethics of the culture needs to be recognised as I have shown elsewhere (Jarvis 1997) and to which we will return later in this study. O'Sullivan (1999) has shown quite convincingly why education needs to be transformative and learning critically aware of the environment in which we live.

Secondary socialisation

As we grow and develop so we enter other groups having their own sub-cultures, such as schools, leisure clubs and work, and in each of these we go through a process of secondary socialisation. We learn to be a student, a club member and a worker; in other words, we learn specific behaviour associated with our position. However, as Turner (1962) showed, the process of secondary socialisation is not merely a process of imitating the behaviour of other role players; that is behaviourist learning. He showed that 'role behavior in formal organizations becomes a working compromise between the formalized role prescriptions and the more flexible operation of the role-taking process' (1962: 38). It is interactive rather than merely imitative, as has been often assumed, pointing to a more complex interaction between 'ego' and the generalised or selected other in learning to perform organisational roles. Moreover, the fact that 'alter' validates the role behaviour indicates that the role player is an accepted member of the organisation and that the role behaviour is likely to conform to certain norms and social expectations. In each status change and personal development there is social identity transformation, although our personal identity remains a continuous and a less frequently changing phenomenon.

None of us remain in the same social position and play the same role throughout the whole of our life span (see, for instance, Erikson 1963), so that we change both roles and statuses – and with it social identities, and so on. When the change is gradual it is possible for both the individual and society to cope with it in the normal course of things, but when it is sudden or dramatic then both the individual being changed and the immediate social group have to be prepared for it. Consequently, status change is often ritualised by the social group through rites of passage, initiation rituals, and so on. From the work of van Gennap (1960 [1908]), these in-between periods in status change have been regarded as liminal periods. Victor Turner (1969: 81) described the ritual process whereby young people were initiated into adulthood amongst the Ndembu people in central Africa:

> Liminal entities, such as neophytes in initiation or puberty rites, may be represented as having nothing. They may be disguised as monsters, wear only a strip of clothing, or even go naked to demonstrate that, as liminal beings, they have no status, property, insignia, secular clothing indicating rank or role, position in the kinship system – in short, nothing that may distinguish them from their fellow neophytes or initiands. Their behaviour is normally passive or humble; they must obey their instructors implicitly, and accept arbitrary punishment without complaint. It is as though they are being reduced or ground down to a uniform condition to be fashioned anew and endowed with additional powers to enable them to cope with their new situation in life.

Here then we see that the initiands were treated as if they had to have their old culture removed and a new 'second nature' provided for them, so that they could fit into society in their new position. Their new learning had to be free from the influences of previous learning. These teaching methods might be regarded as immoral and unsophisticated but they were totally symbolic of 'unlearning' a previously learned culture. This might be seen as a form of brainwashing; an endeavour to remove the effects of a culture upon a person through physical and psychological techniques. Our status rituals are by no means so harsh or as clearly structured since we live in a more open society, but they likewise symbolise the new position and therefore the new learning that has to occur in such social change. Indeed, such writers as Lave and Wenger (1991) borrow the language of anthropology when they discuss situated learning, which in their study is basically a description and analysis of secondary socialisation as a learning process.

Once we have internalised the external culture and made it our 'second nature' it becomes a basis for our own interpretation of our experiences and for our giving them meaning. In other words, this is the psychological consciousness. This consciousness is both learned and validated within the culture and points us to the way that our own interpretation of our own experiences is socially constructed. Thus we can begin to see the significance in understanding the culture into which the learners are born and within which they live if we are to understand their learning processes, but we have already pointed to the significance of space in this process since we have indicated how globalisation affects local cultures.

However, socialised individuals also continue to learn, albeit within a more restricted framework. The Club of Rome Report *No Limits to Learning* (Botkin *et al.* 1979) illustrates this by dividing learning into two types: maintenance learning which is 'the acquisition of fixed outlooks, methods and rules for dealing with known and recurring situations . . . and is indispensable for the functioning and stability of every society' and innovative learning which is 'the type of learning that can bring change, renewal, restructuring, and problem reformulation' (Botkin *et al.* 1979: 10). In other words, innovative learning results in changes in the way individuals act and ultimately change in culture. We are continually doing both in our own learning and the more we seek to maintain the patterns of behaviour with which we are familiar, the more we will tend to resist learning. Therefore, rejection and failure to consider learning opportunities – discussed in the opening chapter – become a feature of our daily life and experience.

Brainwashing and indoctrination

The socialisation processes imply that we learn what is expected of us in morally acceptable situations, but there are many situations when undue pressure is exerted upon us to learn what is expected of us. Wilson (1972: 18) defines indoctrination thus:

> indoctrinated beliefs are those which a person may think that he has accepted freely, for good reasons, but which he has in fact accepted when

his will or reason have been put to sleep or by-passed by some other person, who has some sort of moral . . . hold over him, by virtue of his authority or some other power-bestowing psychological factor.

Wilson goes on immediately after this quotation to say that this is a state which Sartre would call self-deception. Throughout our socialisation and education we may well be exposed to this type of social pressure, which, naturally enough, results in both social and culture reproduction so that our learning might be seen as no more than maintaining the status quo. Whilst frequently applied to religious belief situations, it might be more true to claim that within this so-called learning society indoctrination is much more prevalent, and secular, than it is religious. Indeed, one of the problems with indoctrination is that we may well be unaware that we have been indoctrinated; for instance, in the way that we accept the ethos of consumer society generated through the media at the behest of advanced capitalism. Indeed, we do not always realise just how profoundly changed we are by the ethos of the organisations within which we work, or just how they are affected by the social pressures of advanced market capitalism. Naturally, this occurs most frequently and overtly through advertising – advertising both seeks to create specific desires in us but, paradoxically, it also reinforces a sense of local identity since advertising is tailored to reflect local cultures, and so on.

While the exterior forces producing indoctrination might be quite gentle and not very intrusive, there are other situations where these pressures are much greater and forced upon the recipient. The removal of overt freedom might be the distinguishing feature between indoctrination and brainwashing. The latter (Lifton 1961) might be regarded as thought reform or re-education and has been practised by oppressive totalitarian political regimes. The process is designed to make individuals feel that their previous learning is wrong and so they are forced through manipulative psychological techniques to confess to this and, having done so, they open themselves to re-education. However, the process does not produce a façade of change but a genuine sense of self-change, which, as Lifton discovered, has lasting effects even after the process has been completed and the brainwashed person freed.

Both of these are generally regarded as being morally unacceptable, although it would be true to say that less concern is expressed about the former since there is a sense in which the indoctrinated person has a greater degree of freedom to reject the pressures than does the brainwashed one. Even so, the latter know that they have been brainwashed whilst the former might not be aware that they have been indoctrinated and perhaps there is little worse than being imprisoned behind the bars of our own minds!

Social and cultural capital

Culture is, therefore, most significant in both the creation of the self and in our understanding of human learning. It is perhaps not surprising that its value has been translated into the concept of 'capital' in the West, which in itself demonstrates the power of the global substructure to colonise language and social thought with the riches of the human and personal being translated into economic concepts, and judged as economic value. Bourdieu (1973) was amongst the first to use the term in this way, although it has subsequently been as widely, and as influentially, used by Coleman (1990) and Putnam (2000). Each, however, has used it in different ways: Bourdieu in relation to a materialist conception of culture; Coleman in relation to education and inequality; Putnam as a combination of networks, norms and trust that allows participants to achieve their desired goals. This distinction is nicely discussed by Schuller *et al.* (2000), although it is not necessary to pursue it further here. We are treating social capital here more like the way that Putnam does in as much as it refers to the wealth of resources inherent in the culture of the life-world, all of which affect and contribute to human learning and, in fact, to every learning episode. We will return to this discussion later in the book, but we do not accept that social capital should actually be translated into economic value: the fact that it is illustrates the way that both our language and our culture has been colonised by the forces of advanced capitalism. In this anthropological sense, we can relate it to discussions of community and association (Toennies 1957) which themselves reflect the way that culture changes from more closed to more open society and the differing personal relationships that have occurred in different forms of society. As Bauman (2000) has shown in his discussion of liquid modernity, society is now even more open and changing more rapidly than ever before and we might now say that association has continued to change in the direction of individuation. Now individuals are more responsible for their own actions, and their own learning, than ever before. Human learning is, therefore, profoundly affected by all of these changes since we are-in-the-world and we share its culture through relationship and narrative. However, we do not merely learn the culture and reflect it; our learning is much more complex than this as we seek to navigate our way through the complexities of this multi-level, multi-cultural global society and so it is now necessary to relate this discussion to structure and agency.

Structure and agency

One of the significant issues within sociological thought is the relationship between the social structures and individual actions. For instance, in the foregoing discussion culture is assumed and, in that sense, it seems to be suggesting that individuals emerge as a result of culture and, therefore, the social structures that exist. At the same time, as we have noted, societies are now much more open and so there is a greater degree of freedom to act as individuals than ever before. Nevertheless, we are all still affected by the social structures and they do help mould us in a variety of ways. But ultimately that would imply that the structures exist independently of the person. Alternatively, it might be argued that individuals develop social structures as a result of their interactions and that individuals exist independently of the structures. However, it is clear that neither of these positions is tenable and that both agency and structure are in some way mutually dependent and that the process of learning is quite significant to our understanding of it. In a well-known argument Giddens (1979: 53) suggested that 'the notions of action and structure *presuppose one another*' (italics in original). Indeed, culture is not independent of either agency or structure and so we have three mutually dependent phenomena.

At this point it is necessary to return to the two models of learning discussed in the opening chapter. In novel situations (Figure 1.1) the person often learns the socially 'given' answers to disjunctural situations and, consequently, learns to fit into the existing structures. In this sense, individuals are determined by the social structures. But this does not occur totally throughout the whole of life, or in every learning situation, as Figure 1.2 implies. When individuals have already learned cultural responses to social situations and are then confronted with a new disjuncture, they cannot take it for granted and new responses are demanded (Figure 1.2). Once they have learned a new response and are changed persons, they externalise through action, speech and so forth and, in a sense, influence others. Consequently, the social relationships that exist between the actors involved are in some way transformed through learning and the outcome of which might generate a slightly different relationship – one that is transformed. Giddens (1979: 61) distinguishes here between the patterns of social relationships, which he calls situated practices, and which are reproduced in our taken-for-granted situations, and the systems which are the functioning of these relationships. In this sense, as Giddens argues, this functioning of the relationships is both the medium and the outcome of our relationships. But, as we have already seen, learning results either in maintenance or in innovation (Botkin *et al.* 1979) of social practices and this depends on the actors concerned, so that we can transform the situation through our learning and acting since, as we have argued, individuals not only memorise but they think innovatively, critically, and so on. As Archer (2000: 307) says:

> Each new 'generation' of agents either reproduces or transforms its structural inheritance, but this heritage itself conditions their vested interests in doing so, their aspirations for stasis or change, the resources that they can bring to bear, and the strategies which are conducive to structural morphostasis or further morphogenesis.

Structure, however, is not a static phenomenon and over the ages social structures have loosened and society has become more open. In their different ways both Durkheim (1964 [1933]) and Toennies (1957) have demonstrated this: the former in his discussion from mechanical to organic solidarity and the latter from community to association. However, the process has continued since then, so it would now be possible to say that the process has resulted in some forms of individuation (Beck 1992; Beck and Beck-Gernsheim 2002).[4] There has been a concentration of the individual, individual rights, and so on. Beck (1992: 91) suggests that the 'notion of a class society remains useful only as a notion of the past' but he still acknowledges that this is an unequal world and that individuation in some ways exacerbates inequality (Beck and Beck-Gernsheim 2002: 46–50). Certain social forms such as the extended family play a less significant role and organised religion is no longer at the core of everyday life for most people. This does not deny the importance of social groups and organisations, only to say that individual actors have more freedom, within limits, than ever before to do their own thing. At the same time, the apparent loss of the concept of social class does present the notion that there is greater opportunity for individuals to move their position in the social structures – yet the extent to which they do so is a much more open question. Perhaps the idea of individualisation actually results in the loss of a valuable technique for demonstrating social inequality and that there still is a stasis in the social structures that relates to the idea of social class, especially at the lower echelons of society. Consequently, it might well be necessary to modify the simple Marxist notion of socio-economic class but it may not be advisable to replace it entirely with the notion of social networks since it is necessary to recognise that power is more diffuse because of the fact that it is vested in a much more amorphous grouping of people in society, only some of whom have come from the traditional upper classes. We can begin to detect this in the way the concept of 'education' is being replaced by that of 'learning', although the reasons for the change are more complex than merely a structural change, as we shall explore in the next chapter.

The point is that the person, the self, who has emerged through the process of learning, has the freedom either to act in accord with established social procedures or to innovate upon them through thinking about those disjunctural experiences that lead to learning and the ensuing action; that freedom comes through the interplay of thought, emotion and action. The significant aspect of this discussion is that the self, the person, who emerged in primary socialisation, becomes an agent – with will power – in future processes and acts back on the structures transforming them through learning and being transformed through the learning. It is through this sense of self that individuals have the freedom to think about their experiences rather than merely accept them and be changed by them.

In this sense, the debate about the relationship between agency and structure is one within which learning theory can help us understand the complexity of the process. Indeed, each major social theory presupposes specific theories of learning and in the final section of this chapter we will briefly explore this relationship.

Conclusion

Human learning is inextricably related to the ideas of agency and structure; it also reflects ideas of autonomy and free will and the more interactionist, or critical, the perspective adopted the easier it is to see the place of the human agent within the social context. Nevertheless, we are confronted with a major problem about the nature of the human being and this is reflected in Figures 1.1 and 1.2. It is clear that in Figure 1.1. persons are much more the outcome of the social processes and individuals are seen as fitting within their social context. However, Figure 1.2 assumes that the recipients of those sensations are people who are able to process them and control them to some extent. Hence we have introduced the concept of non-learning into our theory of lifelong learning. In all learning, however, the person is both being and becoming. But the real problem lies with the questions: When did the person become a self? When were the learners able to transcend their social surrounds and become agents? Were they always agents or did agency emerge as a result of learning?

It was argued in the first volume, following Mead (Strauss 1964), that the self emerges as a result of learning experiences (Figure 1.1) in which the mind stores the outcomes of the learning and orders them in such a way as to become critically independent of those experiences and learn from them in a variety of ways. At the same time, we recognised the significance of a metaphysical self over and above the psychological one. For Mead, however, it was through interaction with significant others and within the wider culture that the Me and then the self-identity are formed. He specifically endeavoured to eschew the religious implications of this approach, but this was also the question that Luckmann (1967) confronted when he argued that we become individuals when we learn to transcend our biological nature and that this is a profoundly religious event – an act of creation. It is at this point that we can recognise the metaphysical self. What is clear, however, is that during the early processes of maturation, individuals emerge who are more than just their experiences for they have emotions, commitments, values and beliefs that are not just reactions to their learning experiences (see also Archer 2000). The person is born and develops in and through relationship and continues to exist within the social context; more than nature and more than nurture – a self with inestimable value. But, significantly, one who is learned and who continues to learn throughout the whole of life.

Thus far, we have pointed to the fact that the social context of human learning is undergoing considerable change and so in the next chapter we will examine the global forces of social change which have been seen as globalisation.

Chapter 3

Human learning within a global context

In this third chapter we extend our discussion to the global context within which lifelong learning has emerged. Globalisation is itself about social change and so in the first section of this chapter we will examine the forces of social change, and then look at theories of globalisation and produce a model of the process.

Social change

Since the Industrial Revolution society has witnessed a gradual speeding up of social change and, in a real sense, education has been affected by each major change that has occurred. Indeed, it could be argued that without the Industrial Revolution there would have been little or no growth in education, although we have to recognise that education itself had been stimulated in European society by the churches which were, until that time, the core of society. It was their Christian understanding that pervaded a great deal of education and which remained the main rationale for its existence in Europe – this would also be true in many ways for Jewish and Muslim countries. However, the Industrial Revolution brought about major changes in society including a greater emphasis on technological production, work and rational knowledge. Toennies (1957; first published in German in 1887), writing in the nineteenth century, recognised that these changes were producing changes in human relationships which he described as a move from community to association: community being long lasting whilst association might be regarded as a 'society' which was more open and had more flexible social structures. It is perhaps not surprising that the term 'community' has subsequently become quite an ideological term idealising the past in some way, pointing to the type of society which was static and personal but one in which people could 'feel at home' – safe and secure. In the community individuals learned – usually through socialisation – the norms and mores of social living and then there was little need to learn a great deal more, apart from the fact that during the ageing process, *rites de passage* were practised in order to prepare individuals for their next role in the community and to give the community time to make the necessary adjustments.[1]

Prior to the Industrial Revolution, societies were local, predominantly agricultural. Their forms of knowledge were cultural and they were legitimated either by claims of revelation, or by the priestly, or priest-kingly, social hierarchy. Since the knowledge was cultural and changed slowly, it could be regarded as truth. This is a cyclical position, ultimately, where the cultural knowledge legitimates the social structures that, in turn, legitimate the knowledge! The social structures were fixed by decree and children were initially socialised into their position within them, but all the society's members continue to learn – maintenance learning – as Botkin *et al.* (1979) would assert. But as individuals aged they changed and their position within the static social structures also had to change. Most primitive societies recognise this transition and have 'rites de passage' (van Gennep, 1960 [1908]) which have three stages: a leaving of the initial social status, a period of liminality (betwixt and between) in which innovative learning occurs and a ritual of re-incorporation into the new status. These times of transition, for instance, are birth, from child to adult, single to married, married to widowhood and death. During the period of liminality the community was able to prepare itself for the change and, more significantly, it prepared those who were changing their status for their new role – in other words it is a time of learning. Liminality is a time when the participants have no fixed social status, it is a time of innovative learning since the initiands are free from the inhibiting elements of the social structure and they gradually acquire a new status, new role, new identity, and so on, which become integrated into their biography, or total life experience. During liminality those being initiated into their new position are excluded from the everyday life of the people and undergo a period of learning.

We quoted Turner's (1969: 81) description of this period for puberty in Chapter 2 (see p. 29); this liminal period is one of being prepared for the new status and role in society, which in its turn reinforces the social structures themselves and, as Turner (1969: 89–90) points out:

> The wisdom (*mana*) that is imparted in sacred liminality is not just an aggregate of words and sentences; it has ontological value, it refashions the very being of the neophyte . . .
> The neophyte in liminality must be *tabula rasa*, a blank sheet, on which is inscribed the knowledge and wisdom of the group, in those respects that pertain to the new status.

The humiliation that the neophytes undergo is a symbolic destruction of the previous status and identity and a preparation for their new position. Innovative learning is socially structured but offered within a 'safe' situation as far as the social group is concerned – beyond the structures of society.

It might be regarded as a sacred act that has its own specific set of pedagogics. This social exclusion is necessary because the structures of society are clearly defined and legitimated and are at risk as individuals pass through them, but all the knowledge learned during this period might still be regarded as cultural since it remains the same for succeeding generations. Once re-incorporated into the new status, the transformed individual conforms to the new role, and society and its structures are re-established and reinforced, and then maintenance learning is re-established.

Community living has been idealised though it might actually be a lifestyle which contemporary persons might find a little more claustrophobic than they would like. But it was Durkheim who argued that the changes in social structures were due to the division of labour (Durkheim 1964 [1933]) when he distinguished between mechanical and organic solidarity. The former was due to similarity but the latter was as a result of the division of labour. He also pointed towards a contractual form of solidarity which stemmed entirely from contract and was free of all regulation – which actually comes very close to today's society. Recognition of these fundamental changes in society also points us towards the fact that as society has become more open, so the individual has featured more centrally. There was, as it were, a process of individuation taking place over a period of a few hundred years. Now society is so open that Bauman (2000) can both describe it as 'liquid' and one in which he sees society as being something under siege and individualised. Clearly it is one in which the social demands for learning have changed out of all recognition! Now the important knowledge is scientific and is legitimated by pragmatism rather than a religion, and advertising is the new form of preaching/teaching designed to ensure that the liquid system survives intact and continues to grow.

In this society, the individual is more 'alone' in the world and structures, even in the deepest of relationships – such as marriage and the family, are becoming more transient. The individual takes precedence over the relationship – individual rights at times appear to be more significant than the demands of society; individual responsibility may be regarded as subservient to individual wants; information gained from people is more important than relating to them, and so on. Yet, through the use of information technology, especially the mobile telephone and e-mail, the ability to continue relationships of an associational kind at a distance is being recreated. It will be recalled from the opening chapter that Lukes's (2005) analysis of power pointed to a much more complex process of getting people to accept the domination of others rather than the exercise of coercion in a direct person-to-person type of relationship.

Traditionally, power was defined as an exercise of legitimate force and it was recognised that the State alone had the legitimate right to exercise such force so that power was seen as political. It was Marx who argued that the dominant elite had the ability to ensure that their ideas dominated so that power is not merely political or coercive and in the hands of the political elite. In this individualised, complex society, power is the ability to secure compliance – it is not just an unwilling compliance, but because we are individualised it is a desire to comply, to conform and be like all the other individuals with whom we are in association. Indeed, the loss of community has generated a desire to be like other people, to create a sense of common-ness which in its own way lends itself to responding to trends and being conscious of what the trendsetters are doing, wearing, eating, drinking, and so on. The exercise of this power, unsurprisingly in contemporary society, is frequently through technological means – such as advertising though televi-sion, through personal computers and even mobile phones. The control of that information technology is where a great deal of power lies and, again unsurprisingly, it rests to a considerable extent with producers of the com-modities that need to be consumed if the advanced capitalist enterprise is to survive intact.

A number of conclusions can be drawn from this analysis. First, because society is fluid and always changing, learning itself is changing and needs to become lifelong rather than recurrent at times of status change; lifelong learning is an individual necessity for all people, so that they can each play their roles in this rapidly changing society and feel part of it. It is only with disengagement from the wider society that people gradually attenuate the need for individual lifelong learning. Second, we can see from this perspec-tive that neither education nor learning is an initiator of social change but responsive to it. Having claimed this, it has to be recognised that when gov-ernment or education introduces a new policy or practice, it is frequently in response to perceived needs to the substructure. But, third, we each have the individual power to resist the exercise of the social pressures upon us, and if we resist them in any way we live in a state of tension with the wider society. There will be times when we conform and those, far less frequent, when we resist that temptation. In a sense, there are those who are more inner or tradition directed and those who are more other directed, as Reisman (1950) so tellingly reminded us, we live in a 'lonely crowd'. Seeking to be like others, as well as being invaded with biased information (advertising) about pro-ducts, we tend to 'go with the crowd' more often than perhaps we are 'true to ourselves'. But we do have that power to resist and so we are not mirrors of culture, even though we might all reflect a great deal of it and have much in common. Fourth, in this rapidly changing world, we are frequently in a state of disjuncture and so we are forced to learn, or to reject the opportunity to learn and learn to live in ignorance. But, as we will argue below, not every-thing changes rapidly although many things are made to appear out of date (past their sell-by date) by the power of the social forces for change. It is in this world that lifelong learning must be seen as crucial to everyday life – so that both individual and structural lifelong learning is necessary. Fifth, that the prevalence of information technology is one of the major causes for the realignment of both time and space in contemporary society, for we are now able to be in contact with people throughout the world almost instantaneously and travel around the world in a few hours, so that time and space are no longer major barriers to interpersonal relationships, or even to trading or aiding. But, also, these relationships do not always have to be instantaneous since we can access the World Wide Web at times convenient to ourselves, and so we can access past communications as well as present ones, and so on. Sixth, communities tended to be rather small societies; as nation states appeared societies grew in size and now, finally, we are talking about the world. Globalisation is a contemporary reality which must be at the heart of our understanding structural lifelong learning and the learning society, so that we now examine its meaning and the way that it functions.

Globalisation

Globalisation is a much-used word with a variety of meanings; we will use it here in a specific politic-socio-economic manner. Beck (2000:11) suggests that globalisation is 'the *processes* through which sovereign national states are criss-crossed and undermined by transnational actors with varying prospects of power, orientations, identities and networks' (italics in original). In this he distinguishes globalisation from the idea of the global. Friedman (1999: 7) makes the point that 'Globalization is not a phenomenon. It is not just some passing trend. Today it is the overarching international system shaping the domestic politics and foreign relations of virtually every country.' He claims that it has replaced the 'Cold War system' as the world order but what it is precisely is a more complex matter. There are a number of theories about globalisation and while it may be inappropriate to explore them in any depth here it is necessary to be aware of them. At the same time, it needs to be recognised that many of the definitions tend to omit the political implications of the process and, therefore, reach different conclusions about the process and, even more significantly for this study, different conclusions about the place of education within it. Sklair (1991: 27–36) suggested five classifications of theories of globalisation:

- imperialist and neo-imperialist;
- modernisation and neo-evolutionalist;
- neo-Marxist (including dependency theories);
- world system (and the new international division of labour theory);
- modes of production theory.

The imperialist theory argues that the major powers have struggled for new markets and opportunities to extend their political, cultural and economic influence (see Galtung 1971). The modernisation approach suggests that underdeveloped societies are constrained by their traditions whereas modern societies are able to reach beyond the tradition and this latter perspective has probably emerged as a result of the Industrial Revolution. This has enabled the modern societies to grow and develop since they are led by innovators, usually those whose cultural heritage stems from the Protestant Ethic (see Weber 1930). The most prominent form of neo-Marxist theory is the dependency theories. Sklair suggests that there are theories of dependent underdevelopment, dependent development and dependency reversal (see Bornschier 1980). Clearly these theories are closely linked to the imperialist theories. However, other neo-Marxist perspectives put less emphasis on dependency whilst still recognising its significance. Wallenstein's (1974) world system is one in which he argued for an international division of labour based upon a centre-periphery model of the world, but like the modernisation theory the significance of power is played down in the analysis. Finally, the mode of production theories argue that the reasons for underdevelopment lie in the countries themselves rather than in the position of the countries in relation to the global structures. In a way all of these recognise the centrality of the economic institution of society, although it is only the imperialist and Marxist models that focus on the power of those who control that institution. It is a combination of these that we now see as explaining adequately global power in contemporary society. All of them, however, offer some explanations that are valuable in seeking to understand the globalisation process.

Starting with a neo-Marxian perspective, we would want to argue that the economic institution alone no longer lies at the heart of globalisation since technology and information technology are now part of that core. Indeed, information technology has enabled the realignment of space and time. Together they form the major elements of the global substructure. In accepting this Marxian analysis of social structure, there is no implication that other aspects of Marxist theory are necessarily adopted here, such as the Hegelian dialectic or the emergence of the classless society. The combination of the economic institution and information technology points us in the direction of where global power lies, since it lies in considerable part with those who control both. Indeed, when this is combined with rapid transport systems, the world has been changed into a global village, although the term 'village' is also a little misleading since the world cultures are far less homogeneous than those of a single village. Even so, the imperialist approach has had considerable validity in the past decade since the USA has exerted itself as the single global imperial power. The relationship between the imperialism of the political and military might of America and those who control the economic and technology substructure is perhaps difficult to determine but it is clear that the two work hand in glove in many things, but whether the technical-economic substructure actually controls the USA's political and military activities is a more open question. Nevertheless, American imperialism upholds and supports the socio-technological substructure to such an extent that I would argue that it has become part of it but that this is but a temporary phase in the development of the world. Nevertheless, the capitalist system and the international division of labour do affect a great many of the countries of the world. In many ways, it is this dominance of American political and military might and the advanced capitalist culture that lead to a process of standardisation (Beck 1992) or 'McDonaldization' (Ritzer 1993).

Consequently, the concept of globalisation might best be understood as a socio-technological phenomenon having profound political and cultural implications. It is interesting to note that having discussed globalisation from an economic, political and cultural perspective, King (2004: 50) defines it in a non-economic and non-political way as 'a spatial concept within which time and space is compressed'. Such a definition removes any value judgements about the process. In the same book, Gibbons (2004: 101) suggests that globalisation is 'the imitation and adaptation of knowledge solutions, or innovations, as they are diffused from one country to another'. Such definitions omit major issues in the process and so the conclusions reached from such arguments are sometimes less than incisive. A more thorough examination of the process is called for and this is one of the purposes of this study.

From an oversimplistic perspective, globalisation can be understood by thinking of the *world* as having a substructure and a superstructure, whereas the simple Marxist model of society was one in which each *society* had its own substructure and a superstructure. For Marx, the substructure was the economic institution and the superstructure everything else in social and cultural life – including the state, culture, and so on. Those who owned the capital, and therefore the means of production, were able to exercise power throughout the whole of their society. But over the years the significance of ownership declined as more mechanisms to control un-owned capital have emerged. More recently, the capital has become intellectual as well as financial, over which the centre also seeks control (Prichard *et al.* 2000; Jarvis 2005a). However, one other major change has been that this substructure now includes technology, especially information technology. But, significantly, this substructure is not the substructure of a single society anymore – it is now the substructure of the entire world.

The process of globalisation has been supported by the political and military might of America – Americanisation. Consequently we can see global forces exercising standardising pressures on all societies. Once the power of the state has been seen to be diminished, as it has everywhere except in the USA, it is hardly surprising that the public recognises that politicians are forced to respond to the demands of the substructure, especially those of the large transnational companies whose economies are greater than those of many countries in the world. As a result the public begins to lose respect for its politicians, as the European Commission (EC 2001a) has recognised.[2] The politicians now talk of power sharing but few people who have power are prepared to share it unless they are forced to do so, and those who actually exercise considerable power behind the scenes care little for what others claim in public! If states and cultures are affected by this process, it becomes self-evident that the educational process is also affected by it and we will demonstrate some of these changes throughout this book.

Globalisation has at least two main elements: the first is the way that those who have control of the substructure in the countries of the dominant West, especially America, have been enabled to extend their control over the substructures of all the other countries in the world and consequently over their structures and resources; the second is the effects that these substructural changes are having on the superstructure of each society since the common substructure means that similar forces are being exerted on every people and society despite each having different histories, cultures, languages, and so on. This gives rise to both convergence and difference. The fact that it is not entirely a convergent argument is important since this is not a theory of over-determination or one of determinism itself since it recognises that states and national governments still exist and that they sometimes seek to oppose or modify the forces of globalisation. This approach is neo-Marxian rather than neo-Marxist – Marx's approach to structural analysis is adopted without assenting to every aspect of the Marxist ideology. Indeed, the approach adopted here is much more influenced by the social and prophetic values of Christianity and reflects these values;[3] before we can evaluate it we have to understand it which is the purpose of this study.

It is important to note here that economic competition – the market – is at the heart of the global substructure. It is the market competition that is a major factor in creating a fast moving world since every competitor, and not all are transnational corporations, has to sell its products in order to survive – a consumer society is inevitable in this situation. Consequently, we can see how the world has individualised and has become fluid. Globalisation and the focus on the global has, paradoxically, given rise to a re-emphasis on the local, which Robertson (1995) regarded as glocalisation. He tended to see this as something of a mutual balancing act between the global and the local, but as time passes it would be true to say that a variety of peoples and societies are resisting this process and its standardising effects by endeavouring, to differing extents, to retain their uniqueness and independence which has given rise to a different understanding of the phenomenon of glocalisation. The global–local relationship is now also one of tension since those who control the substructure seek to dominate the local cultures whereas some societies and cultures endeavour to retain their uniqueness. The global superstructure is now more like a latticework in which the various parts are fluid and changing as some lose their distinctiveness within the sea of change, whilst others fight to retain their difference. Hence the local cultures are 'liquid' in many ways but there is a stable substructure which, in its own way, is a major cause of the liquidity of contemporary society.

Factors contributing to globalisation

The process of globalisation, as we know it, has been revolutionary in that suddenly the speed of change has increased dramatically and new priorities and lifestyles have emerged. There have always been global processes and global aspirations; these were often expressions of military might and imperialist aspirations, such as the Greek and Roman empires, and those many other empires before them. As we have already noted, the imperialist aspiration is still a theory that has considerable support and it is one that we have incorporated into our argument here, when we consider the political and military power of the United States, but it took a number of factors occurring at approximately the same time to start off this process. Change is rarely, if ever, triggered by a single factor and so, before we actually examine the process itself, it is necessary to ask what occurred and why it occurred at this time in human history. The process of globalisation, as we know it today, began in the West (USA followed by Western Europe) in the early 1970s, which is the period of post-Fordism, when it was beginning to be recognised that the modern period was, in some way, being superseded by new developments in a period generally referred to as late or postmodernity. There were a number of contributory factors at this time which speeded up this process, such as:

- the nature of capitalism itself and the need to make a profit on commodities produced;
- the recognition that modernity itself was being questioned;
- the oil crisis in the 1970s, which dented the confidence of the West;
- the demise of the Bretton Woods Agreement, that eventually led to the General Agreement on Tariffs and Trade (GATT), enabled both free trade and the flow of financial capital to develop throughout the world;
- the prevalence of the idea of the minimal state and of neo-liberal economics allowed for power to pass from the State to the capitalist institution;
- the development of sophisticated information technology through the Star Wars programme, through which the information technology revolution took off, with one development leading to another, as Castells (1996: 51f.) demonstrates. He (1996: 52) makes the point that 'to some extent, the availability of new technologies constituted as a system in the 1970s was a fundamental basis for the process of socio-economic restructuring in the 1980s'.
- the economic competition from Japan, which challenged the West;
- using scientific knowledge in the production of commodities in the global market;
- the fall of the Berlin Wall – the democratisation of the Eastern Bloc – for, from the time it occurred, there has literally been 'no alternative'

(Bauman 1992) to global capitalism or comparable political opposition to the USA and so it reinforced the process.

I do not want to spend time here expounding each of these because that would detract us from the primary purpose of this study – the examination of lifelong learning and the learning society. However, we do see that during the immediate decades after the Second World War, especially after the demise of the Bretton Woods Agreement, corporations began to relocate manufacturing and to transfer capital around the world, seeking the cheapest places and the most efficient means to manufacture, and the best markets in which to sell their products. They were being forced to do this because of the loss of Western confidence, when the oil crisis demonstrated that the West was vulnerable to those who controlled oil production, and because, as the Japanese economy took off, the West realised that it would be forced to compete with another very efficient economic enterprise. This process was exacerbated in the Thatcher–Reagan era by the belief in a minimal state (Nozick 1974) and through the process of privatisation not only of companies but of public assets, such as water. It was perhaps not recognised by many who supported this process that it was not just a transfer of economic processes 'for the sake of efficiency' but it was also providing a power base for those corporations which were given ownership of public assets. Corporations were able to use the functions that the State had specified to build up their own power base and as they have expanded so they have become the transnational corporations that form the substructure of the global world. Privatisation was, thereafter, quite central to the economic policies of the World Bank. With the fall of the Berlin Wall, the USA remained the only superpower; as its governments have been inextricably intertwined with the large multinational corporations, it has lent political and military might to support the capitalist system, which in turned furthered its own imperialist aspirations.

Hence we see that one of the driving forces of the capitalist market was, in one way or another, to conquer the whole world: the market is not a level playing field and so those who can control the market through production and retailing already exercise considerable power in the world. At the same time, we are seeing that the global forces do not always operate in an unopposed manner – there are some regulating forces that we will examine in the next chapter and again towards the end of the book.

The globalisation process

In order to understand how the substructure can exert a standardising effect on the world and yet each country retain something of its own independence, even something of its own sovereignty, Figures 3.1 and 3.2 depict the way in which the global world may be understood. The significance of

Substructure

Multilayered superstructure

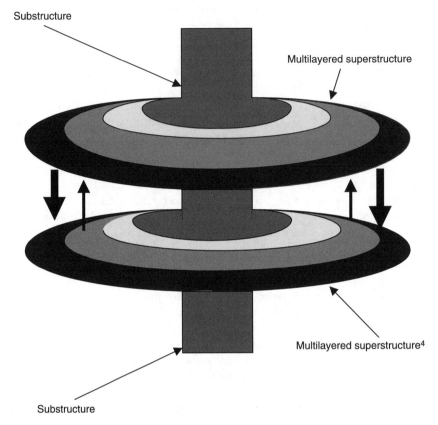

Multilayered superstructure[4]

Substructure

Figure 3.1 **A global model of societies.**

the model in Figure 3.1 is that there is a global substructure represented here by the core running through all the different countries – it exercises a centralised power over each of the countries and, in this sense, it is a force for convergence between the different countries of the world. It consists, first, of the economic system but also of the technological one, especially information technology. Those who control it exercise global power and that control rests with large transnational corporations whose directors are unelected and very powerful throughout the world through the power they exercise in controlling their companies. But these forces are supported by the one superpower, the USA, and so it would be possible to place the USA at the top of the hierarchy of countries, represented by the hierarchical multicoloured discs, or as part of the substructure. I personally regard the USA as part of the global substructure, at this moment in history, although its position could change with the growth of China, and maybe India. Power, then, resides in the global substructure but it can also be exercised between countries through political, trade, aid and other international mechanisms.

The large downward pointing arrows illustrate that there is a relationship of power between the 203 countries of the world (this is the number recorded by UNESCO 2006), while the two small upward pointing arrows depict the resistance to the forces of globalisation. However, it would be true to say that there are probably blocks of countries at different levels of the global power structure, with the G8 countries being the most powerful stratum. However, the global meeting point for these economic and techno-logical forces is the World Economic Forum held in Davos, in Switzerland, in the winter (ski season!) each year. In Figure 3.1 each layer represents a country which is penetrated through the centre by the substructure, and each country can be represented by Figure 3.2. It would have been quite possible to put a few more circles around the layers to illustrate the complexity of the whole but, for the sake of clarity, we have retained a simpler model. At the same time, we have depicted the layers hierarchically in order to illustrate that, it is not merely a geographical matter, there is also a hierarchy of power stemming from the core to the periphery. It has to be recognised that power is not a one-way process since, by the nature of democracy, the 'lower orders' can and should be proactive as well, and we are also aware of passive resistance amongst individuals to the pressures coming from the hierarchy. Naturally, individuals can exercise more power but only within an

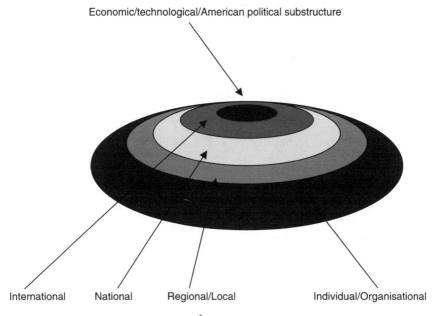

Figure 3.2 Multilayered model of society.[5]

organisational context in one of the other layers of society. However, we can see that individuals' social position and the power that they can exercise within society as a result depends to some extent on their relation to the substructure. This is neither a determinist position nor is it a simple class one since society is so much more open than it was when Marx wrote.

The first thing to note about these two diagrams is that the substructure is united and runs through all the different countries. We must also recognise that there are over two hundred countries, and so the four layers here depict only a few of the many, that have to negotiate between themselves in order to co-operate. Now this core is united in a manner that the individual countries are not – it runs through each making similar demands on each – as Beck (2000) puts it, it criss-crosses national boundaries. At the same time as there is an apparent unity of the core, there is also internal competition since each transnational company that makes up the core is competing with every other one in order to produce products that can be marketed throughout the world. The fact that there is internal competition means that the speed of change within the core is fast, driven by the demands of the market which it is both creating and to which it is seeking to respond. It is, therefore, changing faster than those aspects of the global system that are not so market-driven. Additionally, it is necessary to recognise that change is neither gradual nor even, since new discoveries tend to generate change in fits and starts. At the same time, change itself has profound effects on lifelong learning, as we shall see below.

The second fact to recognise is that these companies, and this technological-economic core, are protected by the political and military might of America and the institutions over which it exercises hegemonic control – such as the World Bank and the International Monetary Fund (IMF). There is considerable confusion within America itself between the core and the political – this confusion has been exacerbated during the presidency of George W. Bush whose government does not always seem entirely divorced from the corporate sector and seems always to act in favour of the economic system of the core. The third factor to note is that because the core controls information technology, as well as technology for production, and so on, it has the power to advertise its products globally and generate both a huge market for its products but also to produce a considerable degree of standardisation across the globe. Fourth, each society is a separate entity and, consequently, co-operation between countries/states is a matter of political negotiation and agreement, something that takes time – as the working of the United Nations (UN) and the European Union (EU) show. However, I have shown a separate international layer since it is not only governments which act internationally but also non-governmental organisations. Nevertheless, it is clear that countries are less able to change as rapidly as the global core and so there is almost an international global situation of 'divide and rule', with the global core exercising a degree of dominance. This means that the law, democracy and civil society are all exposed to a source of power other than the State – that of the global market; a transnational civil society is still a long way from reality, even though we live in a world society (Beck 2000). Habermas (2001: 61) suggests that: 'There is a crippling sense that national politics have dwindled to more or less intelligent management of a process of forced adaptation to the pressure to shore up purely local positional advantages.'

The fifth factor to recognise is that some societies are more accessible to this process than others, so that social change does not spread completely evenly across the globe, with countries like those of sub-Saharan Africa and Nepal not able to respond to the changes at the same speed as does the United Kingdom, and so on. These poorer countries get poorer whilst the richer ones prosper – indeed, enticing them into the World Trade Organisation (WTO) may not be altogether beneficial to them in the long run since they lose their own protection against the might of the global powers. However, it should also be noted that even in the first world, the poor continue to be excluded and get poorer. In the USA, for instance, 16.5 per cent of the population live in poverty, 20 per cent of the adult population are illiterate and 13 per cent have a life expectancy of shorter than 60 years, according to Bauman (1999) citing a United Nations development report. In the UK, 17 per cent of the population live below the low income threshold (*Social Trends 2006*: 79–80) and the most deprived 10 per cent of the population have a life expectancy six years lower than those of the least deprived 10 per cent (*Social Trends 2006*: 100). In a sense, then, we can see that the core is the driving force of each society, to some degree or other, but we have to recognise that within the national and local cultures there are both wider interests and concerns than those to be found in the core and also in some instances a degree of resistance to the changes that are occurring and these are to be found at every level, including the international.

We can see that each country relates to others and although Figure 3.1 has depicted only two countries, we could have put over two hundred different ones in relation to each other. The external arrows now take on major significance because they represent unequal relationships between each country. For instance, the dominant downwardly pointing arrow represents trade, aid, consultations, and so on. The development of information technology, rapid travel, and so on means that people throughout the world are much more aware of what occurs elsewhere and are much more able to affect it. It is possible, therefore, for people at different levels in the hierarchy to communicate across national boundaries electronically and to travel rapidly and cheaply between different countries, so that there is inter-cultural sharing. Nevertheless, there may be more giving by the more powerful to the less powerful countries. In this way it still depicts a hegemonic relationship in which the dominant cultures of the West still export their culture and

commodities through a different mechanism. At the same time, the less dominant cultures have more opportunity to resist the process and have more
chances of retaining their independence. The relationships that exist at this
level are more diplomatic and interactive, and open, on occasions, for the less
powerful cultures to export aspects of their culture to more dominant cultures – much of this comes through international migration of people in
search of employment and the better life, although we know others flee from
political persecution, and so on. Hence the second, smaller arrow upwards in
the diagram illustrates this process.

That there can be some cultural exchange is important and through this
political mechanism there is greater respect for cultural diversity than there is
through the change that is introduced through the global technical-economic
substructure. Respect for individual cultures still plays a significant role in
the political trade and aid relationship. Such a relationship calls for informed
dialogue (Crossley 2006) between countries enabling the bridging of cultures
and a greater exercise in relationship.

As we can see, power need not be exercised in a simple one-dimensional
form, but that there are three dimensions; Lukes (2005: 29) suggests that
the three-dimensional view of power means that it can be exercised over
decision-taking and by controlling the political agenda, over issues and
potential issues, in observable and latent conflict, and in subjective and real
interests. It is in these different ways that the substructure (core) exercises
power over super-structure (the international, national, local and individual):
in the same way the national does the same over the local and the individual,
and the local over the organisational and individual. Consequently, countries
can still be studied as individual entities and we can see how hierarchical
power results in social and cultural reproduction, and education has traditionally played a major role in this process. For instance, Bourdieu (1973:
84) wrote:

> By making social hierarchies and the reproduction of these hierarchies
> appear to be based upon the hierarchy of 'gifts', merits or skills estab-
> lished and ratified by its sanctions, or, in a word, by converting social
> hierarchies into academic hierarchies, the educational system fulfils a
> function of legitimation which is more and more necessary to the per-
> petuation of the 'social order' as the evolution of the power relationship
> between classes tends more completely to exclude the imposition of a
> hierarchy based upon the crude and ruthless affirmation of the power
> relationship.

At the same time, individuals know that they have the ability to resist the
social pressures if they have the confidence, courage, commitment, and so
on – they are also able to forms groups and organisations that can do the
same, as studies of social movements demonstrate.

From Figures 3.1 and 3.2 we can begin to outline a theory of social change. The capitalist competition within the substructure generates change in the levels of knowledge, technology and, ultimately, commodities, work patterns and lifestyle. This spreads through each country affected by the globalisation process. There is a standardisation effect, although countries at the periphery of the global process – poor countries and those dominated by religious systems that have not been exposed to the Industrial Revolution – are more likely to resist the standardisation process that the global substructure generates. At the same time, within each country the powerful still dominate and introduce change either through democratic or through non-democratic means and the more that the powerful are exposed to the global process the more they might try to introduce change, although it is possible that they may simply cut themselves off from the remainder of the population and live their Western lifestyle without too much reference to the people and their culture. However, at the political level there is still dialogue and debate about cultural diversity, but even here the more powerful are likely to dominate and their cultures transported to lesser powerful countries, although there is some opportunity for cultural sharing. However, there is resistance to cultural standardisation both within and between countries, so that social movements have been formed that seek to resist both globalisation and cultural standardisation. In other words, power does not flow smoothly from the top of the hierarchy to lower levels and there is always tension between the levels that in previous times were depicted through class relations. Now the tensions might not only be socio-economic class based but intercultural, and this gives rise to new social movements that seek to resist the process and, unfortunately, international tension that on occasions has manifest itself in both terrorist activities and the so-called war against terror which might be perceived as a war between fundamentalist factions in the West (Christian) and the Middle East (Muslim).

Factors influencing the globalisation process

As we have seen, the core partly comprises transnational corporations and other companies seeking to produce and sell their commodities in the global market, and it exercises power and control through foreign investment in a country. Consequently, it is necessary to determine what factors influence these corporations to invest in any society and we want to suggest ten fundamental reasons:

- opportunity to acquire land/plant cheaply;
- an efficient infrastructure, such as good transport systems;
- a relatively stable government;
- the proximity of raw materials;
- low taxation and wages – which would include weak trades unions;

- cheap and efficient means of production;
- educated workforce;
- flexible workforce which can easily be retrained;
- opportunities for continuing education for workers;
- a market to sell products.

Clearly such investment is welcome to many countries since it brings in foreign capital, provides jobs and the money earned by the workers has a multiplier effect throughout local communities. Consequently, initial investment may be regarded as a considerable advantage to many poorer countries, so that national governments are prone to offer inducements to large corporations to invest capital and expertise – often those inducements include the opportunity to acquire land cheaply, or freely, and the assurance that an efficient infrastructure is in place. However, once a corporation has invested in a country it is able to exercise more power than that which the original investment would have merited since threats to withdraw investment and move it elsewhere put many more jobs in the local area at risk than those provided by the corporation itself. Being seen as a cause of unemployment would make a democratically elected government, local or national, unpopular which, in turn, might jeopardise its chances of retaining power in future elections. Consequently, governments, national and local, are often caught on the horns of a dilemma – either to give in to the demands of the core or to respond to the local people's demands at the risk of alienating the powers of the substructure. Governments frequently bow to the demands of the sub-structural forces even though these are actually opposed by the local population who have other priorities for their areas (Monbiot 2000). If they do not give in, then the companies might move the operations elsewhere to the economic detriment of the local area, but if governments do acquiesce then they are accused of not listening to the local people. When this occurs, the population eventually becomes cynical about politicians and the power they exercise, as the European Commission has recognised. Indeed, the European Commission's White Paper on governance tells us that:

> Today, political leaders throughout Europe are facing a real paradox. On the one hand, Europeans want them to find solutions to the major problems confronting our societies. On the other hand, people increasingly distrust institutions and politics or are simply not interested in them.
>
> (EC 2001a: 3)

The paper might have also added that the politicians are also distrusted. Consequently we see how a great deal of power has been transferred from the political process to the economic. Marx was correct when he recognised this in the nineteenth century but now the process is much more overt and transparent.

In contrast, those societies that are unable to meet these demands lose out: the corporations do not invest in them. It is the law of the market that the rich get richer and the poor poorer.[6] Although it is beyond the scope of this study to discuss most of the above points fully, four are central to this book:

- low taxation since it means that governments do not have the finance to offer a welfare state or even to fund the lifelong learning necessary for this form of society to exist;
- an educated workforce which must, therefore, impinge upon initial education;
- a flexible workforce which can easily be retrained;
- opportunities for continuing education for workers.

What is significant about these, however, is that the substructure in any country excludes both the workings of national governments and the education system which is organised by the State. Tension must exist between the substructure and the national governments which also have loyalties to their populations and so it is hardly surprising that politicians talk of power sharing even though actually they do not have the power to be able to act independently of the sub-structural forces of society.

The political process, however, is even less deterministic than this since democracy demands respect for cultural diversity and dialogue. Through the sharing of problems it is possible to generate new forms of knowledge and new answers to major problems, so that while there is still a trickle-down cultural effect, there is also the respect of difference and so standardisation is not the response to every situation. In some way the political process has to accommodate the standardisation effects of economic globalisation which generates a covert tension between the two which many political documents choose to ignore.

Conclusion

In this chapter we have demonstrated how globalisation has spread throughout the world since the Second World War and we have produced a model of the process in which we demonstrate something of the interrelationship between nation states and the power of the global corporations. It is now necessary to examine the outcomes of this process and to some extent we will concentrate on the outcomes of the sub-structural processes in the next chapter.

Chapter 4

Outcomes of the globalisation process

If the substructure always determined the shape of the superstructure there would be absolute standardisation, but this has not occurred. Clearly, as we saw in the last chapter, governments do seek to attract capital in order to enrich their own countries and once this process begins, since there is a common core, there is a good likelihood there will be a degree of standardisation between countries in the superstructure. In our everyday experience we are aware of the same products, the same shops and the same brands almost wherever we go in the world. But we are also aware of cultural differences, that there are people fighting to preserve cultural diversity and seeking to oppose the process of globalisation by active demonstration. We are also aware that national governmental policies rarely reinforce uncritically the global pressure; rather they try to modify them or avert them in some way. In this chapter we will examine some of the outcomes of globalisation and we will then look at the way that States have tried to regulate the 'free market' and have even resisted some of the globalising tendencies. In addition, we have to recognise that governments' briefs are much wider than those of the global corporations so that with their different policies and ideologies the inevitable result will be difference – even though they will always recognise the power, often covert, of the substructure. In the final section of this chapter we will show how the globalisation process has affected education.

The outcomes of globalisation

In order to analyse both forms of lifelong learning and the learning society sociologically, we need to highlight some of the more relevant outcomes of the globalisation process and I want to do so under five sub-headings: economic, technological, political (the substructure in Figure 3.2), cultural and ecological.

Economic

Marx always argued that the state was controlled by those who exercised economic power and there is a real sense in which this situation has been exacerbated by the global processes. Now the transnational corporations exercise such power. These corporations may be defined as being those that produce goods and services in more than one country. Held *et al.* (1999: 237) suggest that the transnational corporation is in 'its narrowest sense . . . an enterprise which, through foreign direct investment . . . controls and manages subsidiaries in a number of countries outside its home base'. In other words, through investment it exercises power in different countries. Some analysts (see Korten 1995; Monbiot 2000) see some of the larger corporations as world powers in their own right; this power has not been ceded to the corporations democratically but obtained through the mechanism of the market. Indeed, Robinson (1996: 20–1, cited in McLaren 2005: 85) claimed in 1996 that some '400 transnational corporations own two-thirds of the planet's fixed assets and control 70 per cent of world trade'. And in order to extend this economic power, transnational corporations co-operate with repressive regimes to the detriment of some people's human rights. Allen (2006: 8) writes: 'The internet is big business, but in the search of profits some companies have encroached on their own principles and those on which the internet was founded: free access of information'. Basically she maintains that although these Internet firms argue that it is better for them to exist and to be censored than for them not to exist at all in these non-democratic countries, it is an argument that she cannot accept. For the purpose of my argument here, this merely illustrates both the power that corporations have and the lengths to which they will go to increase their own profits. This does not mean, however, that all economic power resides in the large corporations because, as we have already suggested, there is an openness in the competitive market that encourages innovation and, therefore, small and medium capitalist enterprises to take their place within it and governments exercise power over a wider spread of private and public life than do the corporations – albeit always influenced by them.

Nevertheless, where the transnational corporations have invested capital, it has immediate beneficial effects in providing employment for the local population who can then spend their earnings on other commodities. Consequently, there is both an increased standard of living and more wealth for a greater number of people. At the same time, since corporations own so much capital, they can never be ignored in the policy debates of the countries in which they are involved. Moreover, they exercise tremendous influence over populations because if they, and the market, are to survive and grow, as many people as possible are needed to purchase the commodities that are offered. Without sales there will be an economic recession and with it the possibility that the market will collapse. Often we hear phrases like 'consumer-led recovery', but while this indicates the potential power of consumers, at present they are disorganised and disunited and controlled through the power of advertising, and so on. By contrast, the market is proactive in creating sales through advertising – as Baudrillard (1988: 38), summarising Galbraith, says:

> the fundamental problem of contemporary capitalism is . . . a contradiction between a virtually unlimited productivity (at the level of the technostructure) and the need to dispose of the product. It becomes vital for the system at this stage to control not only the mechanism of production, but also the consumer demand.

Baudrillard goes on to argue that needs are produced as part of the system and are not a 'relation between an individual and an object' (p. 42). Basically consumption is a necessary part of the production process – and it must be total consumption, so that more demand can be created and the system can continue to function and even to expand. In this sense, the system creates the desires in the consumers that it needs and this process is now a global one. The same products can be purchased at the same retail outlets in the greater majority of countries of the world – this is the 'McDonaldization thesis' (Ritzer 1998). Ritzer shows how there are new products that need to be consumed – but not all the new products are standardised. The idea of 'tailor-made' products and niche markets shows that new companies can break into the market and produce their own brands and products. Nevertheless, there is a pressure to standardise all the products and above all there are a number of standardised ways of advertising and selling them. Mass production has created mass selling and mass consumption; in precisely the same way, production produces consumption as much, or even more, than consumption generates production.

But the market is not a level playing field; it is not good for everyone. Corporations do not invest in those countries that do not fulfil the criteria outlined in Chapter 3, and so those countries that receive no investment get comparatively poorer. In the same way, not everyone can afford to play their allotted role as consumers in the more wealthy countries and so the poor in every country get poorer. But as we live in an individualised society, so the blame for the poverty is no longer placed upon the structures of society but on those who have not 'exercised' their responsibility to acquire the necessary learning to be employable – 'why should they receive handouts?' is an often-heard denunciation of the poor in the more wealthy countries, and those in the poorer countries are accused of being lazy and unprepared for work. As Bauman (1998: 38) puts it:

> In a society of consumers, it is above all the inadequacy of the person as a consumer that leads to social degradation and 'internal exile'. It is

this inadequacy, this inability to acquit oneself of a consumer's duties that turns into bitterness at being left behind, disinherited or degraded, shut off or excluded from the social feast to which others gained entry. Overcoming that consumer inadequacy is likely to be seen as the only remedy – the sole exit from a humiliating plight.

This is a global phenomenon – it is not only individuals, it is peoples and nations that are in the same situation: the greater part of sub-Saharan Africa, much of the South in general and the poor underclass of whatever colour or creed in first world countries, and so on. A large proportion of humanity is excluded from the benefits of the industrialisation process. It is the transnational corporations which are engaged in this process of creating consumers that gain enormous wealth and power in the global world and the flip side of the coin is that they aid the creation of the poor.

That such power lies with these transnational corporations raises considerable political difficulties. We have already referred to the fact that these corporations have weakened the power of states and politicians but they have become a major force in our thinking about citizenship and democratic politics as a whole, and these are points to which we will return below – but now we need to look at the second of the three elements of the substructure

Technology and information technology

While capital might provide the motive for the sub-structural domination, it is the technology that provides the means through which this is achieved. There are at least three ways in which this is done: through generating the necessary knowledge for new products, or for new versions of existing ones; through providing the necessary knowledge to ensure that the production process is both efficient and cheap – and, consequently, this form of knowledge also includes the necessary social science knowledge to ensure that the production processes are organised efficiently; and through providing ways by which the products can be advertised and the desire to purchase can be stimulated. Technological knowledge is a significant factor in this process.

It is clear that underlying technology and information technology is at the heart of the practical knowledge that makes production and the global transmission of information possible. Control of both the knowledge and the capital to produce the commodities for the market underlie this society and, increasingly, control of the research that generates the knowledge is important. The ability to travel around the globe rapidly also generates the sense that we now live in a united world, even though the political laws have not yet caught up with the laws of the market.

Political

Since the fall of the Berlin Wall there has only been one superpower – the USA. In the past decade, the USA has exerted its military and political might almost at will and even when its friends have not always supported it, it has still gone ahead. It might well be claimed that the fall of the Wall was itself a victory for capitalism over central planning, but what has also happened is the continued expansion of global capitalism to that part of the world where it had previously not had free access. At the same time, the American cultural hegemony has been extended significantly and it may now be placed within the global substructure, as we have done in Figure 3.2. In contrast, Europe has embarked upon 'an unfinished adventure' (Bauman 2005b) to create a more united and harmonious continent while trying, but not succeeding, in keeping up with the rest of the world (Kok 2004). But Europeanisation, a process of generating international forces within the countries of Europe, has also necessarily weakened the strength of each individual nation state as it cedes some of its power to the central European system in Brussels. Being 'betwixt and between' means that Europe cannot devote all its energies in one direction or another, and so it is not the superpower that it might clearly be if it were a united nation nor is it able to compete with the might of America. The heart of Europe is still the common market although, just gradually, it is inching towards greater things. Consequently, we see that the third dimension of the substructure and intimately intertwined with the other two is the American political and military state.

At the same time, the globalisation process has neither destroyed the State nor local government; indeed, while they have had their economic powers reduced as the advanced capitalist global forces criss-cross (Beck 2000: 11) their borders, the nation states still exercise political power. This power is often exercised in support of the economic substructure but it also seeks to regulate the activities of the market, and in other spheres of public life the State still takes its own initiatives so that there is a sense of limited sovereignty. Many of these initiatives will be supportive of the substructure whilst others will not. It is, however, sometimes hard to prove when the State has been the handmaiden of capitalism and when it has been its regulator.

Culture

In many discussions about culture in this period reference is made to postmodernism. Overall, postmodernism refers primarily to the Arts and as such we will not discuss it here. We do, however, live in a period of late modernity, rather than postmodernity – a modern world generated by advanced capitalism. This is a world in which many cultural institutions have become industries in which as they market their own products they also 'sell' their own culture in a wide variety of ways. The market has not only generated consumers and new products; it has transformed traditional institutions into marketable products, with education and health care and welfare being amongst the most significant. It has also changed our language, and with it our understanding of these institutions; for example, the more privileged travellers in trains and planes travel in the business class, education is now a product, the education and health care institutions are now industries and people are now resources and even capital. In this we can see how the sub-structure of global society is commodifying cultural phenomena and colonising language and thereby generating a culture which people learn to treat as objective reality but it is also the culture which the young will learn and internalise during their primary socialisation and then take for granted. Baudrillard (Poster 1988: 32) describes this process thus:

> The cultural center becomes . . . an integral part of the shopping mall. This is not to say that culture is here 'prostituted'; that is too simple. It is *culturalized*. Consequently, the commodity (clothing, food, restaurant, etc.) is culturalized, since it is transformed into a distinctive and idle substance, a luxury, and an item, among others, in the general display of consumables.
>
> (italics in original)

Education and learning materials are to be found amongst these consumables. This is the consumer culture that is produced by the advanced capitalism underlying the global process. It is important to note that if the product is to be sold worldwide, i.e. for mass consumption, then it has to be attractive to the majority of potential purchasers which means that minority interests will not necessarily be catered for and so there is a sense in which global capitalism must be opposed to, or uninterested in, any form of minority or elite phenomenon – a point to which we will return when we examine lifelong learning as a commodity. However, this consumer culture is not only capitalist, it is also largely American. As America is dominant politically and economically, it might be claimed that the process of globalisation has become one of Americanisation. Clearly the dominance of American culture can be found through the mass media transmitting many American television programmes and characters in the American English language, as well as advertising American products and the American way of life – despite Bloom's (1987) *The Closing of the American Mind*. These concerns are echoed by Furedi (2004) who has incisively argued that there are philistine attitudes towards culture in this world of instrumentalism: he actually suggests that there is a cult of banality. It is certainly a society where celebrities are celebrated and experts are neglected in the world of competences.

Yet, all of the remainder of the world does not necessarily embrace such a culture with open arms, as we can see from protests against globalisation and even bigger political and terrorist threats by those who oppose this way. Part of the end of history debate is recognition that there is not a single history of the world, that each society has its own history and its own culture and what we are now seeing is that there is a gradual colonisation of many aspects of different societies' cultures into the Western way, especially in economic and technological spheres, but that some indigenous cultures and histories are fighting – sometimes unsuccessfully – to retain their own identity. Local cultures are affecting the spread of Western culture but simultaneously they are being affected by the encroaching culture being carried by the forces of globalisation. This is also leading to local cultures rediscovering themselves and fighting to emphasise their own distinctiveness – this we see in the way that fundamentalism has reasserted itself in both the Middle East (Muslim) and the West – especially the USA (Christian) – but in an age of migration these are asserting themselves in host countries, such as parts of Europe and potentially America. In these situations we see the potential conflict inherent in cultural differences when one culture encroaches upon another.

Barber (2003: xii), for instance, calls societies that have adopted the knowledge and beliefs of late modern society 'McWorld' – 'integrative modernism and aggressive economic and cultural globalization' – whereas those societies that still espouse the characteristics of primitive societies he calls 'Jihadic', which he defines as 'disintegral tribalism and reactionary fundamentalism' (p. xii). Consequently, it is possible to describe all forms of religious fundamentalism as Jihadic and, therefore, American fundamentalists, for instance, might be regarded as a combination of both McWorld and Jihadic, since such individuals act in different sectors of the same society simultaneously. Hence they learn from different social situations and have different experiences, and people are free to choose from which social situation they learn at any time, but with those who espouse fundamentalist religion, the religious setting may take precedence. In McWorld, innovative types of learning are located within the boundaries of a dominant scientific knowledge, whilst in the Jihadic, maintenance learning and cultural forms of knowledge legitimated by religion and revelation are the more significant.

Clearly the Jihadic movements in Jihadic societies have opposed both globalisation and McWorld, with all its artificial forms of knowledge and innovative learning and all the economic exploitation and social inequalities that have accompanied the neglect of cultural forms of knowledge. While some of these countries tolerate the situation because they are powerless to do anything about it – or even because some countries, like India for instance, are benefiting from it; others have declared war on McWorld, and we see the growth of what we, in the West, define as terrorist activities. However, late modern society is now a segmented society and some people may have both McWorld and Jihadic responses to it. When the late modern societies respond in a tolerant manner it may lead to innovative learning and responses to the situation but when it responds in a Jihadic fashion, because those in power choose this response, whatever the excuse they give for it, we have a holy war, or a 'war on terror'.

Ecological

Corporations need to get raw materials at the cheapest cost and to produce their commodities in the cheapest and the most efficient manner if they are to get high returns on the capital that has been invested. Consequently, they plunder the world's resources for raw materials, often with little or no respect (despite their claims) for either the people who live in the land or for the land itself. Then through the processes of production they pollute the atmosphere and help destroy the ozone layer. Such activities have caused some seriously minded people to question the very future of humanity (see Grayling 2004: 221–9). Governments try to intervene and regulate the activities of these corporations but their success has been limited, despite the publicity about the ecological dangers that these activities are causing.

Regulators and resistance to globalisation

The mere fact that politicians talk of power sharing illustrates the fact that they recognise that they no longer have sovereign power – as realists, they recognise that the dominant power lies with those who control the global substructure. Nevertheless, the states have not disappeared entirely despite the fact that, as Beck has shown, their boundaries are open to be criss-crossed by the dominant economic forces. The strength of the global forces resides in an unregulated free market, but in their different ways governments have tried to regulate it, and in this sense they act as resistors slowing down the onward spread of global capitalism – what at present appears to be an inevitable trend. But in only a few instances has a government opposed its spread since it brings immense benefits to some but by no means all the people in their countries – wealth, employment, health, enriched lifestyle, and so on. Some countries, like the UK, have claimed to have adopted a 'third way' which in the first instance seemed to offer a middle route between socialism and Thatcherist neo-liberalism – but it is really quite hard to discover how the UK's 'third way' has affected the exercise of the economic power of the substructure or even prevented its colonising a wider sector of society. Indeed, it could be claimed that the UK is continuing to be colonised by free-market capitalism and that New Labour is but another manifestation of neo-liberalism.

However, power does not reside absolutely in the global economic system and as we have seen earlier in this book it is a complex and diffuse phenomenon, found in every layer of society. In the first of these levels, power resides in those few organisations that transcend the state – UNESCO and the European Union, and so on, and they are free to present and pursue policies that make little or no reference to the power of the sub-structure, although some times such policies do appear either as idealistic or unrealistic.

The second level is the nation state, which continues to exist but without complete sovereignty. In Europe, for instance, some degree of power has also been ceded to the EU by each member state – but neither the state no the EU has the power to resist the economic might of the advanced capitalist system. Nevertheless, they do seek to regulate activities within their territories – they have control of both the military and legal forces, plus the control of many of the health and welfare functions of the society. Unlike the substructure, there is a degree of democracy at this level with politicians being voted into office in regulated elections. But as the economic system in advanced capital-ist society is not entirely divorced from the political or social systems, politi-cians then can exercise power to regulate the market or, on the other hand, they can fight for an open and unregulated market – which gives those who are beneficiaries of the free market even more opportunity to benefit in the distribution of scarce resources since the market, while open, is not equit-able. Nevertheless, the government in most societies is not powerless, even though there are times when it is unable to resist the powers of the unregulated market forces of global capitalism. However, governments often collude with the corporations in order to give them greater opportunities to exercise their businesses – often in the face of the people's protests. Monbiot (2000) goes further than the argument of this chapter and sees governments as 'captive states', but if it is captivity it is in an open prison!

In the same manner, regional and local governments also exist and they have certain delegated powers from the national government. They also serve as a focus for the local community and are supporters of many of the initia-tives to rediscover local culture. Consequently, we can see how globalisation has helped re-focus upon the local. Local government powers are carefully regulated and in recent years in the UK some of their functions, such as the control of education, have been removed by national government and some of it given to businesses both in owning and running schools, serving on governing boards, administering other aspects of educational life, and so on. Local governments are effective in some of their local activities although there is often a sense of powerlessness in many of their activities.

Individuals, while they may have their desires moulded to some extent by the prevailing ideas of advanced capitalist society through advertising, do not mirror their social culture perfectly and so they are able to act freely: that individuals can act freely and morally is recognised but it is also understood that people often find it easier to conform to prevailing norms. Nevertheless, when individuals band together in common causes, such as with non-governmental organisations (NGOs), they can exercise considerable resist-ance to the dominant forces of global capitalism – they can even become global forces in their own right. This, we have witnessed, in some of the big public demonstrations against globalisation in recent years, but we are also aware of the activities of many NGOs at various layers in each society which oppose the spread of advanced capitalism, although in the West, unfortunately, such organisations as the churches have been less active in this pursuit than they might have been. In addition, we have seen the call for more radical and transformative forms of education to equip individuals to fight this apparently inevitable process (O'Sullivan 1999; McLaren 2005).

Consequently, we can see that while there is not an equal balance of power, there are different levels at which resistance might be exercised against the dominant forces – resistance that endeavours to retain local cultures, belief systems, and even languages. For the sake of simplicity, we can say that there are global forces that stem from the substructure and which are reinforced at other levels by some politicians and practitioners. By contrast, there are forces resisting global capitalism that can be found in all levels of society – national and regional, local and individual. Hence we have to recognise the constant tension between the social forces that operate in global society.

Once we differentiate global society in this way, we can see the complexity of the system and of the power structures – a complexity that causes great problems when we seek to conceptualise, amongst other phenomena, citizenship, and especially active citizenship. We will return to this problem when we discuss the aims and functions of lifelong learning, but before that we need to examine the way that the education of adults has been affected by the social forces of advanced capitalism.

From adult education to lifelong learning[1]

The global forces have also demanded a more educated, and continually educated, workforce and over the last third of the twentieth century these demands became more strident. The fact that adult education, in its traditional sense, has begun to disappear as it has been replaced by lifelong learning reflects the changes that advanced capitalism has been demanding. At the same time, some of the outcomes of these changes have embodied some of the hopes and aspirations of early adult educators, although not in quite the way that they would have envisaged. It is also significant to recognise that the changes that they sought were not being achieved by their own efforts; they only emerged when the social conditions were right for them, which was when advanced capitalism needed them.

Traditionally education has been regarded as the institutionalisation of learning – learning is the process which occurred in individuals and education is the social provision of the opportunities to learn (and be taught) formally. The latter is social and implies a responsibility of the State, in the first instance, but later the employing organisation as well, to provide teaching and learning opportunities to prepare the child for adult life. Later, education referred to those forms of education that were provided to prepare children or young people for adult life at work. However, education has always stretched beyond the limits of formal schooling and university education; consequently, the term had to be qualified by a number of adjectives to describe these other practices – two were especially prevalent – 'adult' and 'further'. In English, adult education came to imply 'liberal' education for adults, whereas further education assumed a more vocational meaning. This was not true in the USA, for instance, where adult education embraced both terms. It was for this reason that in 1981 I started to use the term 'education for adults' rather than adult education because the educational process is the same whatever the topic, whether it is vocational or non-vocational.

Both adult and further education implied that the school–university formal education system was insufficient and that the provision needed to be considerably broader, so that gradually the idea of lifelong education gained popularity. Lifelong education had been on the margins of adult education for many years, especially since the famous 1919 Report argued that

> the necessary condition is that adult education must not be regarded as a luxury for the few exceptional persons here and there, nor as a thing that concerns only a short span of early manhood, but that adult education is a permanent national necessity, an inseparable aspect of citizenship, and therefore should be universal and lifelong.
>
> (Smith 1919, Introductory letter, para. xi: 5)

Some ten years later Yeaxlee, who actually served on the committee that produced the report, wrote the first book in the English language on lifelong education. In it, he (1929: 31) claimed that:

> The case for lifelong education rests ultimately upon the nature and needs of the human personality in such a way that no individual can rightly be regarded as outside its scope, the social reasons for fostering it are as powerful as the personal.

Now, however, we might not totally concur with this claim since the emergence of lifelong education in its present form is much more because of social conditions than individual nature. For instance, the idea did not really gain currency until it was adopted by UNESCO, and written about by Lengrand (1975). Even then, however, it was not the term 'lifelong education' that gained currency, but two others: recurrent education and continuing education. In addition, other new concepts began to appear and in a sense each reflected the changes that had already occurred in the social structures and showed that education was adjusting to try to catch up with the structural changes.

Recurrent education

Recurrent education was the concept espoused by OECD (1973: 7) and defined as 'the distribution of education over the lifespan of the individual in a recurring way'. One of its connotations was that everybody should have a free educational entitlement beyond compulsory schooling. Such an idea was expensive to put into practice and so it is not surprising that it rapidly disappeared from many of the official documents, although the idea of paid educational leave has remained its legacy in the thinking about lifelong education.

Continuing education

In a sense continuing education was rather like 'further education' but it did not carry the institutionalised connotations of educational entitlements that the previous term carried. In the early days there was a debate about whether continuing education implied all education after full-time compulsory education (Venables 1976) or after post-initial education (McIntosh [Sargant] 1979). What was clear, however, was that it combined both vocational and non-vocational education. It was not long, however, before the vocational aspect gained additional emphasis as the terms continuing professional education and continuing professional development gained currency and it was these latter terms that gained funding preference over the liberal forms of continuing education.

Human resource development

The employing organisations espoused the idea of continuing professional development, and it rapidly became human resource development – a term that was initially regarded as morally questionable.

> The mere thought of investment in human beings is offensive to some among us. Our values and beliefs inhibit us from looking on human beings as capital goods except in slavery, and this we abhor. We are not unaffected by the long struggle to rid society of indentured service and to evolve political and legal institutions to keep men free from bondage. These are achievements that we prize highly. Hence to treat human beings as wealth that can be augmented by investment runs counter to deeply held values. It seems to reduce man, once again, to a mere material component, to something akin to property.
> (Schutz 1961 – reprinted in Jarvis with Griffin 2003: 246)

Schutz was among the first to use the term human capital, or human resources, and in the above quotation he notes the moral objections that some people held, and still hold, to treating people as means rather than ends – to use Kantian terminology. Nevertheless, human resource development has taken its place within the plethora of terms used to describe some aspects of vocational education.

Community education

In sharp contrast to human resource development, community education is a form of liberal adult education – a term that gained more currency in Scotland that anywhere else in the UK and is the term still frequently employed for liberal adult education but one that certainly does not receive as much interest. However, there are a variety of meanings for this term, such as education for the community and education in the community. Initially, it had two major meanings: education of people in the community so that they could work for the people's benefit and liberal adult education of an extra-mural nature. Now, adult and community education has taken on the latter meaning and the former is something that is practised by non-governmental organisations, but only occasionally as a result of State provision.

Lifelong education

Each of the terms used above are about lifelong education although one of them, human resource development, implies that the 'resource' will only be developed for as long as people are working. But by the mid-1990s the idea of lifelong education was widely accepted in society but by this time the idea of 'education' had been questioned. There were many reasons for this, such as:

- education was seen as something different from training but in a world where practical knowledge is important and where theory no longer took precedence over practice, education was a questionable concept;
- practical knowledge has to be learned in practice and not in theory;
- education is a provision, the responsibility of the State or the employing organisation, but opposition to the idea of the 'nanny state' had really taken hold as the neo-liberal minimal state beliefs became popular and so it became the responsibility of individuals to seek out their own development;
- education is about the provision of learning opportunities to groups of people but much human development is individual – reflecting the individualisation of contemporary society;
- education is more about teaching whereas, in a rapidly changing world, it is learning that is more important;
- it was widely recognised that a great deal of learning beyond the educational institution was taking place and that it needed to be accredited within the formal system, but it was learning and not education.

Hence a new term had to be found, one that captured the individuality and responsibility and combined the practical and the theoretical, and so 'lifelong learning' came to the fore.

Lifelong learning

By the mid-1990s the term lifelong learning had gained ascendancy over all the other terms and with it came all the associated ideas of the learning society, learning organisation, and so on. While lifelong education and lifelong learning have been regarded by some as synonymous, there are profound differences in the implications of the two terms, as we can see from the questions raised about the concept of 'education' above. Now lifelong learning is:

- not the responsibility of the State;
- the responsibility of individuals to find and undertake it;
- about learning and teaching;
- about learning materials being commodities to be purchased (digested, consumed in the consumer society);
- a recognition of the significance of practical knowledge;
- an acknowledgement that learning that is acquired outside of the educational institution is valid and should be accredited in the same way as knowledge gained and tested within the educational institution;
- a recognition that the educational institution has to change rapidly to cope with this new world;
- a recognition that society, or parts of it, are changing rapidly and so it is necessary for individuals to learn (adjust, be flexible) to cope with the precarious conditions of their daily lives;
- becoming institutionalised without the formal structures of previous times – it is now occurring in an open market and learners can choose whatever provision suits their needs best so long as it can be accredited and socially recognised.

As I argued in the first volume, learning is co-terminal with conscious living and it is something that is very individual and personal, but lifelong learning has also become a social phenomenon – it is about learning but it is also about education. In a sense, it falls between the individual learning process and the formal bureaucratic educational process – it is something of a market – one of learning opportunities and one of opportunities to enrol on courses! Nevertheless, it must be recognised that any market favours those who have rather than those who do not have, so that while it is the responsibility of the learners to acquire their lifelong learning, it disadvantages those who are already disadvantaged. Indeed, it might be argued that there is a double disadvantage since the idea of personal responsibility carries with it the connotation of irresponsibility for those who do not, and those who cannot, acquire that learning. The welfare state, at least, offered more opportunity for those who cannot exercise their responsibility for social and personal reasons. Nevertheless, lifelong learning is still institutionalised although the institution might be better suited for this rapidly changing flexible society than is any form of bureaucracy, although it must be recognised that special provision still needs to be made for the disadvantaged.

Lifelong learning and globalisation

In the previous chapter we saw that advanced capitalism, and with it the phenomenon we now call globalisation, developed in the 1960s and 1970s and so it perhaps comes as no surprise to see lifelong learning developing at about the same time. In this section we will demonstrate the influence of the substructure on the development of lifelong learning at both the international and the national level.

International level

In the 1960s and 1970s, as we also noted above, recurrent and continuing education were the terms that were coming to the fore in the adult education vocabulary. In 1972 UNESCO published the influential Faure Report (1972), which had four underlying assumptions: the existence of the international community, which was a global assumption; a belief in democracy; the aim of development is the complete fulfilment of the human being; only lifelong education can produce this complete fulfilment. The report's idealistic optimism reflects the euphoria of the late 1960s – a period of romanticism. Although we have argued for the necessity of learning per se for human fulfilment (Jarvis 2006), we do now need to recognise the ambiguity in the term lifelong learning which was not apparent in 1972. Soon after this lifelong education was to become a UNESCO ideal; it is in this ideal that we can find a basis for the type of uncritical and evangelical zeal that we find in some of lifelong learning's major exponents, such as Longworth and Davies (1996). Throughout the 1970s and 1980s, lifelong education, in the form of continuing education and especially continuing professional education, formed the basis of many educational policies. Indeed, in the UK, politicians frequently claimed that there is no difference between education and training and that it was all about learning. In the mid-1980s, adult education was also subsumed within continuing education[2] and so there were two movements afoot – to incorporate both adult education and professional training into continuing education, which was already being seen as a form of lifelong education. We cannot really agree, therefore, with Field's (2000: 3) claim that 'lifelong learning has emerged onto the policy scene with the suddenness of a new fashion'; the foundations underlying this policy shift were carefully laid for many years but they went unrecognised by many of us. The only thing that was new, however, was the term and, as we showed earlier, this had to be introduced to enable training to be incorporated into the educational vocabulary. It was a gradual colonisation of education by the world of work.

In 1996, UNESCO returned to the scene with the Delors Report (1996). Like the Faure Report, this was a balanced and humanistic report which, while it recognised the significance of learning for work, also understood the human potential in learning. It started by recalling UNESCO's own foundation: there existed a hope 'for a world that is a better place to live in' (Delors 1996: 14) but it was critical of the emphasis on 'all-out economic growth' (p. 15). In a sense this report was critical of the way that lifelong education had been colonised by the world of work, seeing that education could actually be a dimension of all human living:

> There is a need to rethink and broaden the notion of lifelong education, not only must it adapt to changes in the world of work, but it must also constitute a continuous process of forming whole human beings – their knowledge and aptitudes, as well as the critical faculty and the ability to act. It should enable people to develop awareness of themselves and their environment and encourage them to play their social role at work and in the community.
>
> (Delors 1996: 21)

Throughout the report, there is both a recognition of the social forces of globalisation and a plea for the humanity of each person. Indeed, the report makes the point that there are four pillars of education: learning to know; learning to do; learning to live together; learning to be (pp. 85–97).[3] While UNESCO is an international body, it is not a governing body and so it is not exposed to the pressures of the social structure in quite the same way as are governments, and so on. Consequently, it can spell out a realistic and idealistic programme and, at the same time, it can offer a critique of what is happening in the world and even seek to modify the harshness of the global pressures. This is precisely what this report does, for we only have to look at the European Union to see how the emphases are different.

It was in 1995 that the European Union also entered the policy field of lifelong learning through its work on education and training with its White Paper *Teaching and Learning: Towards the Learning Society* (EC 1995). Indeed, this paper directed European policies on lifelong education. By this time the debate on globalisation was far advanced and the EU document reflects the need being felt for education in Europe to respond to the demands of the economic substructure, and there were many references to the learning society, learning organisation, and so on. Significantly most of these came from management and human resource development and mostly from the USA (e.g. Allee 1997; Carnevale *et al.* 1990; Casner-Lotto and Associates 1988; Nadler and Wiggs 1986; Pedlar *et al.* 1991; Robinson and Robinson 1989; Senge 1990; Watkins and Marsick 1993, *inter alia*). It was 1994 before an educational book that did not stem from management and human resource development on the learning society appeared (Ranson 1994), although four visionary futurist books had been published many years earlier (Hutchins 1968; Illich 1971; Schön 1971; Hussén 1974). In 1995, the first policy statement on the learning society from the European Union argued 'that in a modern Europe the three essential requirements of social integration, the enhancement of employability and personal fufilment' were not incompatible (p. 4).

Nevertheless, the greatest emphasis was on employability in discussions of the learning society. The following year was declared the European Year of Lifelong Learning. However, it was the *Memorandum* (EC 2000a: 5) that claimed that the changes in contemporary society, which we have discussed above, underlie the 'two equally important aims for lifelong learning: promoting active citizenship and promoting employability'. Comments were invited on this memorandum and when they came (about 3,000 responses) many were critical of these rather limited aims of lifelong learning and the EC was forced to revise them. The aims of personal fulfilment and social inclusion were incorporated, so that there were then four aims: active citizenship, social inclusion, personal fulfilment and employability/adaptability (*Making a European Area of Lifelong Learning a Reality*, EC 2001b). While the aims were changed, the general tenor of the document still couples lifelong learning with employability. Nevertheless, there was one significant acknowledgement in the 2001 policy statement: that the Europe of Knowledge threatens to bring about 'greater inequalities and social exclusion' (p. 6) and it claimed that lifelong learning

> is much more than economics. It also promotes the goals and ambitions of the European countries to become more inclusive, tolerant and democratic. And it promises a Europe in which citizens have the opportunity and ability to realise their ambitions and to participate in building a better society.
>
> (EC 2001b: 7).

We have demonstrated the validity of this statement in the above pages. Significantly, the emphasis on the relationship between active citizenship and employability is explicitly downplayed as the statement sought to respond to the criticisms that it defined lifelong learning far too narrowly. At the same time, building a 'better society' become an aim of citizenship and unless the good society is only materialistic, and the EC documents do not really read this way, then space is implicitly being made for political action in the public sphere.

Although UNESCO has championed lifelong learning throughout the period of globalisation, it has maintained a balanced approach, whereas when the European Union entered the scene, it was with a much more vocational interpretation of lifelong learning, even though it did not define it in quite the same manner. However, the European Union was forced to broaden its interpretation of lifelong learning, in just the way that the Delors Report had suggested. Nevertheless, the EU policy documents still do not present a balanced approach to lifelong learning, emphasising employability and active citizenship far more than the other two aims, but this may be because the EU espoused the Lisbon ideal of becoming the most advanced and competitive economy by 2010. At the same time, it should not be thought that the EU has only been active along these rather narrow lines for it has contributed a great deal to the expansion of lifelong learning at every level through its many programmes for the education of adults and young adults. Its programmes have reflected the breadth of the aims of lifelong learning specified in the policy document *Making a European Area of Lifelong Learning a Reality* (EC 2001b).

National level

We suggested that among the reasons why a transnational corporation should invest in a country there are three that have educational significance: educated workforce; flexible workforce which can easily be retrained; opportunities for continuing education for workers. We will look briefly both at some of the policy statements of national governments and also some of the practices.

Over the years the length of initial education has been expanding and while this is not all attributable to globalisation, a great deal of it relates to the increasing demands that industry and commerce have had for an educated workforce. In the more recent period of advanced capitalism we have seen the emphasis being placed on more young people staying at school until beyond compulsory school leaving age. In the UK, for instance, the policy is for 50 per cent of school leavers to obtain a university education – even if only a two-year foundation degree. (The proportion of population of young people entering higher education between 1990/91 and 2001/02 rose from 19 per cent to 35 per cent – DfES, *Trends in Education and Skills*). Other countries, e.g. South Korea and Finland, already have a far higher rate of young people completing their university education. Significantly, the emerging economies are recording far higher enrolments in tertiary education (77 per cent of young people) than the rich countries of the West (43 per cent) (UNESCO Institute for Statistics 2005). Naturally, the high level of tertiary education reflects the way that the West has evolved since the Industrial Revolution, but as this need for higher education has increased dramatically over the past half a century, it is the emerging economies that are changing the more rapidly. This either means that the West will need to attract more highly educated people from the emerging countries into work, which is a morally questionable practice in some ways but one which is going on all the time, or that eventually the emerging economies will overtake the West. India, for instance, with its youthful highly educated population and an inexpensive workforce is attracting an increasing number of transnational corporations to invest both their production and their services (call centres), and so on. Countries wishing to attract inward investment are being forced to increase their initial educational provision because once the country has opened itself to the globalisation process and capitalism begins to colonise the educational system, as Kerr *et al.* (1973: 47) point out, education becomes the handmaiden of industry; and we could extend this to handmaid to the world of work, or the global substructure.

In the UK we are seeing this greater involvement in initial education from the core of society: we find representatives of industry and commerce serving on school governing boards, the creation of corporation-sponsored city colleges (schools often with a technical orientation), sponsorship of a variety of other initial education activities, the provision of work experience for school children and advertising of commercial products within schools themselves. More generally, McLaren (2005: 31) makes the point that

> the business agenda for schools can be seen in growing public–private partnerships, the burgeoning business sponsorships for schools, and business 'mentoring' and corporatization of the curriculum . . . and for calls for national standards, regular national tests, voucher systems, accountability schemes, financial incentives for high performance schools, and 'quality control' of teaching. Schools are encouraged to provide better 'value for money' and must seek to learn from the entrepreneurial world of business or risk going into receivership. In short, the neo-liberal educational policy operates from the premise that education is primarily a sub-sector of the economy.

Of course many of the changes that are occurring in education do improve the educational system but, overall, his claim that education 'is primarily a sub-sector of the economy' fits into this model of globalisation presented here.

In further education this is even more marked. In the UK, for instance, the first report of a national advisory group on adult education in 1997 (Fryer 1997) produced a far more balanced document in respect to lifelong learning than the employability-dominated EU policy statements. But the tenor soon changed and by the time that the Foster Report was published in 2005 (pp. 6–7), it was claimed that further education lacked 'a clearly recognised and shared purpose' and it was recommended that it needed, amongst other things:

- an appetite to catch up with competitive international economies;
- a consequential core focus on skills and employability;
- to increase the pool of employable people and share with other providers the role of enhancing business productivity;
- to acquire an identifiable brand;
- an evolutionary change;
- to learn from the strategic and management arrangements of other public services, both in the UK and abroad.

While students should receive impartial advice, financial incentives should be developed 'to steer students onto courses valuable to the economy' (p. 7). It states quite clearly that its primary purpose is 'to improve employability and skills in its local area contributing to economic growth and social inclusion' (p. 10). Perhaps the influence of the substructure shows very clearly in the section on improving teaching, where we read that:

> Teachers and managers need to ensure that those who come into FE colleges with technical skills are enabled to keep those skills up to date. Representations from business suggest that some teachers do not have a sound understanding of the latest industry developments.
>
> (Foster 2005: 33)

Clearly there are many places in the report where it seeks to recognise the human potential of education but, overall, the above summary indicates clearly the direction that was being advocated. State-provided further education has been fully and freely colonised by the economic system.

Even before Foster reported the Learning and Skills Council (LSC) announced the funding allocation for further education: funding for the 16–18 year olds for vocational types of education was increased by 10.3 per cent while that for the 19+ age groups was decreased by 3 per cent (cited in *Adults Learning* 2005, no. 1: 7). It is the hegemonic power of the core that is producing these changes in the educational system and government grants are being made available for vocational education especially for young adults; substantial cuts in government grants for non-vocational education is having dire results. Tuckett (2005: 6), commenting on the UK scene, writes:

> if policies remained unchanged a million to a million and a half opportunities for adults will be lost over the next three years. And, as a result, once again questions are being raised about what public money should be spent on the field of adult learning.

Naturally, governments could claim that they are doing this in the national interest since it is fundamentally important that there should be an educated workforce in the UK or else business and industry will go elsewhere if the

UK does not keep abreast of its competitors. But it is also the hegemonic power of the substructure that produced the changes in the educational system. While lifelong learning is both vocational and non-vocational, it is the former that is favoured rather than the latter. Low taxation, which means that there are insufficient resources to spend on non-vocational education, and even welfare provision, and the demands for an educated workforce means that government is forced to give priority to vocational education, so that public money is being selectively allocated in favour of the economic interests

It is also important to note that much adult literacy started as an altruistic effort to help the poor in many undeveloped countries to read and write, and campaigns, like 'Feed the Minds', provided literature for people to read. Indeed, the UNESCO policy statements on adult literacy emphasise that its fundamental rationale lies in human rights (UNESCO 1990, 2000a, b) and work, while mentioned, is not a dominant concern. The same types of emphases occur in the studies on adult literacy by Freire and Macedo (1987) and Flecha (2000). Now adult literacy is the first step to lifelong education and is a route into employability. In the OECD report (1996) *Lifelong Learning for All*, two of its five arguments for lifelong learning refer specifically to the economic institution. Indeed, it (OECD 1996: 15) states quite specifically that:

> A new focus for education and training policies is needed now, to develop capacities and realise the potential of the global information economy, and to contribute to employment, culture, democracy and above all, social cohesion.

The same argument that the university system has moved in the same direction has also been well documented (Aronowitz 2000; Jarvis 2001a). Indeed, the British government recognises that 'higher education must expand to meet rising skill needs' and that 'universities need stronger links with business and the economy' (DfES, *The Future of Higher Education*, Executive Summary). Aronowitz (2000: 11) also argues the same for American higher education:

> Far from the image of the ivory tower where, monk-like, scholars ponder the status of the stars and other distant things, the universities tend to mirror the rest of society. Some have become big business, employing thousands and collecting millions in tuition fees, receiving grants from government and private sources, and, for a select few, raising billions in huge endowments.

Every grant that a university receives from business and industry makes it more dependent on the core for future funding in order to keep academics in employment. Indeed, there are now instances where corporations sponsoring university departments have influenced the appointment of academic staff, even to the extent of threatening to withdraw funding support if certain academics were appointed. At this point universities have lost their independence. There have always been sponsored professorial chairs but the number has increased dramatically over recent years and the amount of commissioned research has likewise increased. But, like the transnational corporations, universities are themselves becoming transnational – not in the sense that academics have always been cosmopolitan – in opening campuses in different countries and having their sales teams in those countries to attract fee-paying students to enrol in their courses. In addition, distance education is attracting increasing numbers of students to study with them, and here we see how the control of information technology adds power to the multinational corporations. Universities are becoming corporations. Indeed, they are slowly becoming transnational corporations and, as such, being incorporated into the substructures of global society. Indeed, the Society for College and University Planning (2005: 6) reports that in 2002 US universities earned $1.3 billion in patent revenues. In addition, the commodities that they sell are research and learning materials (and even the accreditation that the material has been studied). Not only are universities seeking to attract great numbers of students, as clients, but they are changing their own practices in order to do this – running part-time degrees, increasing the number of postgraduate taught courses, restructuring the courses into modules that can be sold and accredited by a finite amount of time devoted to studying (not to be confused with learning although the vocabulary of learning is often employed!), exercising their own quality assessment and control mechanisms and making it possible to transfer credit from one university to another, and so on.

In precisely the same way there has been a tremendous increase in part-time study at lower levels, so that further education colleges and their equivalents in other countries are offering an increasing number of courses to a wider section of the population than in previous generations. Naturally this is a continued inducement to insure that global corporations do not move their operations from the UK and, as such, it saves corporations from having to spend on these aspects of workforce training. We might ask what happens if governments do not respond sufficiently quickly to the learning demands of the substructure and we note another new phenomenon – the corporate university (Eurich 1984; Meister 1998; Jarvis 2001a). In these instances, some of the large corporations, such as Motorola, have started their own universities, or training programmes.

Significantly, governments claim to work in partnership with the politico-economic substructure so that when they initiate reforms or introduce educational innovations, they never have to acknowledge that they have bowed to pressure from the substructure but, as we see from our model, each country can be studied separately and as governments' concerns are wider than those of industry and commerce, we can see other aspects of lifelong learning being introduced without reference to the global forces. Significantly, for instance, employability does not loom so large in some other national policy statements about lifelong education. In Ireland (*Learning for Life* 2000: 12), for instance, six priority areas for adult education were identified:

- consciousness raising
- citizenship
- cohesion
- competitiveness
- cultural development
- community building.

But the same report notes that in both *The National Development Plan* (1999) and *The National Employment Action Plan* (2000) lifelong education is elevated to 'a pivotal role in labour market policy' (*Learning for Life* 2000: 17). In contrast, Hong Kong's report (*Learning for Life* 2000) does not mention employability but focuses much more on learner development and enrichment although the growth and development of the education of adults in Hong Kong is extremely vocationally oriented. The fact that different societies with different levels of development and different forms of government adopt different policy approaches to lifelong education is not surprising.

Whether the UK, following the USA, is 'leading the way' and other countries will follow is not altogether clear, although it does appear that the substructure is exercising an increasing amount of influence on the educational system in more countries.

Conclusion

We started this chapter by pointing out there is not a deterministic relationship between the substructure and the superstructure and, apart from human nature itself, education is one of the reasons why this is not so. It is possible to educate children and adults to be critical of the present situation and to desire a different approach to society. Whilst education is a very necessary factor of the knowledge economy, it is potentially a weak link in the capitalist chain of production so that it is not surprising that it has been targeted by the substructure for both of these reasons. Lifelong learning has become quite central to contemporary globalised advanced capitalist society and so now it is necessary to turn our attention to lifelong learning, knowledge and information.

Chapter 5

The information and the knowledge society

Two concepts that are inextricably intertwined with lifelong learning are the information society and the knowledge society and it is important for our understanding of lifelong learning and the learning society to understand both of them. Whilst I am separating them here, they are confused in some of the literature which is unsurprising since they almost always refer to precisely the same societies. Nevertheless, UNESCO is clear that they are not the same:

> Today, as we are witnessing the advent of the global information society where technology has increased the amount of information available and the speed of its transmission beyond all expectations, there is still along way to go before we achieve genuine knowledge societies.
>
> (UNESCO 2005: 19)

For the sake of convenience in this study I am also separating them conceptually: information society refers to those societies which utilise advanced technology to transmit knowledge; knowledge societies utilise knowledge as a major resource in the production of commodities and services. Consequently, I am defining information societies as those societies *that utilise advanced technologies to convey knowledge (information) within or between societies*, whereas knowledge societies are those societies that *utilise specific forms of knowledge in order to function or produce commodities*, so that it is not surprising that the term *knowledge economies* is frequently used. It should be noted that once we objectify these two concepts, as we are bound to do in sociological analyses, we lose the personal basis of knowledge as something learned and the idea of interpersonal interaction in the process of exchanging or transmitting knowledge.

However, for knowledge to be objectified in this manner implies that it has been accepted socially and is, in some way, embedded in either the culture or the practices of a society or a social or cultural group and so we might ask – What constitutes knowledge? Dictionary definitions of knowledge almost inevitably relate it to information or to learning, so that it is not surprising that the terms are used almost interchangeably in places. In order to try to clarify this distinction, we might start with the ideas of facts or data. A fact is something that has been, or is capable of being, empirically verified but has not necessarily been learned; it has no meaning until it has been studied and understood and given meaning by the learner. Data are the outcomes of investigations that, likewise, have not yet been learned and assimilated – for instance a computer printout contains data but until it is read and digested it cannot become knowledge. Knowledge, then, is the outcome of learning and information is the transmission of data, facts or learning between persons. It can only be treated objectively when it has become embedded in the practices or culture of a social group, and so on.

There are fundamentally three ways by which data can become treated as knowledge: rationally, empirically or pragmatically. Rationality, something upon which great emphasis was placed from the times of the Protestant Reformation and the Industrial Revolution, is based upon the idea that starting with a premise a rational or logical argument can be constructed that results in a final position, or truth – or something that might be learned as knowledge. Empiricism is based upon the ideas of experimentation or observation, from which can be derived data that can then be studied and given meaning. Pragmatism is based upon the idea of the practical consequences of applying knowledge (a theory) and achieving the expected results. This approach has been made popular by Lyotard's (1984) assertion that legitimate knowledge needs to be performative in contemporary society, in other words – it must work!

Once we locate this approach to knowledge within the framework of advanced capitalism, we can see that pragmatism underlies the types of society we are discussing and the globalisation process that we have outlined in previous chapters. Lyotard (1984: 5) outlines this position clearly:

> Knowledge in the form of an informational commodity, indispensable to productive power is already, and will continue to be, a major – perhaps *the* major stake in the worldwide competition for power. It is conceivable that the nation-states will one day fight for control of information, just as they battled in the past for control of territory, and afterward for control of access to and exploitation of raw materials and cheap labor. A new field for industrial and commercial strategies on the one hand, and political and military strategies on the other.
>
> (italics in the original)

While Lyotard focused on the nation state, in this globalised society we could replace this with transnational corporations. In today's society, industrial espionage is not unknown; nor is the poaching of knowledgeable individuals from one employer by another in order to acquire the knowledge possessed by that person. Certain forms of, but by no means all, knowledge underlie the types of society that we are discussing here.

However, the data underlying the knowledge, or the information, may be value-free but its use-value is more significant. If that knowledge can be used to produce new marketable commodities, or be used to make the production of such commodities more efficent and therefore cheaper, then it is valuable to the producers; that is to a considerable extent the substructure. Consequently, it has to be recognised from the outset that while facts may be value-free because they have no intrinsic meaning, their use and the meaning placed upon them do have value. Now value is not a private thing and values tend to relate to use-value, as Arendt (1958: 154) wrote: 'Value is the quality a thing never possesses in privacy but acquires automatically the moment it appears in public.' Data may have no value but information may have real use-value and the greater the use-value of information to corporations in the global substructure the more likelihood there will be competition, industrial espionage, etc. to gain it.

While knowledge and information are such intertwined concepts it is easy to understand how they become confused but we will treat information and knowledge societies separately in this chapter for the sake of clarity, starting with the former.

The information society

The process of conveying information between people begins with language (first body and then verbal language) and this was enhanced when literacy was developed. This allowed for written information to be conveyed between people at great distances through a variety of means of transport but it was with the invention of the wireless and the telegraph that information could be conveyed at speed over vast distances. Conveyence of information, therefore, depended upon the level of technology developed and utilised for this purpose and so it was with the development of the computer and electronic means of transfer that the information society, as we now know it, came into being and with it, what Castells (1996) called, the network society. Castells (1996: 65) rightly reminds us of Kranzberg's first law that technology is neither good nor bad in itself.

However, we do have to recognise that the information that is carried and transmitted by that technology almost always has use-value and in this sense it is far from value-free. Those who provide that information and those who seek it are in a market exchange situation and so we see that the predominant culture of the capitalist system prevails. The information that has potentially the most use-value is most valuable. This position is one that has caused academic researchers a great deal of anguish: for the academic, knowledge and, therefore, the information contained in teaching and learning materials and in research reports has instrinsic value rather than use-value and, as we will see below, there has been a considerable unwillingness to accept the changes being forced upon the universities by the social forces of the sub-structure. In this sense the culture of academia is opposed to the prevailing culture of global society.

In our model of globalisation (Figure 3.2), we can see that technology, especially information technology, is one of the three strands of the sub-structure and so it is at the heart of the globalisation process. The other two strands are the economic institution, namely advanced capitalism, and the supporting might of America. Capitalism is the driving force of change and even for the introduction of advanced technology. The competition between transnational corporations means that the more they can produce commod-ities cheaply and the wider their markets the greater their profitability. As Castells (1996: 81) puts it: 'Profitability and competitiveness are the actual determinants of technological innovation and productivity growth.'

Consequently, in the 1960s and 1970s we saw the introduction of the network society in which there was an internationalisation of capital. Castells (1996: 85) writes:

> By extending its global outreach, integrating markets, and maximizing advantages of location, capital, capitalists, and capitalist firms have, as a whole, substantially increased their profitability in the last decade, and particularly in the 1980s, restoring for the time being the preconditions for investment on which the capitalist economy depends.

The introduction of advanced technology, information technology, facili-tated the further development of capitalism and legitimated the network, and therefore, the information society. This movement towards technology led wrongly to a downgrading of industrial production and so ideas such as the post-industrial society emerged. For Daniel Bell (1973), for instance, 'knowledge and information ... [became] ... the strategic resource and transforming agent of the post-industrial society' (Bell 1980: 531).

Webster (2002) suggests that there are five theories of the information society: technological, economic, occupational, spatial and cultural. He discusses all five approaches:

- a vast array of innovatons that have appeared since the late 1970s;
- the economic worth of informational activities;
- the preponderance of occupations are to be found in knowledge work;
- information networks that connect locations and consequently affect the way that time and space are organised;
- contemporary culture is information-laden.

He concludes that as definitions they are 'either or both underdeveloped or imprecise' (p. 21). He goes on to suggest that whilst these descriptions are a useful device for exploring features of the contemporary world, they are unacceptable as definitions and after a very full discussion on the idea of the information society he concludes that he (p. 261) has 'quite forcefully rejected the concept of the information society, even though it is much used in and outside the social sciences'. This is an important observation since there is a tendency to accept a definition and forget those aspects which it omits – this is certainly true of the knowledge society, as we will demonstrate below. Webster rightly acknowledges that it is not an entirely worthless concept but it is one that does not define today's society. Nevertheless it does describe aspects of one of its dominant characteristics. Indeed, we can see how the phenomenon fits into the model of globalisation that we discussed in chapters 3 and 4.

Webster (2002: 141) refers to the work of Schiller (1981: 25) whose discussion comes very close to our model:

> What is called the 'information society' is, in fact, the production, processing, and transmission of a very large amount of data about all sorts of matters – individual and national, social and commercial, economic and military. Most of the data are produced to meet very specific needs of super-corporations, national and government bureaucracies, and the military establishments of the advanced industrial state.

Once these communication technologies have been established a new medium exists for the domination of society and its peoples – advertising. Basically, advertising offers information to people about the products that have been produced by the corporations, although it is very clear that its functions are more fundamental than this. Through psychological techniques, advertising creates desires and demands, it serves as an agency for imposing lifestyes on people and, consequently, for perpetuating the advanced capitalist system since without sales the system would collapse. The information society, because of its advanced capitalist basis, must be the foundation upon which the consumer society is built.

While Webster might be unhappy with a conceptual definition of the information society, UNESCO embraced the idea and held a World Summit on the Information Society. Its basic texts (UNESCO 2003) cover such areas as education, culture, science, communication and information, and freedom of expression. UNESCO's basic concern in all of its policy documents is that there should be a fundamental equality between the peoples of the world and the opportunities that the information society offers, although it recognises that globalisation is most likely to result in inequality:

> Globalization is both an opportunity and a challenge. It is a process which must be shaped and managed so as to ensure equity and sustainability. Globalization is generating new wealth and resulting in the

greater interconnectedness and interdependence of economies and societies. Driven by the revolution in information technologies and the increased mobility of capital, it has the potential to help reduce poverty and inequality throughout the world, and to harness new technologies for basic education. Yet globalization carries with it the danger of creating a market place in knowledge that excludes the poor and the disadvantaged. Countries and households denied access to opportunities for basic education in an increasingly knowledge-based economy face the prospect of deepening marginalization within an increasingly prosperous international economy.

(UNESCO 2000b, para. 26)

Clearly UNESCO states the possible positive outcomes from globalisation although the negative aspect is recognised. What is not discussed in these documents is both the structures of society and the power relationships within it. The documents, therefore, lack something of the reality and an analytical cutting edge because of these omissions. From an analysis of the UNESCO documents, there is a considerable emphasis on the possibilities of enhancing the opportunities of the underprivileged, and the themes of the information society echo through many conferences during these years; strangely enough, however, there is not a great deal of emphasis on distance learning, despite it being an innovatory approach to the transmission of information for educational purposes. The European Commission (Campano et al. 2004: 32–3), on the other hand, has identified ways in which information technology can be used for educational purposes both in business and commerce and also in community learning. Basically it is suggested that information society technologies can 'provide tools that empower learners in many areas of activity' but that 'it becomes a learning topic in its own right' (p. 33).

Fundamentally, education has always involved the transmission of information and in traditional education this has occurred in face-to-face interaction. Only with the invention of the printing press did technology enter into the process to any extent. Distance education, as we know it today, began in the latter half of the nineteenth century but more significantly the catalyst for its growth occurred in the late 1960s with the idea for a University of the Air, which was to become the British Open University. Significantly, this was at the time when globalisation was taking off and so politicians recognised early the potential of information technology in education. The first four faculties of the British Open University were Arts and Humanities, Education, Social Sciences and the Sciences; it was a liberal arts university. However, that was soon to change with the introduction of the Technology Faculty, the School of Management, and so on. In the early years the university actually received generous government funding, but it still charged a fee for each of its courses – education was becoming a commodity.

As government funding decreased proportionately, so the Open University began to utilise its expertise to sell its courses abroad and, gradually, the liberal arts emphases in the Open University has become less significant as vocational courses have increased. It has also entered the commercial market in research.

The British Open University was the immediate forerunner of many distance education universities around the world, as Rumble and Harry (1982) noted. At the same time, traditional universities slowly began to move into flexi-study and distance education. The University of Surrey, for instance, ran an international distance education course in adult education at Masters degree level from the mid-1980s. Now, universities are not only using distance education, they are relocating some of their expertise in areas where there is a market for students and universities are building second and third campuses in different parts of the world.

With the development of information technology, universities and other institutions of education are able to co-operate across the globe. This becomes increasingly important as topic areas grow in complexity and as a more multidisciplinary approach is applied to them. Few single university departments are large and diverse enough to employ academic staff to cover all areas, nor are they sufficiently large to research these complex areas, so that networks of universities are appearing. This is also advantageous for a mobile population. Once it becomes beneficial to work in a co-operative manner like this, it becomes necessary to develop assessment systems that allow the transfer of credit between courses and even between universities. The European Union has also utilised this approach in its big research projects in Framework 5 and Framework 6.

Distance education has become more significant and in the emerging countries of the world distance education universities grew with tremendous rapidity, so that by the early part of the twenty-first century there were many distance education universities employing even more sophisticated technology. In India, for instance, the distance learning university – Indira Ghandhi University – has about 1.5 million students and delivers some of it programmes by its own satellite to 17 different countries. Is there any other university in the world that has its own satellite? In the mid-1960s the Shanghai Television University was founded; it now has 350,000 students, but is by no means the largest university in China. Indeed, in 2003 there was a world summit conference of 17 mega-universities in Shanghai Television University – only four came from the West, one from each of South Africa, Spain, UK and USA (*Joint Action for the Future of Distance Education* 2003).

Slowly we are aware that in the West there are movements towards using technology more efficiently in education – but the universities, for instance, are very slow to change, assuming that there are no rivals to their supremacy. But this is not necessarily the case and soon the emerging countries' universities may not only reach more students by more technologically efficient means, but produce more students working at advanced levels. In the West, some scholars have doubted traditional universities' ability to utilise technology efficiently (Katz *et al.* 1999) and have suggested that it is 'Dancing with the Devil'. Perhaps dancing with the devil is actually one of the only ways of achieving the desired end of widening participation and giving everybody the opportunity to participate in learning and so grow and develop themselves as human beings. But we can still see that information technology has been a major instrument in the commercialisation of university education, so that Aronowitz (2000) can now refer to them as 'knowledge factories', and other scholars are also voicing their concerns about the way that universities are developing (Slaughter and Leslie 1997; Bok 2003; *inter alia*). As universities are relocating and building campuses in different parts of the world, and as networks of universities are developing, there will soon be mergers between some of them, and takeovers of some by others, and it will not be long before we see the development of multinational universities and even transnational ones.

Once universities, and other educational institutions, enter the marketplace, they are dependent on customers so that the more popular and more instrumental courses grow and develop whereas minority subjects either get priced out of the market or dropped altogether, so that the direction of research and teaching is controlled more by the markets than by the inner demands of the subject under deliberation.

But there is another major problem and this makes universities dependent upon commercial funding agencies. Universities are not joint-stock companies and they have few means of raising capital from the market, so that they need sponsorship if the governments do not provide 100 per cent funding – which they do not do in the majority of cases. If government does not fund students and research at a level sufficiently high for the institutions to be independent of the market, then higher education institutions seek funding from business and commerce, which is often forthcoming – but at a price. There are instances of sponsoring companies influencing staff selection procedures and even vetoing new appointments. Companies sponsor certain research and seek all patenting rights from the work that they sponsor, even to the extent of controlling precisely what is, or is not, published as a result of sponsored research. Basically, what we see is that the power that rests with capital means that educational and research institutions cannot remain independent of the substructure. The substructure can wield considerable power over the workings of the educational system but, in another way, its demands on the remainder of society results in the market controlling the teaching and learning materials that higher education can offer on the market.

At the same time, universities are being forced to create companies, even public companies, in order to develop and market their own new discoveries.

University companies are no longer new phenomena in the knowledge society and, indeed, they become a vital part of the innovation process that keeps capitalism alive. Moreover, the market actually ensures that universities concentrate on certain forms of knowledge that are practical and can lead to marketable products so that, paradoxically, the innovation in knowledge and production results in a process of reinforcing the social and cultural structures of contemporary society.

In contrast to the way that this control is operated, the World Wide Web offers free access to a great deal of information and has become a 'global library'. Accessing information from a multitude of sources is now possible to anybody who has access to the Web and the skills to search for it: e-learning is now a reality. However, that information, like most other information, is not value-free and so it has to be acquired critically, knowing that the authors of the material may be giving free access to it in order to influence those who acquire it in some way or other. Learning information transforms it into knowledge.

The knowledge society

UNESCO has clearly differentiated between information societies and knowledge societies:

> The new information and communication technologies have created new conditions for the emergence of knowledge societies. Added to this, the emerging global information society only finds its *raison d'être* if it served to bring about a higher and more desirable goal, namely the building, on a global scale, of *knowledge societies* that are the source of development for all.
>
> (UNESCO 2005: 27, italics in original)

The UNESCO team recognise that their vision and what is occurring are not always in harmony with the contemporary world but they offer an idealistic scenario. For the report's authors, knowledge is a common public good (UNESCO 2005: 170–2). For them, the knowledge society means that we now have the means to achieve equal and universal access to knowledge and development that should come from a genuine knowledge-sharing. They are concerned that indigenous knowledge will be omitted as a result of the dominance of the North. It is are clear that the North–South divide indicates that there is social exclusion and knowledge-sharing almost non-existent. They warn against the commoditisation of knowledge:

> An excessive appropriation or commoditization of knowledge in the global information society would be a serious threat to the diversity of cognitive cultures. In an economy where the focus is scientific and

technological, what role might certain forms of indigenous know-how and knowledge play? They are already often deemed less valuable than technological and scientific knowledge. Is there a chance that they might simply vanish, even though they are a priceless heritage and a precious tool for sustainable development?

(UNESCO 2005: 22–3)

For UNESCO, knowledge societies are a source for development and can enhance well-being for all people and they must, therefore, change their cultures in order to respond to the new social, political, economic and ethical dimensions that arise. But the North–South divide – a digital divide – is a major obstacle in achieving these humanistic aims. The report realistically recognises that knowledge-sharing is 'the cornerstone of the practices and values that should be at the heart of knowledge societies' (p. 170). In precisely the same way, concern is expressed about the gender divide. Here, then, we see an idealistic picture of a knowledge society in which knowledge opens up the possibility for human and social development, in which all the peoples of the world can participate in the benefits that knowledge brings. It is a utopian vision – one which serves to remind us that we are not always developing in the right direction.[1] Despite its utopianism, it is a realistic report about some of the problems in achieving such goals.

While the UNESCO report recognises the place of capitalism in the knowledge societies, it does not include the dimensions of power within its considerations, neither, unfortunately, does it thoroughly examine the public–private divide in societies although knowledge is seen as a public good. In the remainder of this section we will analyse what is widely assumed to be the knowledge society.

Conceptually, knowledge itself presents problems, as we have already implied; while we do not want to pursue the epistemological issues here, we have to be aware that there is a movement away from the idea of epistemology to that of cognitive science (Williams 2001). Williams suggests five problems with knowledge: analytical, demarcation, method, scepticism and value. Each it seems is a relevant issue when we discuss the idea of the knowledge society, although space forbids that discussion here. Nevertheless, we have already implied some of these when we sought to differentiate between fact, data, information and knowledge. We also examined what legitimates knowledge – rational, empirical or pragmatic bases. Clearly, in this society pragmatism, i.e. practical knowledge, has come to the fore but this does not mean that there are no other grounds for knowledge, although the dominant one might be seen to prevail for a short period in history. But not all knowledge can be verified by pragmatic approaches nor is all knowledge immediately and verifiably useful, a point that Scheler (1980 [1926]: 76) raised as early as the mid-1920s when he tried to classify knowledge into seven types:

- myth and legend;
- everyday knowledge, implicit in everyday language;
- religious knowledge;
- mystical knowledge;
- philosophical, metaphysical knowledge;
- positive knowledge of mathematics and the sciences;
- technological knowledge.

Scheler was also concerned to demonstrate that each of these types of knowledge changed at different speeds which he suggested constituted different degrees of artificiality – by this he meant their speeds of change in relationship to the natural world view which changes most slowly. Now we can certainly argue with Scheler's classification in many different ways. For instance, the social sciences hardly feature at all in it, but it would be possible to include them within positive knowledge, except that not all social science knowledge is positive! In the same way, we can say that certain empirically based scientific knowledge is far from artificial: for instance, the speed of light does not change but our understanding of the nature of light might. In addition, we could argue that some forms of indigenous knowledge are pragmatic and do change as the social conditions change. Scheler differentiated between the first five forms of knowledge and the bottom two – which he regarded as the most artificial. He suggested, even in the mid-1920s, that as a result of research, positive knowledge changes hour by hour – perhaps we might now say that it changes minute by minute, or even second by second.

Scheler's classification is not correct when we consider our contemporary understanding of knowledge, nor can knowledge be so simply classified, but he does raise a number of significant issues for our discussion of the knowledge society: that there are different forms of knowledge; that not all knowledge changes at the same speed; that certain forms of scientific and technological knowledge change exceedingly rapidly; that knowledge in the arts and human sciences changes more slowly; that relativity is much more complex than is usually understood. Indeed, it could well be argued that some values do not change at all over time (Jarvis 1997). However, the dominant forms of knowledge do fall within Scheler's later categories and, by and large, are those which are assumed to be knowledge in today's society. It is perhaps significant here to recognise that although power lies at the heart of the global society, the capitalist market is, to some extent, open for new forms of knowledge. It is not only the large transnational companies that are producing this new knowledge, in many cases it is small and medium-sized companies – even university companies – that seek to market their new commodities. If they are successful, then some of the companies can and do expand and some go public and offer shares on the Stock Market. Eventually, some of these successful companies are incorporated into the core, either by acceptance or by being taken over by the larger transnational companies.

The market, therefore, fosters rapid growth of both new knowledge and new commodities – indeed, it feeds on them. Change in knowledge and commodity production does not alter the power structures of society but, in a sense, it actually reinforces them.

In the UNESCO report (2005), there is a certain assumption that all forms of knowledge should underlie the knowledge society, but Stehr (1994: 92) suggests that underlying the knowledge society is scientific knowledge and that knowledge itself has been treated as a 'black box' – that is that any major debates about what it is, how it is justified and what are the outcomes of its implementation are not really analysed and discussed, as we have just suggested with the concept of relativity. Nevertheless, Stehr is suggesting that the foundations of the knowledge society are the outcomes of what Scheler regarded as the most artificial forms of knowledge – those that change 'hour by hour'. Stehr (1994: 101) says that 'Scientific knowledge as productive knowledge becomes the dominant type of knowledge'. Scientific knowledge has certainly become the most dominant form of knowledge and this rational and research approach to knowledge has become the generally accepted way in which we think about knowledge. But the flip side of this is simply not that there are no other forms of knowledge but that they do not feature on the agenda of the knowledge society to the extent that perhaps they might.[2] The emergence of this phenomenon was noted long before talk of the knowledge society, when industrialisation was beginning to assume significance. Kerr et al. (1973: 47), for instance, noted that:

> The higher education of industrial society stresses the natural sciences, engineering, medicine, managerial training – whether private or public – and administrative law. It must steadily adapt to new disciplines and new fields of specialization. There is a relatively smaller place for the humanities and the arts, while the social sciences are strongly related to the training of managerial groups and technicians for the enterprise and the government. The increased leisure time of industrialism, however, can afford a broader public appreciation of the humanities and the arts.

Of course, they were wrong about the nature of society but they were right about the emphasis being placed on scientific and useful subjects, albeit in the post-industrial society. The dominant discourse about knowledge in knowledge societies is scientific, so that it appears that all knowledge has to be scientific, or at least social scientific.

This is the hegemony of those who exercise control over the agenda of global capitalism. Coupled with this is that those forms of knowledge that do not conform to the scientific criteria for knowledge are sometimes no longer considered to be valid knowledge: this can be demonstrated, for instance, by the questions raised about epistemology above. In addition, indigenous, or local, knowledge is reduced to folklore and knowledge is lost in this globalising process. UNESCO (2005: 149) points out, for instance, that indigenous knowledge is rarely documented or legitimated by scientific studies but that when its value is recognised it results in bio-piracy, that is that those who control the substructure plunder local cultures, patent indigenous recipes and treatments for illness, for capital gain, despite international agreements to the contrary. Hence, we can see that UNESCO's formulation of the knowledge society and the type of society discussed by Stehr differ, and one of the reasons for this is that their approaches to knowledge itself differ. Indeed, if the knowledge society described by Stehr represents the way that policies about knowledge and society are formulated, as it almost certainly does, then those formulations are founded upon a restricted and not very full understanding of knowledge itself, but it is one that is championed by those who control society's substructures. It is this power that puts at risk the future of traditional societies founded on indigenous and traditional knowledge and even in the long term the future of the planet.

Stehr (1994: 10–11) suggests that the advance of science into the life-world and the economy can be described in various ways:

- the penetration of most spheres of social action;
- the displacement, but not elimination, of other forms of knowledge;
- the emergence of science as a productive force;
- the differentiation of new forms of political action;
- the development of new sectors of production;
- the change of power structures with the creation of technocracy;
- the trend to base authority on expertise;
- the shift in the nature of social conflict from allocation of income to generalised human needs.

These claims have to be carefully examined and it might well be asked:

- whether most spheres of social and political action have been penetrated by scientific knowledge;
- whether the power structures of society have really changed;
- whether authority is really based on expertise;
- whether there has been a shift in the nature of social conflict, and so on.

These seem to be unsubstantiated claims based upon the apparently likely or idealised outcomes of the introduction of more scientific knowledge into society, but each of them is profoundly questionable in today's society. Indeed, Stehr (1994: 5–17) also suggests that the structures of the economy are changed by the knowledge society and that knowledge itself is the driving force for change. But knowledge per se cannot be the driving force for change because knowledge has no internal will; in other words, it is not a person but it is an outcome of individuals' learning and change is a result of their actions. One of the major driving forces for change, as Castells (1996) argued so convincingly, is capitalism's need to produce a profit and it is the control of knowledge and the desire to create new knowledge that lies at the heart of social change. The fact that scientific knowledge changes so rapidly, is primarily because of the drive to produce more performative knowledge and since its products are worldwide, it is hardly surprising that the idea of 'knowledge without boundaries' (Walshok 1995) has emerged. But we also noted that the third strand of the global substructure is the United States with its rather imperialistic approach to the world, so that a second force for the production of new scientific knowledge lies with the military might of America – it is always seeking to strengthen both its defences and its attack potential and so it sponsors research which can lead to even greater military might.

Both of these approaches to research are pragmatic and differ profoundly from the academic desire to know, which is another driving force in research leading to the development of new knowledge. However, it is recognised here that the funding for this form of research – while very important and highly esteemed since much of it comes from government and the research councils – constitutes only a fraction of the funding going into research per se and much of the remainder comes from business, industry and government for specifically defined purposes. Social change comes from the introduction into society of the outcomes of new knowledge. The really useful knowledge in contemporary society is that which those who control the global sub-structures can use for production purposes which will lead to a profit or increased military might.

Once social change is recognised as stemming from sources other than knowledge itself, some of Stehr's other claims about the nature of the knowledge society can be seen to be open to question, and this takes us back to our model of globalisation (see Figure 3.1). As we argued above, the generation of new knowledge occurs in the global substructures of society and it allows for the production of new products that can be sold in the global market and/or the more efficient, and therefore cheap, production of those goods. The control of research is, therefore, a vital element in the global society and this is why universities and their research and teaching are so significant to those who control the global substructure. Research universities are crucial factors in the development of new knowledge. Walshok (1995: 20) writes:

> the university as a whole, not just individual faculty members within the institution, needs to be measured on the extent to which it serves the knowledge needs of society as a whole, as well as how it serves basic teaching and research.

It appears that there is a confusion here between the needs of society and the needs that capital perceives or seeks to create in people and, as we have already suggested, the academic approach to knowledge and the commercial pragmatic ones differ widely and so it is not surprising that many academics are concerned about the direction in which university teaching and research is being taken. Some academics, however, are able to utilise their knowledge in this knowledge society and market their own inventions successfully, although:

> One thing remains clear about millionnaire entrepreneurs and spin-off successes . . . their top priority is to invent, not to swell their purses. Their goal is to see their ideas developed and taken up by industry or commerce. They are dedicated to their discipline and their roles as educators and researchers first; making money and being an entrepreneur comes second.
>
> (Shepherd 2006: 9)

It is also hardly surprising now that knowledge is regarded as 'intellectual capital' and that contemporary societies are referred to as 'knowledge economies' that those who manage the financial capital need to manage the intellectual capital in the knowledge society – knowledge is a private good not a public one. Capital, however, needs to be managed. Indeed, Drucker (1994: 10) concluded that because the knowledge society has to be an organised one then its distinctive organ is management and we have seen how there has been a tremendous growth in the emphasis of management as an area of study and as a necessary qualification to progress in many forms of business life. However, there are different levels of management and it is only at the upper echelons that management is answerable to others beyond the corporation – the shareholders. It is important to recognise that lower and middle management are by no means the ultimate source of power in the organisations or in the knowledge society; they are the employees of advanced capitalism in the same way as are other knowledge workers. At the same time, management is, amongst other things, always an exercise in power.

Managers, however, are not managing as many people as perhaps they used to, but they are managing processes. Corporations using knowledge strip themselves of as many fixed assets as they can but seek to retain the knowledge workers – the intellectual capital of the company. Stewart (1997: 40) pointed out that at the turn of the twentieth century 17 per cent of America's workforce worked with knowledge but by the turn of the twenty-first century that figure had risen to 59 per cent. He (1997: 43) goes on to point out that:

> Not surprisingly, manufacturers are hiring better educated workers to perform these knowledge intensive jobs. Before 1947, Ford's personnel department didn't even bother how much education its employees had.

Today, between a third and two-fifths of car makers new hires have at least some post-high school education, a number twice as high as it was less than a decade ago.

Certainly, the use of Ford as an example is very important since the assembly line is well documented as an alienating process (Beynon 1975), whereas the loss of the highly skilled crafts jobs are rarely referred to in discussing the knowledge society. The dignity of some work, not assembly line work, has been lost in the process. But education must respond to the knowledge demands of the business and industry. It is the way that the knowledge economy is maintained. In an interesting way this function of education has not changed greatly over this past century, for John Stuart Mill claimed that the content of education was to be found in the 'culture which each generation purposely gives to those who are to be its successors' (cited in Lester-Smith 1966: 9). The function remains the same, it is just that the purpose has become restricted much more to the world of work and the content has altered! Clearly, the nature of work has changed with the utilisation of knowledge and the knowledge workers, as has education. More young people have to stay at school for a longer period in order to gain initial qualifications but, as we have already shown, really useful scientific knowledge changes rapidly, so that it becomes incumbent on knowledge workers to keep up with these changes and so they need to continue their education beyond school.

Consequently, we can see that the structure of the workforce in such societies also revolves around knowledge work. Two well-known formulations of the structure of the workforce for the future are Reich (1991) and Rifkin (1995). Reich (1991: 171–84) suggested that there would be three dominant types of worker in this new global knowledge society: routine production workers, in-person service workers and symbolic-analytical service workers. Rifkin (1995) suggested that the knowledge workers would predominate because of advanced technology and he looks at such futuristic scenarios as 'No More Farmers', 'Hanging-up the Blue Collar', 'The Last Service Worker' (pp. 109–62), which takes the argument much further than Reich. Nevertheless, he is making a point! Clearly the emphasis of both on the knowledge worker (symbolic-analyst) and the significance of their education is something that affects the structures of both the formal educational system and our understanding of lifelong learning and the learning society.

The major resource that most corporations which compete in the knowledge economy have, then, is their knowledge workers, which they regard as their intellectual capital. As Stewart (1997: 61) says:

> When a company is bought for more than its book value . . . that premium usually consists of intellectual assets – anticiated revenue from patents, customer relationships, brand equity, etc plus the premium for

obtaining management control. The knowledge becomes capital – intellectual capital.

This is the really useful knowledge in today's society. Stewart (1997: 67) cites Klein and Prusak's definition of intellectual capital as: 'Intellectual material that has been formalized, captured, and leveraged to produce a higher value asset.' Certain forms of knowledge have become a capital asset to the corporations/organisations which manage it in the knowledge society. Consequently, Tuomi (1999: 84), citing several authors, suggests that organisations are 'stocks of "knowledge capital"'.

Assets have to be operationalised in order to realise their value and so we see that this really useful knowledge is practical knowledge, or at least its application has to have practical outcomes. Knowledge workers have to work within an organisational context which enables the knowledge to be used to produce the desired output. Hence workers need more than just the requisite knowledge, they need the skill as well and this mixture of knowledge and skill might be called a competence, but as Tuomi (1999: 84) makes clear the emphasis upon individual competence is not the whole story: core competences emerge which are the pool of knowledge and skills integrated within the organisation's structures. Consequently, education has become competency based. Competency itself is an interesting word. When there were only 17 per cent of America's workforce using knowledge, their ability might have been referred to as expertise. Certainly the highly skilled crafts people would be referred to as experts; now the idea of expertise has been replaced by competence. Competence is the ability to perform, not the ability to do something well. As a result of the introduction of technology in the production process, expertise, as such, is no longer a premium in many occupations. This certainly means that more people would be expected to be able to undertake a job because it does not demand the same level of expertise, which is both an inclusive idea and one which encourages forms of equity. But it also carries the connotation that it is not expertise that is required, and the expert craftsman is relegated to the sidelines in many areas of the technological knowledge-based society. Giddens (1994) offers other reasons why expertise, as a concept, has fallen into disfavour, such as the fact that experts offer universalising knowledge and are regarded as the final authorities, neither of which are acceptable in non-traditional society. Of the few writers who have focused on expertise, Benner (1984), following Dreyfus and Dreyfus (1980), places competency at the mid-point on a five-point scale of expertise, with proficiency to follow. Expertise takes time to achieve, but clearly many organisations only require competence, the acquisition of which is less time consuming. Competency has become part of the contemporary vocabulary. The core competences have always included 'learning how to learn' since knowledge is changing so rapidly and global competition means that corporations must always be at the forefront (Dubin 1990: 9–43).

In the knowledge society, is knowledge owned or controlled by organisations? It is owned in the terms of patents and procedures and it is controlled or managed in the way that the corporations manage and utilise their knowledge workers (structural and human capital). However, human capital is also a risk since the workers who have that special knowledge might resign, or be poached by other organisations, so that 'part of the task of the practice of intellectual capital is to enforce routines of documentation, of transferring knowledge from humans to machines where it can be articulated into more endurable and stable forms' (Yakhlef and Salzer-Morling 2000: 30), that is, the building of corporate databases. But this argument might be taken a little further because a great deal of human knowledge within organisations is tacit:

> Tapping into tacit knowledge of gatekeepers between the different functions, project teams and phases of the development programme has become the focus of major corporate investment. Knowledge management, one American corporate planner reflected, will have succeeded to the extent that it 'really *drills* down into the experience'.
>
> (McKinlay 2000: 114, italics in original)

However, if this control is too tight, then the human capital will seek other opportunities to work and exercise that knowledge; McKinlay (2000: 120) records how a manager noted that that control has to be bearable. Basically, this is reducing knowledge to information so that other employees in the same corporation can learn it – hence, workplace learning; but this also raises interesting moral questions about the ownership and control of knowledge. It even demands an answer to the more personal question – who owns the workers' learning? It does, however, point to the significance of power in the organisations/corporations that relates back to our original model in Chapter 3. Indeed, Thompson *et al.* (2000: 136) conclude from their research that:

> The fact remains that most companies 'lever' knowledge in ways that bear little resemblance to the literature or official corporate and governmental pronouncements . . . companies typically lever knowledge in routine work situations, including assembly and low-end service work. Managers seek to identify employee competencies, systematically utilise what has traditionally remained tacit, then abstract from knowledgeable practice regulatory systems that seek to formalise and assess that knowledge.

In a sense, tacit knowledge is used here in a similar way to practical wisdom but wisdom is another of those words that have tended to disappear from the vocabulary of the knowledge society. The power to utilise another's practical wisdom in this way is covert but, nevertheless, exercised and this fits neatly into Lukes's (2005) three dimensions of power which were discussed in the opening chapter. Tacit knowledge is transformed into documented procedural information, to be learned by others in the workplace.

Two distinct approaches to the knowledge society have emerged and although there is some overlap between them, there are fundamental differences. That which has been formulated by UNESCO is certainly more idealistic and captures a humanistic spirit that is certainly foreign to the approach of advanced capitalism in global society, which we have also discussed here. However, it is the latter form of knowledge society that is emerging since it reflects the ideological perspectives of advanced capitalism which lie at the core of global society. At the same time education has been forced to adapt to the demands of the substructure; education has always had a vocational element but it has also served to prepare the young person for the whole of adult life and older people to be able to play their role in the wider society. Now, however, the main emphases of education, especially the education of adults, have become vocational. Personal spin-offs from the educational process, such as individual development, appear to be incidental.

Conclusion

The existence of knowledge and the many possibilities to acquire it, means that societies that function by the application of knowledge must be learning societies but, unlike these two forms of society, a society that places learning at the heart of its culture is a process-oriented society and, in a sense, since it involves human processes, it should be a humanistic society.

Chapter 6

The learning society

Thus far we have documented the way in which globalisation has resulted in both ideas of information and knowledge societies. We have illustrated how the control of knowledge and information and the means of transmitting information lies at the core of global society and how power operates in instrumental ways to further the ends of capital, even to suggesting that this power operates on occasions contrary to international agreements and certainly not always to the common good, although those people who have been enabled to embrace a Western lifestyle and have become knowledge workers have benefited considerably as a result of it. Yet if knowledge changes rapidly, driven by the needs of capital to produce new marketable commodities and to do so efficiently and cheaply, then new knowledge has both to be discovered and learned. We have noted how the universities have a significant place to play in the knowledge economy even though the changes are not always favoured by those who work in them. We have also noted that this new knowledge has to be learned, as the new workforce is prepared and many members of the existing workforce need to be updated. This has led to the ideas of the learning society, the learning organisation, the learning city and learning networks and these are the subjects of this chapter, while the next one is on lifelong learning itself. In order to discuss these concepts, we are first confronted with a problem with the word 'learning', which is also implicit in 'knowledge' and 'information', and so it needs to be dealt with here. It will form the basis of the first section of this chapter and, thereafter, we will examine the other ideas.

The concept of learning

We are confronted with a conceptual problem when we look at the concept of the 'learning society' which is different in grammatical form from both the information society and the knowledge society: both information and knowledge are nouns that can easily act as an adjective to describe the type of society. 'Learning', however, is a verb and as such cannot become an adjective describing society – it can, however, become a gerund which is a noun formed from a verb denoting an action or a state (*Collins English Dictionary*). But our definition of learning in the first chapter is of a process, i.e. a verb, and not a noun. It would be easy to suggest that we could just restructure the sentence as, 'a society that learns' but we cannot do this because we have defined learning as a personal action and society is not a person, or a thing, although there is a tendency to reify society in discussions of the learning society. In the same way, we cannot actually turn around 'the knowledge society' to 'a society that knows' or the 'information society' to 'a society that informs'. However, with these latter two concepts, it is easy to document that there is a great deal of information transmitted between people and that more people's work depends on the use of scientific or technological knowledge. It is also possible to say that a great many people now attend educational courses – an educative society – but we cannot logically do the same for learning. We can say that many people attend educational courses in order to learn – but it is the people who attend courses who actually undertake the learning, not the society, and we cannot guarantee that attendance is synonymous with learning. Societies cannot inform, know or learn – only people can do that! Societal culture can encourage it but cannot force or control it. Neither can we document the amount of learning that takes place because learning is personal and almost synonymous with life itself. We have also pointed to the fact that in the knowledge society only certain forms of knowledge predominate and that other forms get relegated to folklore, superstition and irrelevancy, but it is not the learning that gets relegated, only the subject learned!

Consequently, we see two different approaches to lifelong learning emerging. Field and Leicester (2000a: xvi–xix) raise this issue quite nicely in the introduction to their edited collection when they ask whether we are dealing with the question of lifelong learning or permanent schooling, although the idea of recurrent schooling might be a more accurate description of the current situation. They do not develop this ambiguity, but it lays the foundation for their book and in the following chapter Edwards (2000) rightly points to recurrent education as the other factor in lifelong learning. Indeed, it was in 1973 that the OECD published a policy paper *Recurrent Education: A Strategy for Lifelong Learning* that combined the two. But because the boundaries between education and learning beyond school are no longer recognised and formal education is being forced to accredit learning that occurs beyond the educational system, lifelong learning may now be regarded as a combination of human learning and recurrent education. It is a question hidden from the debate by the traditional definition of the concept, such as the one given by the European Commission (EC 2001b: 9) that it is: 'all learning activity undertaken throughout life, with the aim of improving knowledge, skills and competences within a personal, civic, social and/or employment-related perspective'. This in an individualistic definition which is open to question on its instrumental perspective; it suggests that lifelong learning must have an aim. But it allows for a personal interpretation of learning itself. However, as we noted above, learning is an existential phenomenon which is coterminous with conscious living, i.e. learning is lifelong because it occurs whenever we are conscious and it needs have no end in itself, although it frequently does have a purpose. In a sense it is neither incidental to living nor instrumental in itself, it is an intrinsic part of the process of living. I have defined lifelong learning (see also Chapter 1) as:

> the combination of processes throughout a lifetime whereby the whole person – body (genetic, physical and biological) and mind (knowledge, skills, attitudes, values, emotions, beliefs and senses) – experiences social situations, the perceived content of which is then transformed cognitively, emotively or practically (or through any combination) and integrated into the individual person's biography resulting in a continually changing (or more experienced) person.
>
> (Jarvis 2006: 134)

Since we all live within time in society, there are times when we can take our life-world for granted and act almost unthinkingly for so long as we respond to the familiar, but once we are confronted with novel situations we can no longer take that world for granted. It is a state of disjuncture, when we become conscious of the situation and are forced to think about it or adapt to it in some way – that is learning. Disjuncture, itself, is a complicated phenomenon as we have demonstrated previously, but briefly it is the gap that occurs between our experience of a situation and our biography which provides us with the knowledge and skill that enable us to act meaningfully. When this gap occurs, we are not able to cope with the experience we have without learning something new. Consequently, in a rapidly changing world we can take less for granted and so disjuncture becomes a more common phenomenon and so throughout our lifetime we are forced to keep on learning – lifelong learning – and it is only when we disengage from social living that the rate at which we learn may slow down.

Learning is also individualistic since it is existential; there is no way that it can be anything other than individual because it is about an individual's life. But when we read much of the literature on lifelong learning, we are certainly not confronted with an existential phenomenon but a social one, so that we have to recognise that the term is used in a totally different manner. This is the point implicit in Fields' and Leicester's question – just how is it related to lifelong education, or even to education itself. While Field and Leicester recognise that lifelong learning transcends schooling, Edwards points to the fact that what we have is recurrent education. In this sense, the intermittent attendance at educational institutions throughout the lifetime – which in policy documents usually means the duration of the work life – indicates that the term is used in a different manner to the learning process but that it also includes that process. In this sense, the non-existential approach to life-long learning also embodies a form of recurrent education – a concept that was popular with the OECD and other institutions in the 1970s, but it also goes beyond it by including initial education.

It might well be asked why the boundaries between education and individual learning disappeared during this period. It was certainly not just a triumph of those adult educators who had been arguing for years that adults learned a great deal more after their initial education which should be recognised by the educational awards system, and Martin (1981: 25) points to an answer: 'The most salient feature of the counter-culture of the 1960s was the symbolism of anti-structure.' This was a period of expressive revolution in which structural boundaries of society were lowered and personal experience increasingly recognised, and so the experience of learning was recognised. This is also true of the boundary between education and work, which was also in accord with the needs of the emerging knowledge economy. Significantly, it also became easier to think of education as lifelong, since the social structures between different stages in the life cycle were lowered and education was no longer limited to certain stages of life. Thereafter, ways had to be found to recognise it, and so the accreditation of prior and experiential learning found its way into the system, as did the uniting of the ideas of education and learning. Since learning was the common feature, it was quite easy to see how lifelong learning took precedence over lifelong education as a term. When the expressive revolution drew to a close and the boundaries were recreated, both the concept and the processes of accreditation were encapsulated within the new structures and have gradually increased in popularity. Lifelong learning, therefore, includes formal and non-formal, as well as informal learning. In addition, third-age learning should be included, although it is frequently omitted in policy documents. Consequently, we need to recognise this combination of learning and recurrent schooling in another way of understanding lifelong learning which can be defined as:

> Every opportunity made available by any social institution for, and every process by which, an individual can acquire knowledge, skills, attitudes, values, emotions, beliefs and senses within global society.

Both of my definitions refer to different approaches to lifelong learning. Learning is always personal but some of the opportunities to learn are provided by social institutions, such as the State and employers. It is, therefore, a definition relevant to the private sphere of life, whereas the second definition, more relevant to the public sphere, might be indicative of the learning society, or the institutionalisation of the learning process. We are faced with not one term but two, of not totally different, but overlapping phenomena – one human and individual and the other both individual and social – or at least institutional; one more likely to be studied by the philosopher and psychologist (although not entirely as Jarvis and Parker 2005 show) and the other to be studied by both of these and also by the economist, the policy theorist and the sociologist. Certainly the study of lifelong learning requires a multidisciplinary approach.

The fact that they are overlapping is important since the person still learns *qua* individual in the vocational setting and in the non-vocational one the individual can learn knowledge and skills that are useful in the vocational. Perhaps they can best be depicted by Figure 6.1. The overlap between vocational and non-vocational lifelong learning illustrates that one type of learning may have functional utility in the other. For instance, non-vocational learning may have beneficial results in the work situation and learning in the workplace may also serve a non-vocational learning function as well. A great deal of vocational education is provided for young adults while traditional non-vocational adult education remains underfunded and much non-vocational learning may occur in non-formal and informal situations.

Consequently, the concept of the learning society is a metaphor to describe the fact that people are encouraged to learn, usually in specific situations and for vocational purposes; when we discuss the learning society, we need to see learning as something other than the learning process – it is about the opportunity to learn specific knowledge and skills. We suggest that it is the provision of learning opportunities that should underlie the idea of the learning society, and in this sense we want to define the learning society as one in *which the majority of social institutions make provision for individuals to acquire knowledge, skills, attitudes, values, emotions, beliefs and senses within global society*. In other words, it is a society in which people are enabled, even encouraged, to learn, but they have to take responsibility for that learning; it is the individuals who learn and not the society, and that society may be changed, even transformed, as a result of the learning of members of its

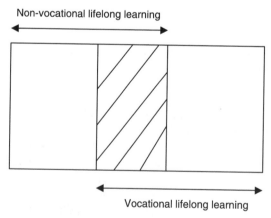

Non-vocational lifelong learning

Vocational lifelong learning

Figure 6.1 Categories of lifelong learning.

population. This definition puts learning but not education at the centre. Perhaps, even more significantly, the degree of change may correlate in some way with the degree of power or influence that the learners may have and those with little or no power or influence, e.g. indigenous peoples and people from non-knowledge-based jobs, have little influence on the societies in which they find themselves – they are in the lower layers of their society. The learning society, like every other society, is defined by those who have the power to define it; it is an unequal society in which opportunities to learn certain things depend upon people's positions in the social structures even though these structures are more fluid than ever before.

The learning society

The concept of the 'learning society' emerged with two authors in the 1960s and 1970s, the period when so much of what we are discussing here found a major impetus. Hutchins (1968) saw it as a society when everybody would have the opportunity to learn and develop themselves through part-time education, as society was organised to facilitate such opportunities. Husén (1974) thought that such a society was possible as the computer revolution would make it possible for everyone to receive information and learn. Two other authors had similar visions but did not use the term in this way: Illich (1971) postulated a time when society could be deschooled and Schön (1971) recognised the significance of individual learning in adaptable learning systems. In their different ways they foresaw some of the opportunities: the liberal educational philosophy that has under girded a great deal of the thinking of UNESCO and the technology that led to the information society. Naturally, their visions were slightly different, but they all looked forward to a society in which learning was placed at the centre. But Illich was more suspicious of what was happening and so he warned us against being imprisoned in a global classroom (Illich and Verne 1976) by learning demanded by employing organisations. One of the only other writers to use the 'learning society' concept during this early period was Boshier (1980), although he did so from the perspective of adult education becoming more prevalent in New Zealand. Although this is a far-sighted book in many ways, Boshier (1980: 2–3) was trying to do little more than to catch the spirit of the times when he suggested that:

> The notion of a learning society stems from third force psychology, widespread disenchantment with traditional education, the writings of educational radicals such as Illich, Reimer, Goodman and Freire, and the unprecedented transformation wrought by economic and social changes associated with evolving technology.

He tried to show the direction that he thought that adult education was moving rather than documenting the emergence of the learning society, as such. By contrast, van der Zee (1991) sought to expound his idea of the learning society by starting with an examination of existing forms of learning, he then showed how learning can be developed and, finally, argued for the unique contribution different agencies could make. For him, learning per se is at the heart of the learning society, although no real attempt to locate this discussion in the wider social context occurred.

Two quite distinct approaches to the learning society, the one private and the other public, as the two definitions imply, are to be found: one which is embodied by UNESCO documents and the other that relates much more to the socio-economic demands of contemporary society. Delors (1996) opens his UNESCO report with a chapter entitled 'Education: the necessary utopia'.[1] The focus of this is on personal and social development – the enriching of people through the learning process and the recognition that:

> The truth is that all-out economic growth can no longer be viewed as the ideal way of reconciling material progress with equity, respect for the human condition and respect for the natural assets that we have a duty to hand on in good condition to future generations.
>
> (Delors 1996: 15)

The word 'utopian' (see Appendix) might sound a strange adjective to describe education, especially coming from such an international statesman as Jacques Delors, but it is also the word that Freire (1972a: 40) used:

> When education is no longer utopian, that is, when it no longer embodies the dramatic unity of denunciation and annunciation, it is either because the future has no more meaning for men, or because men are afraid to risk the future as creative overcoming the present, which has become old.

Freire suggests that the latter is a distinct possibility. But utopianism is not something unrealistic as Horton, in conversation with Freire, makes clear when he says that he looked at all the utopian communities but 'it just became clear that I would never find what I was looking for. The thing to do was just find a place, move in and start, and let it grow' (Bell et al. 1990: 53). And so Highlander was born – the place where Rosa Parks was educated and many of those who were influential in the peaceful protest movement that was the catalyst in the desegregation movement in the southern states of the USA. Utopia is not just something that drops from heaven, but it is a dream, something to be worked for, helping people learn so that they can grow and develop and help change the world.

Perhaps it is unwise to try to describe in detail a utopian vision but this is just what Delors (1996) called it when he and his team concluded that learning – the treasure within – had four pillars: learning to know, learning to do, learning to live together and learning to be. In a different way Ranson (1994) tried to describe what the learning society should be like. It would involve education for democracy in which there would be many active citizens because educated people would join active debate. He (1994: 105) suggests that:

> The creation of a moral and public order that expresses and enables an active citizenship within the public domain is the challenge of the modern era. The task is to generate or constitute more effectively than ever before a public – an educated public – that has the capacity to participate actively in the shaping of a learning society and public. This will require citizens, both as individuals and together, to develop a firmer sense of their agency.

He goes on to look at the components of the learning society and suggests that there are two organising principles: an essential structure of citizenship and practical reason. He then suggests that there are purposes, values and conditions. There are conditions for:

- the learning self – agency, life as discovery, the self in relation to others;
- the social conditions of learning – creating a moral community, widening horizons;
- the polity – justice, participative democracy, public action.

This requires democractic governance at both central and local levels and a reorganised educational system to enable such a society to emerge. More recently, UNESCO (2005: 60) offered the following as a view of the learning society:

> Thus, learning, as a phenomenon may generalize at all levels of our societies and offer a model for organizing the time, work and lives of our institutions. Such an evolution illustrates a paradigm shift. On the one hand, education and learning can no longer be confined to a set and settled space-time, but may develop over a lifetime. On the other hand, the human actor must be put at the heart of the continuing process of knowledge acquisition and communication.

Such an approach demands that everybody should have the opportunity for education and that there should be a degree of equality in society and a genuine concern to put people in the heart of policy and practice. But when we look at both we find that this is not always the case. Indeed, Hughes and Tight (1998) actually suggest that the learning society is a myth since nothing like a learning society actually exists and neither is there a prospect of one emerging in the foreseeable future. Certainly, the vision of the learning society from the perspective of Hutchins, and maybe Delors and Ranson, seems far removed from the reality that we experience, and so what does exist and for what purpose?

Perhaps another attitude towards the learning society and lifelong education is summed up in the title of Ball's chapter in Ranson (1998: 36–41) 'Learning Pays'! Here we see a pragmatic and instrumental approach to learning and the learning society – it pays to learn, although he produces no empirical evidence to support his claims. Walker and Yu Zhu (2003: 149) indicate that 'the returns to education and, in particular, to proceeding from A-levels to a degree are high, but the variation in this across individuals is also high' since it depends on the subject studied, with 'Law, Health, Economics and Business, and Mathematics, considerably higher than Arts, Education and the other Social Sciences'. Consequently, these sweeping claims need to be tempered with evidence. This compares with the approach of the British Economic and Social Research Council's (ESRC) research project 'The Learning Society: Knowledge and Skills for Employment' (Coffield 2000). While there is a genuine research question raised in the project, there is also an assumption that money was given for research into the learning society since it appears that there might be an economic spin-off – which is the other aspect of the assumption made by Ball. However, the outcome of the 14 different pieces of research conducted within this programme was much less conclusive as to precisely what a learning society is. Coffield (2000, vol. 1: 8–27) indicates that ten different models of the learning society can be found:

- skills growth
- personal development
- social learning
- a learning market
- local learning societies
- social control
- self-evaluation
- centrality of learning
- a reformed system of education
- structural change.

In the second volume of the same research report Coffield (2000, vol. 2: 5–23) notes that seven other themes occur, and then there are lessons to be drawn from elsewhere in Europe. The seven themes are:

- learn from work, if you can;
- participation and non-participation;
- an over-reliance on human capital theory;
- the shifting of responsibility to individuals;

- there's precious little society in the learning society;
- the centrality of learning;
- new inequalities.

We have already noted the problems of shifting the responsibility to individuals, new inequalities and the centrality of learning in the learning society, but they and some of the other themes will also be addressed later in this book. It is clear that no simple conception of the learning society is possible, and Coffield's project does not exhaust the possibilities since it only had fourteen pieces of research in it, and so we can conclude that the characteristics of the learning society, if one actually exists, are not self-evident. Consequently, Coffield (2000, vol. 1: 27) quotes Young (1998: 141): 'the learning society has become a contested concept that "the different meanings given to it not only reflect different interests but imply different visions of the future and different policies for getting there".' It can be assumed, however, that those interests and policies that predominate in the discourse about the learning society reflect the interests and policies of the most powerful and influential groups in society.

Nevertheless, one other approach to the learning society has emerged, albeit under a different name – the reflexive society – another metaphor! Reflexive modernity arises out of the risks that some groups in society impose upon all of us. In order to produce innovations in production and/or bring new commodities to the market, producers take risks which have not been fully evaluated and, in a sense, society becomes their research laboratory – this might appear to be a very extreme statement but often the long-term effects of product innovations are not fully known when they are introduced. Beck (1992: 53) writes:

> Risk positions, on the contrary, contain quite a different type of victimization. There is nothing taken for granted about them. They are somehow universal and unspecific. One hears of them or reads of them. The transmission through knowledge means that these groups that tend to be afflicted are *better educated* and *actively inform themselves*. The competition with material need refers to another feature: risk consciousness and activism are more likely to occur where the direct pressure to make a living has been relaxed or broken, that is among the wealthier or more protected groups (or countries).

Basically Beck is arguing that only those who are already educated are conscious of, or able to learn about, the hazards that result from the contemporary production processes. Hence the potentiality for another type of learning society appears – one that is reflexive. For Beck (1994: 5–8) reflexivity implies self-confrontation rather than reflection. He goes on to suggest that this calls for the reinvention of politics since it demands action from the educated, but there is another sense in which reflexivity implies reflection and, therefore, learning. This is an individualised society, so that there is no real mechanism of social class to be activated against those who put the world at risk, there are only individuals who learn to live in times of uncertainty. Is it any wonder that citizenship education has become a major theme in lifelong learning policy? But, as Bauman (1988: 76–7) points out, with the standard of living that the educated enjoy people do not need rights and, therefore, Who is going to protest against these risks? Educated activism will perhaps be the activity of a small number of educated people who have the will and the moral commitment to be active. By reflexive, Beck is suggesting that this process is built into the very structures of society itself – individuals learn to live with risk and to master it to the best of their ability. The risk society, therefore, creates conditions for individual learning (reflection) and there is a sense in which reflexive modernity is a learning society. This, then, is another model of the learning society to add to the other characteristics that Coffield (2000) isolated.

However, taking this point even further, there is another sense in which society might be regarded as a learning society: the mere pace of change in science and technology is introducing change at every level of society – structural change and social and technological innovations are constantly occurring. People are being forced to learn, informally and almost incidentally, in order to live. This is not just the educated; everybody is confronted with the pace of change. The technological innovations are creating new lifestyles and people are being forced to learn. Structural change caused by globalisation results in culture change. A culture of learning has been created. Incidental learning in order to live in rapidly changing technological society is a sign of the learning society – it is one in which we can no longer take the present for granted, one in which we are frequently confronted with disjunctural situations which cause us to adapt our thinking, change our approach, and so on. The culture of a learning society is one that produces changes in behaviour as well as the need to learn in order to survive. But it is not society which is learning, it is the changing structures and situations within which we live that cause us all to learn, unless we disengage with the wider society as some people appear to do. In a sense there is no other single characteristic that is universal apart from learning itself – all the remainder are different characteristics of a rapidly changing society created by the advanced capitalism of the global substructure.

We can also see an significant difference between the private and the public definitions of learning: the former cannot be legislated for and no policy can be formulated to ensure that it happens. By contrast, the latter is social and can occur as a result of policy decisions. Consequently, policy decisions by governments can lead to the formation of this type of learning society.

The learning organisation

Organisational theory began with the founding fathers of sociology: Max Weber's (1947 edition) work on bureaucracy and Michel's (1966) work on oligarchy were among the first. For Michels (cited in Grusky and Miller 1970: 29): 'It is indisputable that the oligarchic and bureaucratic tendency of party organization is a matter of technical and practical necessity. It is the inevitable product of the very principle of organization.' And so, the iron law of oligarchy in organisations was recognised from very early on and with it the recognition that organisation, by definition, implies both power and structures. For Weber, there are three forms of leadership within organisations: charismatic, traditional and rational-legal. Charismatic leaders are those who can command a following because of their beliefs and message, or because of their success in what they do. Their power rests with their followers and if the followers decide that their leaders have lost their charisma and no longer follow them, then there can be no organisation. Successful leaders, however, can establish their own organisation and in the early days their authority lies in the traditions that emerge. In traditional society, the legitimacy and status of leaders, and therefore their authority, rests solely in the acceptance of the traditions, so that they are frequently legitimated by religion but in existing organisations their authority comes either from rules or laws or by order of the ruling body of an organisation. It is in this type of organisation that bureaucracy emerges and for Weber (1947: 333–4) the following characteristics apply:

- office holders are personally free and subject only to the official obligations of their office;
- offices are in a clearly defined hierarchy;
- each office has a clearly defined sphere of competence;
- each office is filled by free contractual relationship;
- candidates for office are selected on their technical qualifications;
- office holders receive a fixed remuneration;
- the office is the primary occupation of the holder;
- there is a system of career promotion between the levels of the hierarchy;
- the office holder is separated from the means of production;
- the office holder is subject to discipline and control in the conduct of the office.

Thus the structures of the organisation are fixed and dominated by rational procedures; once one has entered the organisation and learned the rules and regulations there is little or nothing more to learn about the organisation's operation and most of the work involves the office holder in administering a set of imposed or agreed procedures – impartially or otherwise. Change is inhibited by the structural procedures and those who want to change things are often unable to do so, unless they are amongst the oligarchy. In my own research, for instance, I found an inverse relationship between job satisfaction and professional beliefs and ideologies (Jarvis 1977) in bureaucracies.

Organisational change only really occurs when two sets of forces, those acting upon the organisation from outside and those acting within the organisation, operate in the same direction. In a bureaucracy, however, the forces within the organisation are resistant to change and even when the outside forces put pressure on bureaucratic organisations they are still resistant to change. Consequently, not all organisations responded to the forces of globalisation or to the societal forces of global capitalism within their own societies which have been apparent for the past half a century. Gradually, however, the competition in the global market from countries like Japan and the opportunities to increase profits through extending their markets globally meant that leaders of large organisations recognised the need to change. During the 1960s and 1970s there was a gradual increase in continuing professional education, as we documented earlier, but continuing education in itself did not change organisations. This was seen in a number of organisational studies, such as one by Argyris and Schön (1978: 26) who stated quite specifically that

> Since World War II, it has gradually become apparent not only to business firms but to all types of organizations that the requirements of organizational learning, especially for double-loop learning, are not one-shot but continuing.

Argyris and Schön (1978) were clear that there were major external forces that were affecting organisations and in the introduction to their book (pp. 1–5) they produced a case study that shows how five workers at one level of a company were convinced that a product was a failure six years before the decision by senior management was taken to stop producing it. At first, the subordinates believed that the errors could be corrected by hard work but as they struggled they realised that this was not sufficient, but senior management was still promoting the product as a winner. Eventually, they composed memos to middle management explaining the problems but management found the memos too forthright, and they also doubted them because previous studies had not predicted this situation. Having taken a 'reality check', they then wanted time to see if they could correct the situation. When, finally, they decided that they had to communicate to senior management what they had discovered, they had to compose memos in carefully structured doses so that the bad news could gradually dawn upon senior management, and this actually took a lot of time. The learning of some individuals took nearly six years to permeate to the hierarchy because their learning had to be mediated through the power structures which prevented changes occurring as rapidly as they should have done. Now Argyris and Schön rightly focus upon the need to change procedures, which they incorporate in the idea of organisational learning, but they actually play down discussion of the power relationships within the organisation which prevented the lower hierarchical orders communicating rapidly to the hierarchy without risking their own position. These power relationships become hidden within their discussion of theories of action and organisational learning – both single-loop and double-loop learning which they combine into Bateson's (1972) concept of deutero-learning. Their focus became the need for the organisation to change which they then incorporated into the metaphor of organisational learning (p. 28):

> Organizational learning occurs when members of the organization act as learning agents for the organization, responding to the internal and external environments of the organization by detecting and correcting errors in organizational theory-in-use, and embedding the results of their inquiry in private images and shared maps of organization.

Significantly, the fact that there are hierarchies in organisations and people who exercise power has now disappeared in their writing and nowhere in their summary of the chapter on organisational learning does the idea of a hierarchical power occur. The idea that power is exercised in the learning organisation is also omitted from Watkins and Marsick's study (1993). The question needs to be posed, therefore, as to whether organisations – even facilitative ones – can actually exist without hierarchies of power, or whether these formulations of teams and networks without the recognition that power (even covert power) is exercised in and through the organisation are realistic. Naturally, it is quite possible to discuss organisations in this way when the discussion is between power holders – managers – and then the power is taken for granted, assumed and therefore not a problem to them, but their own leadership may be! Facilitation, however, demands that the facilitator is supported by the organisational structures and as most books on learning organisations are written for managers, the issue of power is not significant, but it is a major omission. Indeed, as we can see, there are a number of assumptions about the nature of the learning organisation already appearing.

However, it is generally accepted within organisations that flatter hierarchies are occurring, structures that facilitate easier and quicker communication between top and bottom and vice versa. However, a flat hierarchy does not preclude power – quite the opposite, as Green (1997: 14) reminds us:

> Flattened hierarchies can often mean the curtailing of middle management leading to increasingly centralized decision-making and the intensification of work among lower grade staff who lack any real autonomy and see their career paths cut off.

Power is a dimension which cannot be omitted from any analyses of organisations, whether or not they are learning organisations. The characteristics of this type of organisation – the learning organisation as it has come to be called – are summarised by Clarke (2001: 3):

- team working and learning;
- a culture of cross-organisational working;
- a system of shared beliefs, goals and objectives;
- individuals, teams and an organisation that learns from experience;
- individual, team and organisational learning are valued;
- development of new ideas, methods and processes are encouraged;
- risk-taking is encouraged;
- responsibility and authority are delegated;
- everybody is encouraged and expected to perform to their maximum ability.

But these characteristics are not the same as those suggested by other theorists. Pedlar *et al.* (1997: 15) suggest the following:

- a learning approach to strategy;
- participative policy-making;
- informating;
- formative accounting and control;
- internal exchange;
- reward flexibility;
- enabling structures;
- boundary workers as environmental scanners;
- inter-company learning;
- a learning climate;
- self-development opportunities for all.

For Longworth (1999: 215) the learning organisation has the following indicators, it is an organisation that:

- needs to improve its performance through learning;
- invests in its future through education and training of its own staff;
- encourages its staff to fulfil their human potential;
- shares its vision of tomorrow with its people and stimulates them to respond to the challenge;
- integrates work and learning and inspires its people to seek excellence;
- mobilises its human talent;
- empowers all its staff to broaden their horizons;
- applies up-to-date delivery technologies to create more learning opportunities;

- responds proactively to the needs of the environment;
- continues to learn and relearn.

While there are similarities between these three lists, there are also pro-found differences, but in none is power a major issue and, therefore, for these and other reasons, the analyses are open to question. Now it could be argued that Pedlar *et al.* have a different audience but they could also be describing different types of organisation under the same title, so that these differences call into question the concept of learning, as it is used here, and we will return to this below. However, we can also see that different writers on learn-ing organisations certainly produce different lists of characteristics, so that the very least we can say is that there is not only one type of organisation to which the term 'learning' might be applied. In addition, a learning organisa-tion, if such a phenomenon actually exists, need not only be a work-based one – churches, for instance, might be learning organisations, as might other non-governmental organisations.

The theorists of these organisations also appear to wish the same types of utopian characteristics as the learning society upon them although it is to be doubted whether any major organisational research, rather than management research, has been conducted into the feasibility of these characteristics being realised within an organisation. Yet it is to be noted that the four types of learning described by Pedlar *et al.* (1997: 59) – learning about things (knowledge), to do things (skills), to become ourselves (personal development) and to achieve things together (collab-orative enquiry) – are the same as the four pillars of learning in the Delors Report. Indeed, the utopian idea again points us to the fact that there are more ideal arrangements for human collaboration than those that are generally practised. But even if we concentrate just on 'organisational learning', we note the definitional problem of learning itself is the same one as we have already highlighted. Hence, this idea of organisational learning itself needs a little further examination before we proceed.

Argyris and Schön (1978) make the point that their approach to learning is related to action, but then they state quite specifically that not all of the changes qualify as organisational learning (pp. 17–18) since some changes in organisational procedure can be regarded as organisational entropy because they result in a deteriorisation in the way that the organisation functions. But learning can result in organisational entropy, although according to this definition, this form of learning is not organisational learning. Hence organ-isational learning, according to their understanding, is something that only has positive results, i.e. that it is instrumental, in that it can be seen to correct situations and allow organisations to respond to both internal and external pressures usually in the way that the managers want. But learning per se need not have positive results and this is now being recognised as managers are taught to accept that innovators are bound to have failures as well as successes and that they still need support.

While Argyris and Schön rightly recognise that learning is personal, so that it appears that this type of organisation is person-centred, they are actually suggesting that when organisational procedures are changed positively as a result of social pressures, then it is what they call organisational learning, so that once more we can conclude that organisational learning, as a concept, is not actually learning per se nor necessarily people-centred – but it is change in the right direction. It is the successful introduction of new procedures into an organisation that enables it to function more efficiently and to respond more effectively to the external social pressures. But who actually introduces the changes and who has the authority so to do is not discussed within their definition. Clearly, only those who occupy hierarchical positions have the power to introduce changes in the procedures and expect others to follow them, even if the suggestions for change come from other levels of the hierarchy. What they appear to be suggesting is that the more permeable the layers of the company, the more the managers can learn from within the organisation, from change agents or entrepreneurs, and the more they can create a change situation either because of what they have learned from within or because of what the socio-economic pressures from the global or local market are demanding. They are equating organisational learning with change and action, which is not human learning, as we defined it in the opening chapter, although it reflects the behaviouristic approach to learning – that is, that it is a process that can be measured by its outcomes. However, behaviourism, as such, is not actually learning, as we argued in the previous volume (Jarvis 2006). It is not actually learning at all but it is changes in organisational procedures and efficiency, as a result of either one or a group of people's learning in the workplace, responding to either internal or external pressures, and implementing new procedures as a result that seem to be the characteristics of the learning organisation. This is similar to the idea suggested by Senge (1990: 14) that learning organisations are 'continually expanding [their] capacity to create [their] future'. He goes on to say that they have not just to survive but to adapt to the changing conditions – or, as I would argue, to the social forces generated by global capitalism or to compete with others who are generating those forces on the wider society. This is also the position implicit in the definition of Pedlar et al. (1997: 3) that: 'A Learning Company is an organization that facilitates the learning of all its members and consciously transforms itself and its context' (emphasis in original).

What is clear in all the three lists of characteristics cited above is that the power to introduce change in procedures is assumed and not discussed. In precisely the same way the ideas of concord and agreement are assumed and the processes by which individuals learn to change to fit into new procedures are not highlighted, and so we need to recall that one of Coffield's (2000, vol. 1: 8) characteristics was social control. Coffield cites Hewison's (Coffield 2000, vol. 1: 167–97) research, and summarises (Coffield 2000, vol. 1: 16) that: '"opportunities for lifelong learning" were viewed by many of the participants in their study as a threat or an obligation imposed by employers rather than a promise'.

A similar sentiment is echoed by Field (1999, cited in Coffield 2000, vol. 1: 18):

> Without anyone much noticing it, a great deal of professional development and skills updating is carried out not because anyone wants to learn, but because they are required to learn. Contract compliance, regulatory frameworks and statutory requirements are the three main culprits.

It is this dimension of power and control that is missing from much of the discussion of the learning organisation, as it is from many of the other evocations for lifelong learning to which we refer throughout this study. While Hewison's study is of the health service, there is no reason to assume that in other organisations embracing lifelong learning similar patterns do not occur, as Field's comment indicates.

It is also the relationship between personal learning and the organisation that Senge (1990) addressed in *The Fifth Discipline*: his first four disciplines are personal – how we think, what we want, how we interact and how we learn from on another (Senge 1990: 11). His fifth discipline is systems thinking, which is social, when through integration of thought and practice a shared vision across the whole organisation can stimulate change and efficiency in an organisation. For Senge (1990: 13) a learning organisation is a place where individuals are 'continually discovering how they can create their reality' – it is a place of discovery, growth and development that results in more dynamic and creative solutions. In this sense, once again the organisational hierarchy has gone, as has the power inherent in it. There is an openness that not only encourages sharing of ideas but of a genuine dialogue that can be really creative, but in order to create such procedures Senge concludes that what is required is a new type of management practitioner, more a leader than a traditional manager, and here Senge clearly recognises the dimension of power. As he (1990: 139) recognises 'Organisations learn only through individuals who learn (but) individual learning does not guarantee organizational learning', and implementing this learning ultimately rests with management which has the requisite authority and leadership expertise to implement and carry through successfully the changes that it feels are necessary. Basically, then, learning in the learning organisation is personal and private and more open, but what is important are the social outcomes of learning that have been implemented in the company in order to make it more competitive in the global market.

Senge's use of systems theory is important since it is a recognised socio-logical theory that has been discussed by many scholars over the years. It is an organisational theory that has not commanded universal acclaim amongst organisation theorists, the way that Senge's book has acquired fame amongst managers. Systems theory is open to critical discussion on at least seven counts according to Abercrombie *et al.* (2000: 354–5):

- it cannot deal adequately with conflict or change;
- its assumptions about equilibrium in society are based on a conservative ideology;
- it is so abstract that its empirical references are hard to detect;
- its assumptions about value consensus are not well grounded;
- it is difficult to reconcile assumptions about structural procedures with a theory of action;
- the teleological assumptions cannot explain underdevelopment or underutilisation;
- it is tautologous and vacuous.

We have already highlighted some of these in the foregoing discussion and we could proceed to argue that the persons within the organisation, and their learning, are not really considered within the framework of power. Indeed, change only happens when power is exerted within the organisation itself – by managers! Hence the learning organisation appears to be a man-agement theory for managers but it is weak conceptually, sociologically and educationally.

It is necessary, therefore, to recognise that power is not the only issue that needs to be understood within the learning organisation – it is also necessary to understand who the trendsetters are and how innovations spread through the company. People are important in the process and it is people, as actors – change agents, who are played down in these discussions and so it is important to return to re-examine the relationship between structure and action and learning.

What many writers on learning organisations do not focus upon is the idea of human capital (Schutz 1961) since they emphasise the way that indi-viduals might grow, not the way that they can be used. But those who control organisations control workers and if the workforce is to be regarded as capital, then they control both the financial and the human capital of the organisation. Consequently, for organisations to become Investors in People makes good sense in the knowledge economy, since it is through ensuring that workers continue to learn that the organisation becomes more effective. But the reason for investing in the workforce is not necessarily for the benefit of the worker – but for the gain of the organisation. The recipients of the investment are not the reason for the investment – the profits are – although the individuals might well benefit themselves through the organised learning that they have undertaken. Some non-governmental organisations, however, which are investors in people, may – but need not – have made their investment mainly for the benefit of their workforce. Clearly, the workers may gain a lot from their learning, but if they are human capital, then they are not ends in themselves but means to other ends – something contrary to Kant's argument that people are ends and not means! Human capital, as a concept, implies power and suggests that workers' learning is a means to another end. Having a flexible workforce, able to respond to the demands of the management and of the external forces is essential to organisations that have to keep adapting to the pressures that global capitalism exercises.

The learning organisation is different from bureaucracy, not because it does not have a hierarchy, but because those in the hierarchy have learned to create more open procedures for information processing so that they can facilitate or implement directly the outcomes that they and others in the organisation have learned. The learning organisation is the antithesis of the bureaucratic organisation in the sense of having a more responsive management in implementing new procedures and, maybe, in creating a slightly flatter organisation so that information can flow from bottom to top, and vice versa, more quickly. But it is not different in the oligarchic sense; the changes have been forced upon those who occupy places in the hierarchy by the forces of global capitalism that demand that productive organisations become more competitive or else they do not survive. It is the hierarchy that has then to implement new procedures and persuade the workers to adopt them, even to go to additional education and training so that they are better equipped to do so. But as most of the literature about learning organisations is written by management theorists for practising managers, the issues of power and control are not as significant since these can be assumed; their concern is in producing results, so that the greater part of most of these studies concentrates on generating the procedures that will enable the organisation to become more profitable – ultimately for their shareholders' benefit. Consequently, the emphasis now transfers to leadership! Nevertheless, we note a fundamental weakness in these as academic studies of organisations. An interesting paradox emerges from this – that in order to be effective and efficient in a competitive world those within the organisation need to be open and share with each other – perhaps it is a lesson that global capitalism needs to take unto itself as we contemplate the world that global capitalism is helping to create!

Having discussed all of these aspects of the learning organisation, it would be false to assume that learning organisations, or at least those that claim to be learning organisations, are necessarily successful in this global capital world. For instance, in the European Foreword of *Lifelong Learning* by Longworth and Davies (1996: ix), John Towers, the chief executive of Rover cars, wrote, 'We at the Rover Group Ltd are proud to be among the world's foremost "Learning Organizations". If that sounds strange coming from a manufacturing company, let me explain' and he went on to outline all the ways in which Rover had changed its bureaucratic structures and how it emphasised the strengths of its workers. Perhaps a decade later, with Rover having been taken over twice and returned to British ownership once, and with there now only being a chance for car manufacturing if the new Chinese owners put in cash, it casts some doubts on the validity of the claims about Rover, or the wisdom of using Rover as an example, especially when Towers actually claims that Rover 'has invested heavily in learning, and knows that that investment pays off' (p. ix). Not all organisations claiming to be learning organisations succeed and, clearly, more research is required into management-speak from the academic world of learning – amongst other research needed into the claims of both management and their gurus.

The learning city/region

One of the outcomes of globalisation has been that we have become more aware of the local – a form of glocalisation. Robertson (1995: 31) makes the point that 'there is an increasingly globe-wide discourse of locality, community, home, and the like' and so it is not surprising that there should be a focus on the local. The information society and its network counterpart have also assisted in this development as the ideas of the learning region and the learning city have arisen, in which local information networks have been established. In fact, we might see the learning region and learning city as new forms of community education and, consequently, we will discuss both of these together since they are very similar in structure.

In the same way as we noted that the concepts of society and organisation are reified in the above discussions, so we see the same process happening with the learning city.

> A learning city is one which strives to learn how to renew itself in a period of extraordinary social change. The rapid spread of new technologies presents considerable opportunities for countries and regions to benefit from the transfer of new knowledge and ideas across national boundaries. At the same time global shifts in capital flows and production are creating uncertainties and risk in managing national and local economies.
>
> (Department for Education and Employment – DfEE 1998: 1)

The DfEE definition of the learning city actually goes on to explain something of the origins of the idea – both global and local use of capital and technology. While many of the initiatives for learning cities and learning regions have come from adult educators, support is necessary from local government and local business and commerce. In fact, Longworth (1999: 114) suggests that the network consists of:

- primary and secondary education;
- universities and tertiary education;
- industry, business and commerce;
- professional bodies and special interest groups;
- adult and vocational education;
- social services and voluntary organisations;
- local government.

In my own experience, one learning region's committee was chaired by the local mayor and in another the idea did not take off apparently because the local mayor could not find sufficient support from educators. It is the partnership that makes it happen because learning cities are fundamentally top-down in as much as they are supported by local and regional governments and organisational leaders. More recently, Partnerships Online is seeking to establish similar online communities in towns and villages.

The learning city idea also comes from the same period as many other concepts discussed in this book – the early 1970s. But the first international meeting about the learning city did not happen until 1990, when one was organised in Barcelona. Thereafter the idea grew and it was one adopted and supported by the British government from the mid-1990s when the first local governments committed their towns and cities to become a learning city. Thereafter a learning city network evolved and the European Commission supported the development of networks to promote and support lifelong learning locally and regionally (EC 2003). Basically this movement towards learning cities and learning regions might be described as a new social movement or, better, as part of a wider new social movement which is lifelong learning itself – and we will discuss lifelong learning as a new social movement in subsequent chapters. But we will analyse learning cities under the same four sub-headings – aims, social base, means of action, organisations – as we will for lifelong learning as a new social movement in Chapter 7. It would probably be true to say that initiators of learning cities and regions are educators although support for the movement locally needs to come from a wider spread of sources. It is significant that while those advocating the learning or ganisation are futuristic, the world of work is more restrictive and less visionary, so that it is not surprising that it is educators who have adopted a more visionary approach and generated a new social movement – which might also be seen as a new way of looking at community learning.

New social movements differ from traditional social movements in that they are not class-based and from interest groups in as much as they are not small groups. Traditionally, a social movement was one which began with the people of working or lower classes, although often inspired and led by middle-class intellectuals and well-wishers, seeking to pressurise the government to act. In the new movements, which are not class-based, the aim is social transformation through the political process and in this case the leaders have emerged from education, often from traditional adult education. As Abercrombie *et al.* (2000) point out, new social movements can be distinguished by four features: aims, social base, means of action and organisation.

Aims

The aims of this movement are to create a culture of learning, of intended learning. Learning per se occurs naturally in the process of living but intended learning is basically vocational, although in learning cities and regions there is a greater emphasis on the non-vocational than there is in learning organisations. The second purpose of learning cities and regions, according to the DfEE (1998: 1) document, are 'to support lifelong learning' and 'to promote social and economic regeneration' through partnerships, participation and performance.

Social base

Unlike traditional social movements, the social base of new social movements is not social class, and in this case it appears to be professional educators, often from an adult education background, who have embraced lifelong learning, and the leadership can stem from one organisation – not necessarily an educational one. For instance, in Hull 'City Vision Ltd is the public/ private partnership charged with taking this ambition forward' (DfEE 1998: 15).

Means of action

Those who propagate the ideas of learning cities do not need action in the forms of social protest so much as lobbying those who are influential in their communities, such as local government, using advertising and other ways of spreading the 'good news' of learning and also seeking sponsorship, often from local business and industry.

Organisation

Usually the learning city is a partnership of educational and other service providers which includes business and industry and which has its own co-ordinating committee and, maybe, part-time or full-time staff. Unlike the learning organisation, the learning city sees itself as a partnership which seeks to provide learning opportunities for its citizens, thereby enriching the life of the people and contributing to the richness of the city. However, it would certainly be true to claim that the initiative has come from lifelong learning as such and that this was stimulated by the perceived need to create a knowledge economy.

Learning cities and learning regions have now become a feature of contemporary society. In the UK literature, nearly every large city seems to be a learning city. As early as 1998, there were 18 learning towns and cities cited by Yarnit (1998). But the same concept has emerged throughout the world, with European Union projects (EC 2003), local government White Papers, in the Basque country and elsewhere in the world, such as Australia. While the learning city need not focus primarily on the economy, it is natural that it should play a significant role and the OECD (2001), for instance, locates the learning city/region within the knowledge-based economy. Now an international network exists for learning towns and cities which illustrates something of the success of this aspect of the new social movement. However, learning cities frequently incorporate a slightly broader perspective. Consequently, it could be argued that learning cities, unlike learning organisations, seek to build the social capital of the region.

Social capital

One of the first writers to discuss social capital was Coleman (1990: 302), although Putnam (2000) points out that it was used as early as 1916, who claims, wrongly in my opinion, that it is a concept that is defined by its function since, as he points out elsewhere, what is functional to one person might be dysfunctional to another. It is, however, a form of social organisation in which personal relationships are significant and which Hanifan (1916) claimed as 'those tangible social relationships [that] count for most in the daily lives of people: namely good will, fellowship, sympathy, and social intercourse among individuals and families who make up the social unit' (cited by Putnam 2000: 19). In other words it reflects some of the ideas of community discussed by Toennies (1957). Hanifan, however, was self-conscious about using the concept and even then he felt that there had been a decline in rural communities in America (cited Putnam 2000: 445–6). Putnam's (2000) work is perhaps the most impressive study of the decline in social capital in America over the past few decades, a decline that reflects the decline in active citizenship. Social capital is the potentiality for social action that resides in groups through their shared norms and values, but it must be noted immediately that groups which do not work for the good of society but for their own ends, e.g. racist groups and fundamentalist religious sects, also possess social capital, so that all social capital is not necessarily socially good. Consequently, Putnam's work is not without its critics and there are, for instance, major problems with measurement of social capital. At the same time, there is widespread agreement that there has been a decline in civic participation over these past few decades, for whatever reasons, and this has allowed the forces of the substructure even more freedom. It is the lack of community that caused Putnam to write his book *Bowling Alone*, which emphasises the individualism of contemporary society.

Social capital and community spirit may be seen to have many similarities, if not be synonymous. It was, according to Durkheim (1915), the division of labour that changed these social structures. Putnam, however, examines a far wider set of data, looking at: civic and religious participation, the workplace, informal relationships, altruism and volunteering. He reaches the conclusion that there is a decline in community in America. Coleman, however, recognises that the term capital means that people can draw upon it in times of need. He goes on to ask why rational actors create social obligations and he claims that people can invest in order to create it but he recognises that it occurs as a by-product of other human actions. Nevertheless, Coleman's perspective is individualistic and instrumentally rationalistic and in many ways is the antithesis of what he is discussing. Coleman also suggests that by creating relevant social structures social capital might be created and in this reflects some of the ideas that were prevalent in city design in the same period. A question remains about the relationship of social capital to the learning city.

The idea of social capital has certainly been used as a yardstick in evaluating local communities. However, Baron *et al.* (2000: 243) suggest that social capital offers 'one way of apprehending and analysing the embeddedness of education in social networks'. But they go on to say that 'it also challenges the dominant human capital approaches . . . which concentrate on narrowly defined, short-term results or tidy analytical devices'. The outset of their argument is that social capital actually provides many opportunities for informal learning but that it is inherently narrowing – which is precisely the same type of argument that has existed for years about the advantages and disadvantages of living in small communities – but they produce considerable evidence.

In a sense, then, part of the research into social capital has taken us back to the ideas of the community and the community spirit, phenomena that have apparently declined tremendously as a result of the division of labour, although the same concern about the decline existed nearly a century ago. It might well be that this reflects the social process of constructing ideal communities, that we either see them as utopian and in the future or locate them in a dim and distant past! In both cases their function is to illustrate that we do not live in a perfect society – but then we may never ever do so! What these studies have shown, however, is that there are community resources that can enrich human living, although they might have their drawbacks; these resources might aid informal learning but through planning and learning we can create conditions and structures through which human living may be enriched but we cannot dictate that the community spirit will be created or learned. We will return to this issue when we examine the functions of lifelong learning which have been researched as unintended benefits of lifelong learning.

The question remains then, why should the term social capital have come to the fore at this particular time, especially as Hanifan (1916) was self-conscious about using the term to refer to social assets. But this is precisely the same point Schutz (1961) raised about using the term human capital: human beings are more than capital; it is just that instrumental rationality in its capitalist form relegates everything to its use-value for capital itself and as capitalism is the dominant ideology in contemporary society it has colonised not only our language but our thinking.

Conclusion

Throughout this study we have pointed to the dominance of advanced capitalism in contemporary society and we have argued that social change occurs as a result of the social pressures exerted by the capitalist system upon the wider society. We have seen how in the learning society and the learning organisation this perspective dominates; we have also seen how when we look at learning towns and regions the economic perspective is still a major player but the social as well as the economic elements have a greater part to play, even though the concepts employed are dominated by the same capitalist vocabulary. However, we have until this point not examined the idea of lifelong learning itself and for the remainder of this book we will analyse lifelong learning from a variety of perspectives.

Chapter 7

Lifelong learning

Thus far in this study we have shown how learning of all forms is affected by the structures of society, so that a sociology of human learning is not only a possible way of understanding learning, but a significant one. We have also argued that globalisation has exerted pressures on the structures of almost every society for change and one of the directions in which societies are being moved is towards the knowledge economy which, in its turn, is having effects on the educational systems of society and also on the lifestyles of members of the population. The social situation of competition, innovation and rapid change generated by globalisation in a knowledge economy have led to the emergence of lifelong learning. In the last chapter we explored the two meanings of the concept, both private and public, and concluded that there was a sense in which it referred to an interrelationship of personal learning and recurrent education. However, that interrelationship is not as simple as it appears on the surface since, as we pointed out, a result of the lowering of barriers between different sectors of society is that there are now many sites for learning and they intermesh. Learning is not only lifelong, it is life-wide. For heuristic purposes only, we are going to separate lifelong and life-wide into two chapters, dealing with lifelong learning here and life-wide learning in the following chapter. In this chapter we will, first, discuss the idea that lifelong learning has become a new social movement, then we will look at lifelong learning as a commodity; third, we will look at recurrent education and its relationship to practice; fourth, relevant types of personal learning as a response to the social forces of globalisation will be examined; fifth the value of lifelong learning is assessed; finally, lifelong learning has a demographic aspect and so we will look at learning and ageing. In the following chapter we will examine learning in relation to the life-world in which life-wide learning features much more prominently than it does in this chapter.

A new social movement

In our contemporary society people are frequently urged to return to learning, to get qualifications, and so on. It has become a new social movement aimed at human development and yet some of the institutions which are urging us to return to learning seem to have totally different motives, such as to try to sell their wares. In some ways this relates back to the two definitions that we have already discussed. It is the first way of viewing lifelong learning that lends itself to being regarded as a new social movement while the second approach allows for it to be seen as a marketable commodity trading on the claims of the former approach.

The private, existential definition of lifelong learning is about the process of transforming experience into knowledge and skills, etc. and resulting in a changed person, one who has grown and developed as a result of the learning. In this sense, learning is essential – indeed, like food and water are essential to the growth and development of the body, learning is an essential ingredient to the growth and development of the human person; it is one of the driving forces of human becoming and enriches human living. In this sense, learning assumes value – it is something self-evidently good, something that human beings must engage in if they are going to grow and develop and, as a result, be useful members of society. Learning, then, is a valuable human process and the more that we learn, the richer we will be as human beings, and the recognition of this has led to many campaigns to encourage learning. Although the main motivator of these campaigns has not always only been a concern to enrich the human person so much as to ensure that society's needs are met. Learning is necessary to ensure that individuals are employable, and it was claimed would enable European societies to achieve the Lisbon goals of making Europe a global leader by 2010 – now acknowledged it will not be achieved (Kok 2004). But some who have espoused this more humanistic and individualistic approach to learning have also embedded it in the social context of the knowledge economy, especially those who are responsive to the European Union's aspirations embodied in the Lisbon Declaration. 'Learning pays!' claims Ball (1998: 36–41): here we see a pragmatic and instrumental approach to learning and the learning society – it pays to learn. Ball actually produces no empirical evidence to support his claims, although there is clear evidence to show a correlation between the level of education and the amount of money earned, as we pointed out in the previous chapter (see also McGivney 2006: 40).

This rather evangelistic approach to lifelong learning, echoed by the writings of Longworth and Davies (1996) which reflects more than an academic approach to analysing the process, has become an ideology and a vision for the future. There are a variety of groups in the UK that fervently encourage learning, such as the Royal Society of Arts' project on Learning, the British Institute of Learning, the European Lifelong Learning Institute, and so on, and their existence suggests that lifelong learning has become a new social movement. This is a different approach to that adopted by Crowther (2006) who asks how lifelong learning should be associated with social movements rather than seeing it as a social movement. As we noted in the previous chapter, the same enthusiasm for lifelong learning occurs in the learning city network which has its own aims, means of action and organisation (Department for Education and Employment 1998). In addition, there are frequent media advertisements to persuade people to return to learning and many slogans like 'Learning is Fun' are publicised. New social movements differ from traditional social movements since they are not class-based interest groups agitating for political change. They tend to be broad movements seeking to change society through the political processes. As we noted in the previous chapter, Abercrombie *et al.* (2000) suggest that new social movements have four main features: aims, social base, means of action and organisation.

Aims

The aims of the lifelong learning movement are to create a culture of learning, or intended learning. Learning per se occurs naturally in the process of living but intended learning is basically vocational, although in learning cities and regions there is a greater emphasis on the non-vocational than there is in learning organisations.

Social base

Unlike traditional social movements, the social base of new social movements is not social class, and in this case it appears to be professional educators, often from an adult education background, who have embraced lifelong learning, and the leadership can stem from one organisation – not necessarily an educational one. For instance, in Hull 'City Vision Ltd is the public/private partnership charged with taking this ambition forward' (DfEE 1998: 15).

Means of action

Those who propagate the ideas of lifelong learning do not need action in the forms of social protest that adult educators were forced to take in the past. Since it has become institutionalised it is easier to lobby those who are influential in the various layers of society, and to spread the 'good news' through international and national conferences, publications and public lectures, and so on. In addition, we find advertising and other ways of spreading its message.

Organisation

Lifelong learning per se has a variety of organisations, as we have already noted and, in addition, there are learning city partnerships of educational and other service providers, which includes business and industry. These organisations are trying to create a greater awareness of the advantages of learning and to get educational establishments to provide more opportunities for adults to learn, so that the social movement has social aims which, in an interesting manner, actually coincide with those of the educational organisations and the government, but not always for precisely the same reasons. Consequently, one major difference between this new social movement and many other social movements is that it is pushing against an already opened door, whereas most traditional social movements seem to push against closed, and even locked, doors because they oppose the dominant sectors of society, as was the experience of many adult educators until the early 1970s.

However, lifelong learning, as we have pointed out, does not cover all academic disciplines and is not really about human learning, so much as a social institution that has also become a commodity on the learning market.

Lifelong learning as a commodity

As governmental funding for education has increased, even though it by no means covers the cost of the education institution, so it has become important that educational institutions continue to recruit fee-paying students and this has changed the ethos of many of these institutions. They now have to market their courses in order to recruit customers rather than students – an employer can pay for an employee to attend a course and then the employer rather than the student is actually the customer. However, this changing ethos is one that many academics do not like and it has been attacked in many publications: in higher education, for example, we get such titles from the USA as *The Knowledge Factory* (Aronowitz 2000), *Universities in the Market Place* (Bok 2003), *Academic Capitalism* (Slaughter and Leslie 1997); and in adult and continuing education (Tuckett 2005, amongst others). Each of these titles reflects precisely the same thing – universities are being forced to market their courses, through a variety of means, in order to gain financial income. In other words, lifelong learning has become a process of consumption in the learning market.

Once we see lifelong learning as a process of consumption we have to recognise the power of the consumers: they will only purchase what they want or what they need, and the more lifelong learning becomes vocational, the more likely it is that only specific teaching and learning commodities will be purchased. Stehr (1994) makes the point very clearly when he shows that the learning society utilises only scientific knowledge. Therefore we can also say that this approach to lifelong learning is generally not about learning a very broad range of knowledge – it tends to be instrumental and narrow, which is an impression that the concept of lifelong learning does not in any manner convey. Once it is recognised that lifelong learning tends to be about vocation, then the question must be raised about those who want or need to learn other forms of knowledge that are not emphasised. Government grants to further and higher education ensure that the vocational subjects are supported but the remainder are open to market forces and so there is a decline in non-vocational and leisure time education. In addition, this raises an issue about social inclusion: social inclusion is only about being included in what already exists and about conforming to the dictates of government and, ultimately, to the dominant forces of globalisation.

Significantly, both government and those who espouse lifelong learning as a new social movement want to know who is actually learning and so we get many surveys seeking to show who is enrolling on courses. In the UK, for example, there have been National Learning Surveys (Beinart and Smith 1998; LaValle and Blake 2001) and the National Institute of Adult and Continuing Education (NIACE) (Sargant 1991; Sargant et al. 1997; Sargant and Aldridge 2002; Aldridge and Tuckett 2004, inter alia) has also conducted surveys of the amount of learning undertaken by the population. These surveys provide excellent marketing information for the adherents to the movement but also for the policy makers and those who are marketing learning materials as a commodity, and we will return to these in a later chapter.

Lifelong learning (recurrent education)

The driving force for the introduction of this approach to lifelong learning is that employers demand an educated workforce in order to respond to a market that demands innovation and efficiency. This has resulted in a knowledge economy in which only specific forms of knowledge are being utilised and this, in its turn, has caused changes in the educational curriculum and well as to the system. However, this is a much more complex process of change than a simple direct cause and effect. Clearly, there are the direct forces of globalisation, but universities and colleges are having to enter the learning market and sell their commodities, so that they are also looking for customers. In addition, this has coincided with the professionalisation aspirations of some of the semi-professions, such as nursing, who have sought to gain university recognition for their training courses, so that the semi-professions are a potentially large source of revenue for the universities and the colleges. The growth of the knowledge economy has also assisted them in their quest, and many universities introduced degree courses for some of the semi-professions. Consequently, the first major change that we see is that the higher education system itself has changed, almost beyond recognition; in the UK, the government has set itself a target of getting 50 per cent of school leavers into higher education – a policy of inclusion. Consequently, both the further education and the higher education systems have changed tremendously and the UK has moved closer to the higher education system in the

USA where many of the semi-professions have long had access to the higher education system. It is perhaps significant to note that the knowledge economy demands, even if it does not need, such highly qualified novices when they embark upon their careers. Livingstone (2002), for instance, argues that there is not the employment for such a highly qualified workforce.

As a result of these changes to the higher educational system, at least three things have followed: the functions of higher education have changed; the nature of knowledge underlying university qualifications has changed; there has been a change on the perceived level of teaching. First, it was Lyotard (1984) who recognised that the functions of higher education would be changed as the knowledge economy became more significant and more professions gained access to it. He (1984: 48) wrote:

> In the context of delegitimation, universities and institutions of higher learning are called upon to create skills, and no longer ideals – so many doctors, so many teachers in a given discipline, so many engineers, so many administrators, etc. The transmission of knowledge is no longer designed to train an elite capable of guiding the nation towards its emancipation, but to supply the system with players capable of acceptably fulfilling their roles at the pragmatic posts required by its institutions.

But, despite this emphasis, we have not destroyed the need for experts, although we have wrongly downplayed it in recent years. Second, the fact that each of these professional groups being educated in the universities has demanded that part of the curriculum should be practical has meant that practical knowledge has assumed a major place in many courses and that the barriers between universities and the fields of practice have had to be broken down and expert practitioners have played a role in training and assessing for university awards. Coupled with this has been the recognition that the traditional relationship between theory and practice – applying theory to practice – is false in many situations. New advances in learning theory also point us to different relationships between theory and practice, including the recognition that in many instances theory might follow practice (Jarvis 1999). The market demands that new products be produced – it does not demand new theories in the first instance, although in some disciplines this might be the way forward. Third, the increase in the proportion of young people entering further and higher education in order to gain work and, significantly, the increase of those entering who are already working, has resulted in a change in the level of the theoretical knowledge being taught.

Indeed, the increase in the number of young people entering further and higher education has changed dramatically, as Table 7.1 indicates. Not only is the growth tremendous but it is significant that women's opportunities have changed so much during this period. However, while I suggest below that the greater the opportunity, the more chance there is for children from socially

Table 7.1 Young people entering further and higher education, 1970/1 and 2003/4 by sex (000s)

	Male		Female	
	1970/1	*2003/4*	*1970/1*	*2003/4*
Further Education				
Full-time	116	534	95	548
Part-time	891	1,434	630	986
Higher Education (undergraduate)				
Full-time	241	543	173	664
Part-time	127	261	19	445

Source: *Social Trends 2006*: 38.

deprived backgrounds to break into the system, education does still serve as a means of social reproduction.

> The socio-economic status of parents can have a significant impact on the GCSE attainments of their children. In England and Wales 76 per cent of pupils whose parents were from higher professional occupations achieved higher grades GCSEs (or the equivalent) in 2004, compared with 33 per cent of those whose parents were in routine operations. Educational attainment of parents can also influence the attainment of their children, 73 per cent of young people who had at least one parent qualified to degree level and 64 per cent who had at least one parent whose highest qualification was a GCE A level achieved five or more GCSEs at grades A* to C. This compares with 41 per cent of young people with parents whose higher qualification was below GCE A level.
>
> (*Social Trends* 2006: 41–2)

This is the pattern that sociologists have long reported and that, more recently, has been a constant theme in NIACE's reports (Sargant 1991; Sargant *et al.* 1997; Sargant and Aldridge 2002; Aldridge and Tuckett 2004). As Sargant and Aldridge make the point, it is a 'persistent pattern' and Aldridge and Tuckett call it, 'business as usual'.

The lowering of standards is an almost inevitable result if there has been a widening the entry level, although the above statistics illustrate that to a large extent it is still children from the same type of socio-economic background who have continued their education beyond compulsory school age. However, the lowering of standards might be found not so much in entry level since there was a vast increase in professional and technological employment in the 1960s to 1980s. By 2005, approximately 35 per cent of both males and females were classified as managerial and professional, and a further 5 per cent of males and 15 per cent females as intermediate and approximately a further 10 per cent of males and 5 per cent of females were self-employed (*Social Trends* 2006: 15)[1] which means that a greater proportion of young people have parents from these occupational categories and are, therefore, more likely to succeed at school. Consequently, the lowering of standards might be found at university level since 58.6 per cent of all students gaining a non-clinical degree in 2003/4 were first class or upper second class honours (McGivney 2006: 87), which is far higher than it has been in the past. Despite government denials, and those of university spokespeople, many academics have claimed that there has been a lowering in the standards of university education and the fact that such a high proportion of students achieve what used to be regarded as a 'good' degree gives credence to this claim.

However, the culture of the era is one in which elitism is apparently frowned upon, so that this cultural change also supports the movement to widen university entrance and to award more good degrees. Nevertheless, as Furedi (2004: 148) writes:

> It is difficult to take the wealthy and cultural mandarins seriously when they argue the case for eliminating elitist privilege and extending the agenda for inclusion. Some commentators take the view that the elites do not really mean what they say in relation to culture and education.

He goes on:

> Through a variety of devices – lifelong learning, certificates of competence, training and development – people's intellectual and cultural life becomes subject to institutional expectations. These trends stimulate the mood for conformity and passivity.
>
> The imperative of social engineering leads to the colonization of people's informal lives. The accreditation of prior learning is presented as an acknowledgement of the important learning experiences which people have acquired through their encounters in their experiences in their communities and at work. And many people are delighted that their lives are taken seriously by educators.
>
> (Furedi 2004: 154)

The danger of this process as Furedi recognises is that education accredits daily life and this becomes a mechanism of control. However, it is not only accreditation of prior learning but on-the-job training which can lead to qualifications through both part-time attendance of colleges and personal learning. It is, perhaps, at this point that an opportunity for those from underprivileged backgrounds to break into the educational system occurs.

Certainly the level of theory taught during many university courses might have changed and the lessening of the emphasis on theory might well give an impression that standards are lowering – they are certainly different. But much of the lowering of standards may merely reflect the fact that the more practical professions do not emphasise literary abilities in the same way as do the more traditional university courses. Indeed, the culture of equality which prevails at the moment, with its emphasis on competence rather than expertise, does raise questions about the nature of society. Among the factors that Furedi neglects is the fact that lifelong learning occurs in different sites and that there are times when learning in non-formal situations contributes to the understanding of the subject being studied in university. Consequently, there is a place for the accreditation of experiential learning and, therefore, the construction of portfolios illustrating and documenting the learning that has occurred. However, it must be pointed out that there is a singular danger that the accreditation of prior experiential learning might be seen as a sales promotion, a discount in the educational marketplace, offered to attract more customers to the educational supplier.

However, this is also only half the story in another way since entry to undergraduate courses is not the end of the lifelong learning process – even within the institutional framework. There has also been a massive increase in continuing professional development through the higher degree system (see Table 7.2). Over this same period we have seen a mushrooming of higher degree courses being offered. The same picture emerges here as we noted in Table 7.1. However, the major changes in postgraduate work have been the diversity of qualification and the amount of that work which is taught, as opposed to pure research. McGivney (2006: 88) notes that in 2002/3:

- 31.7 per cent were undertaking a taught higher degree;
- 22.3 per cent were undertaking a postgraduate diploma or certificate;
- 15.4 per cent were undertaking a professional qualification;
- 8.4 per cent were undertaking a higher degree by research.

At both Masters and doctoral level, there are now taught and research degrees offered and ones which are a combination of both. As the volume of

Table 7.2 Numbers in postgraduate education, 1970/1 and 2003/4 by sex (000s)

	Male		Female	
	1970/1	2003/4	1970/1	2003/4
Full-time	33	110	10	111
Part-time	15	138	3	170

Source: *Social Trends 2006*: 38.

knowledge increases and more specialisms emerge, so the need to teach as opposed to research beyond the first degree level grows and it is in Masters and professional doctorate postgraduate degree courses that the teaching element has increased. Indeed, a taught Masters degree is almost the entry level, or at least the career grade, for some high-status professions in contemporary society. A great deal of the research is also undertaken in the workplace and there has been a considerable interplay between theory and practice and also between the university and the workplace. Work-based learning is, therefore, an important element in lifelong learning and practical knowledge is a more holistic way of understanding knowledge. Aristotle recognised this:

> The cause is that such wisdom is concerned not only with universals but with particulars, which become familiar with experience, but a young man has no experience, for it is length of time that gives experience: indeed, one might ask the question too, why a boy becomes a mathematician, but not a philosopher or a physicist. It is because the objects of mathematics exist by abstraction, while the first principles of these other subjects come from experience.
>
> (Aristotle 1925: 148)

Of course, Aristotle was writing about wisdom, a word that has fallen into some disuse in recent times, as we prefer to talk about knowledge and competence. Perhaps we need to rediscover not only practical knowledge but practical wisdom. Nevertheless, it is in practice that the experience of the practitioner comes to the fore; with it, therefore, must come the learning that has occurred in the practice situation. Consequently, it is hardly surprising that in contemporary society, higher degrees should assume a more practical orientation. Practitioner doctorates are an almost inevitable outcome of this process, especially when the academic qualification is one of the symbols of lifelong learning that is acceptable in the employment market.

Similarly, with an increasing emphasis on practitioners, it is hardly surprising that universities have to change their methods of delivery and also provide opportunities for students to study on a part-time basis. This has also entailed them changing the whole structure of courses; modularisation, for instance, has facilitated both the delivery of courses by distance and part-time face-to-face study. In addition, modular structures are useful since universities can market certain elements of relevant, especially work-based courses rather than the whole degree and give credit for it.

However, as education has been forced to become more practical and expand its brief beyond the realms of theory, the traditional tripartite role of the academic – teaching, research and service (or in some situations, teaching, research and administer) – has changed almost beyond recognition, as we will see in Chapter 8. These changes are also the result of the need for some to undertake their education at a distance; traditional distance or electronic means of delivery has meant that the role of the teacher has expanded. Significantly, the role of the practitioner/manager has also changed. On the one side, we get teacher practitioners (Jarvis and Gibson 1997) and, on the other, practitioners and managers who become fieldwork teachers, coaches, mentors and assessors (Schön 1987, *inter alia*).

Consequently, we can see that the recurrent aspect of lifelong learning has grown tremendously over this period – indeed, the change has occurred much more rapidly since 1990/1. The number of students in both further and higher education in England and Wales more than doubled between then and 2003/4: there were 2.234 million in 1990/1 and 4.850 million in 2003/4 in further education and 1.175 million in 1990/1 and 2.246 million in 2003/2004 in higher education (*Social Trends 2006*: 38). While we know the number of enrolments in formal education, we know far less about those forms of learning that occur throughout life but which do not entail enrolling in educational courses.

The value of lifelong learning

Learning is a driving force in human living, it is one of the major means by which we become ourselves, it is a stimulus enriching our lives and making us truly human. In this sense lifelong learning is good. It is impossible to conceptualise a human being who does not learn. Hence both theorists of learning and those who espouse the social movement encouraging learning have a very moral foundation to their beliefs and practices. Learning is self-evidently good.

This self-evident goodness of learning has also permeated the recurrent education aspects of lifelong learning, often without a great deal of reformulation, so that the second approach to lifelong learning 'trades' on the value intrinsic to the first approach. Nevertheless, this self-evident goodness in learning is less evident in self-directed learning; there are at least two ways in which we might illustrate this: the first is the market and the second is seeing lifelong learning as a means of control. First, the learning market is not driven by concern for the learner but concern for the provider and even the provider's profit and its own and shareholders' interests. This is the nature of the market system but profit is not a self-evidently good concept since its flip side is that it is taking from the consumers more than the cost of manufacturing and marketing the product which might be viewed as a form of exploitation. Increasingly, however, we are finding profit and loss accounts of educational providers being presented to governors' meetings and university courts, although not to the general public, in the way that public corporations have to declare their financial returns publicly.[2] Second, employers are in a position to expect their employees to learn and to keep abreast with changes as work becomes increasingly knowledge-based and employment-based on the level of educational achievement. In other words, it has become an instrument of control that employers can exert, and so, in Illich and Verne's (1976) words, employees can become 'imprisoned in a global classroom'; employees are expected to attend continuing education courses, often, at their own expense and at times which are detrimental to other aspects of their and their family's lives. For instance, in the research of Hewison and her colleagues (2000: 186), they record that:

> Less than half the sample (42 per cent) said that they thought the course was fitting reasonably well with home and family life. Forty-eight percent (n=43) thought that the course was a strain and 10 per cent of the participants (n=9) thought that the course was causing serious detrimental effect to their home and personal lives.

They go on to state:

> The rhetoric of the *learning society* is upbeat and positive. It is about 'opportunities' and the benefits that learning can bring. Lifelong learning promises that there will be many such opportunities, following one after another, throughout an individual's career.
>
> To many of the participants in our study, such a prospect would be a threat not a promise. It is not that they lacked the motivation to learn, but rather that learning opportunities were often offered on very disadvantageous terms.
>
> (Hewison *et al.* 2000: 186, italics in original)

Since Hewison's sample consists of health service employees, many were probably women and this might suggest that in this still male-dominated world, even lifelong learning is not always attractive to everybody and that an element of this value orientation may be male-dominated, which calls for a feminist perspective on lifelong learning to be undertaken. There is clearly an element of social control in the way that lifelong learning opportunities are presented in some work situations and so it can be argued that lifelong learning is no longer self-evidently good. The value of the phenomenon depends on what aspects of lifelong learning are being analysed and the perspective that is being adopted in the analysis. Indeed, the crude claim that 'learning pays' does not do justice to the fact that learning is also costly – not only economically but also socially and personally.

Nevertheless, there remains a market value of lifelong learning and this can be seen in three ways. First, we see it in the fact that there is, amongst other things, an economic return on lifelong learning as McGivney (2006) showed and which was mentioned above. Second, there is an educational value given to personal learning through the accreditation of experiential and prior experiential learning. Third, the accreditation is itself proof that a person has undertaken a course of study or is capable of performing the types of role that are specified in the qualification which, therefore, becomes currency in the labour market. There is, however, one other aspect of accreditation: each qualification is not only currency in the labour market, it is a way by which employers can continue their surveillance and control of employees by requiring it and even rewarding those who continue their studies and are able to report that they have gained another award.

For a wide variety of reasons, such as student mobility in the liquid society, the increasing complexity of society and its knowledge and skills base, the development of education and learning as a commodity on the learning market and the recognition that learning is personal and experiential has meant that the traditional method of attending formal education and sitting examinations to gain an educational qualification has become outmoded. While this traditional approach has still been suitable for full-time students, especially in modularised courses, it was less suitable for students involved in lifelong learning and recurrent education. Recognition had to be given to personal learning outside of the formal education system and so the accreditation of experiential learning (APEL) developed. Significantly, many of the APEL schemes are based upon Kolb's (1984) experiential learning cycle (Baile and O'Hagan 2000).

In addition, as the idea of competence rather than just knowledge became a basis for qualifications, it became more necessary to recognise the experiential learning that occurred during the practical element, so it became accredited. As accreditation of non-formal education within professional education and training courses began to emerge, education itself was being changed during the latter half of the twentieth century. Clearly, both modularisation and accreditation of experiential learning were beneficial to educational organisations as it enabled them to extend the scope of their clientele and to lifelong learners

Lifelong learning and the life cycle

Throughout recorded history society has changed very slowly until recent times, more slowly than human beings matured so that as individuals aged and moved from one period of their lives to another society had to recognise this in the form of *rites de passage* (van Gennap 1960 [1908]). As individuals grew from children to adults, and so on, they had to learn new roles relating to their newly acquired status and so initiation rituals served as periods of learning (see Chapter 2). There have been several well-known life cycles constructed by scholars, such as Erikson (1963), Levinson *et al.* (1978), Levinson and Levinson (1996). They have constituted an area of study in traditional adult education courses and it would still be true to say that age is a factor in the way we learn. As the West has become an ageing society educational gerontology is becoming a more significant field of study.

However, over the last century or two the pace of change has speeded up and change has become a constant feature of this book. Indeed, we have seen that it has almost become synonymous with learning and many of the rituals of status change have almost disappeared or, at least, assumed less social significance. This is not to deny that some status change rituals still retain a great deal of significance for family and friends, because they are the ones who are immediately affected by the changes. Moreover, the formalised learning attached to these rituals has also become less significant and individuals, if they want to learn more about the new roles and statuses into which they enter, are being left with the responsibility for finding out about them for themselves, although in the work organisation a mentor is sometimes appointed to assist the new employee, or new status holder, to learn their role. Consequently, there is a great emphasis placed on non-formal and informal learning in rapidly changing society, some of which has to be recognised more widely in society.

As we have already argued in this book, the idea of lifelong learning has really reflected society's concern for adult learning, especially working adults, so that lifelong learning has effectively not covered the life cycle at all. Consequently, a whole area of lifelong learning has been emerging in Western society and with it a new educational study – older adults learning and educational gerontology.

Learning and demography

The Western world is, by and large, an ageing world. In the UK in 2004, for instance, 9.6 million people, or 16.05 per cent of the population are over the age of 65 years, which is the statutory age of retirement for men at the present time – the third age; in the USA it is about 13 per cent. However, 4.58 million or 7.7 per cent of the population are 75 years and older, which may be termed the fourth age, although another way of looking at this definition is when the older person ceases to be independent (statistics from *Social Trends* 2006). This picture of an ageing population is true for the whole of the European Union (*Social Trends* 2006: 12). Significantly, there are few institutionalised learning opportunities for older adults apart from the traditional liberal adult education. McGivney (2006: 64) notes that in 1996 there were 2 per cent of the 65–74 years age group and none above this age in full-time education, but by 2005 there were 0 per cent of both age groups in full-time education. However, *Social Trends* 2006 (p. 39) reports that there were 7 per cent of the population above 50 years but below 60 years (women) and 65 (men) who were studying for a qualification.[3]

These statistics can be interpreted in at least two different ways: that older people lose the incentive to carry on studying or that employers no longer give older workers the same opportunities for further training that they give younger ones, and in these instances ageism at work becomes an issue – one that will incease in the coming years as the age of retirement is increased.

However, as funding is increasingly directed to young adults and vocational education, we have seen a loss of 1.5 million adult learning places (Tuckett 2005) in liberal adult education and so incidentally the elderly are institutionally discriminated against by government policy. Yet there is an increasing number of active elderly people, many of whom want to continue to learn and one of the institutions that has encouraged this is the University of the Third Age (U3A). Started in Toulouse in 1972 by Pierre Vellas, the universities of the third age have spread rapidly throughout the world. Indeed, there were – at the time of writing – 571 universities of the third age in the UK (*U3A News* 2005/6: 8) and some are growing so fast that they are doubling their membership in a single year. When *Learning in Later Life* in 2001 was written, there were only just over 400 (Jarvis 2001b) in the UK. Naturally, older people do not always want to learn vocational subjects and so, as we witness the decline of liberal adult education within the institutional adult education framework, we might see a new and vibrant basis for human studies in later life. Among the most popular subjects are computer studies, music, social sciences, drama and play reading, history, arts and crafts and other leisure time activities, such as educational visits and walking.

Similar organisations began in 1962 in the USA. The Institute for Retired Professionals was founded in New York at that time, thereafter there was a growth of Elderhostel and then the Institutes for Learning in Retirement came into being, which are now called Lifelong Learning Institutes. Perhaps the rapid growth in these organisations throughout the Western world also reflects the fact that as more people are required to work with knowledge, the more they want to continue to learn as they age, which may be one of the unintended benefits of the knowledge economy. Certainly from my own experience people joining the universities of the third age do have a relatively high level of education.

Chene (1994) showed that community-based learning groups fulfil a number of functions other than learning, all of which are true to my own experience of working with this age group: they enable new friendships to be created; generate mutual aid; allow for the sharing of experiences; generate a family spirit; provide a sense of belonging. Clearly, we see that the incidental learning is as significant as the intended learning for those older people who join in these activities. Amongst the other functions of such activities is the retention of mental fitness: Cussack and Thompson (1998) reported on a project initiated in one older people's centre in Vancouver which consisted of a six-week needs assessment programme and an eight-week programme of workshops, etc. These workshops were all about mental activity and the outcome was that the participants increased in their measured scores for creativity, optimism, openness to new ideas, willingness to take risks, mental flexibility, willingness to speak their minds, ability to learn new things, memory and confidence that they could remember. Other research has demonstrated similar findings, so that we can see that there are hidden benefits of learning in later life and yet we find that nearly all of these activities are organised by non-governmental organisations rather than the State.

Conclusion

Traditionally, it was argued that education should always provide a balanced curriculum, although as lifelong learning grows in popularity, it might be argued that vocational learning will occupy certain periods in the lifespan and learning in the humanity occupy others. For those knowledge workers, used to learning in the workplace, learning is but an extension of work, but on retirement they might feel the need to continue learning and begin to study non-vocational topics. The breadth of the curriculum might be lifespan and not necessarily life-wide; it is to this topic that we now turn.

Chapter 8

Life-wide learning

We all live in our own worlds – our life-world – which Schutz and Luckmann (1974: 21) define as 'that reality the wide-awake, normal, mature person finds given straightforwardly in the natural attitude'. Fundamentally, it is the sense of feeling at home in the world, when our internal sense of reality is in harmony with our perception of the external reality at any given moment in time. Living in harmony, we relate to people in our immediate environment with the assumption that their perceptions of reality are the same as ours: this enables interaction and common speech patterns in such a way as to generate a sense of inter-subjectivity – it is something that we share as a result of our primary socialisation. Our secondary socialisation, however, is the process of becoming members of different groupings that are part of our life-world. Fundamentally there is a shared culture between those with whom interaction occurs in the immediate life-world. It is such that we can take the world for granted and we can do so as a result of our previous learning and memorisation of past events which we have internalised.

> Each step of my explication and understanding of the world is based at any given time on a stock of previous experience, my own immediate experiences as well as such experiences as are transmitted to me from my fellow-men and above all from my parents, teachers, and so on.
>
> (Schutz and Luckmann 1974: 7)

What Schutz and Luckmann fail to say in the above quotation is that it is not just the past experiences but what we learn from them and so it might be more accurate to say not 'stock of previous knowledge' but 'previous learning', so that this includes skills, attitudes, values, beliefs, and so on. Because we can make these assumptions we can act in an almost unthinking manner and, in a sense, we can presume upon our world and we do not need to learn from it. There is a sense, therefore, in that our everyday life is premised upon the fact that reality is static and unchanging and that, therefore, both we and those with whom we interact within our life-world can continue to act in the same way as we have in the past without having to learn anything new. In this sense, continuity is the order of the day, but one of the features of this new global world is of rapid social change – the forces from the substructure of society and from governments introducing new policies, laws, procedures, and so on – and so, in another sense, discontinuity is also a daily situation. Consequently, trying to keep abreast with the social discontinuities created by the advanced capitalist global core means that we can no longer assume that this reality will continue to be unchanging. The fact that individuals are more globally mobile also means that their life-worlds are subject to massive and continuing changes – discontinuities that create a sense of disjuncture between people's internalised perception of reality and their present experience of it. Such a sense of disjuncture is not just something one individual experiences – it is something that everybody experiences, so that it is not just forces from outside the life-world, as it were, forcing change, it is also immediate pressures resulting in interaction between close associates sometimes demanding renegotiation of meanings and practices, and so on. These are what Habermas (1987: 125) refers to as 'problematic situations' since new definitions are required. Consequently, disjuncture is frequent but intermittent during the course of daily living – this is the individual experience – discontinuity is the social situation that causes it.

Disjuncture, the sense of not feeling at home in the world, occurs in a wide variety of ways at one time or another – individuals do not understand, do not know how to behave, cannot understand other's attitudes, beliefs, values, and so on. But it also occurs at different levels of intensity and difficulty, which may be seen on a continuum from a sense of feeling at home at one end to feeling isolated, alienated and anomic at the other. It will be recalled from earlier in this volume (Chapter 1), and in the first volume of this series, that disjuncture is a necessary condition for learning to occur, so that there is a relationship between the type of disjuncture and the learning demanded in order to recreate the conditions of harmony; Table 8.1 shows how this may be depicted.

There are many reasons why people do not respond, such as not having sufficient time, interest, motivation, and so on. Elsewhere I have recognised

Table 8.1 The continuum of disjuncture

	Type of disjuncture				
	Harmony (no disjuncture)	Slight disjuncture	Disjuncture	Major disjuncture	Strangerhood (total disjuncture)
Level of learning required to re-establish harmony	Non-learning	Minor adjustments (incidental learning)	New learning (some will not respond)	New learning effort/motivation necessary (many might not respond)	Almost impossible to bridge the gap in short time Alienation Anomie

that non-consideration and rejection are forms of non-learning (Jarvis 1987, 1992, 2006, *inter alia*). In the same way, migrants might be regarded as strangers but also, for instance, a person without advanced scientific or technological knowledge entering a scientific research laboratory would be a stranger in the situation. Consequently, the continuing failure to learn and accept the language and sub-culture of the group, either through non-learning or through not accepting aspects of that sub-culture, might also result in experiencing a sense of strangerhood that might result in individuals leaving the group.

When we are in a state of non-learning, presuming upon the world, time passes in an almost undefined manner, which Bergson (1999 [1965]) called *durée*. But when disjuncture occurs, then we become conscious of time – we are in a situation in which we may have an episodic experience, and it is from this that learning might occur, or the motivation to learn something new in the future might arise.

Individual learning in everyday life

As a result of globalisation and rapid social change, individuals have to keep on learning to feel at home in the world and this occurs in every aspect of daily living. Apart from the formal learning discussed above, therefore, there is also incidental and self-directed learning.

Incidental learning

Much of our daily life functions on the assumption that society does not change and so we can behave in the same way as we have done previously in similar situations. However, in the globalising world society is changing much more rapidly as, indeed, is the world of work. It is not unfamiliar to hear people say, 'I don't know what this world is coming to these days' and even to hear people at work say 'The place is not what it used to be'. This may reflect the idea that some people no longer wish to keep on learning but for others it suggests that they have to respond to the changes in an unplanned manner and that they maybe are finding it difficult. In contrast, in my own research into human learning, I have frequently asked people to describe a learning incident in their lives and my respondents have often had great difficulty in isolating learning, which suggests that incidental learning may be very frequent and often unacknowledged, even unnoticed.

Incidental learning has assumed a more significant place in our understanding of learning since a greater recognition has been given to experiential learning. This has been enhanced by the fact that much learning in the workplace is incidental (Marsick and Watkins 1990) and occurs because of the context. In fact Marsick and Watkins (1990: 16) believe 'that the context is more important to learning from experience when the nature of the task is interpersonal or social in nature' although they are careful to differentiate it from informal learning. In this sense, it is 'a by-product of some other activity' (p. 127). While this might be true when examining incidental learning in the workplace, it is less likely to be the case when it occurs in non-work situations. The fact that it has assumed a more prominent place in research into learning is clearly because of the rapidity of social change.

Self-directed learning

Self-directed learning is certainly no new phenomenon, even though adult educators were quite surprised to discover how prevalent it was when they began to study it (Johnstone and Rivera 1965; Tough 1979), despite the status of Samuel Smiles's famous book on *Self Help* (1859). Tough discovered that the majority of his respondents were involved in projects – a project was a minimum of seven hours spent in the previous six months. Only 1 per cent of his respondents sought credit from their learning. Candy (1991) rightly regards self-direction as a method of learning in which the learner is in control and he (pp. 32–46) suggests that there are six reasons for the rise in interest in self-directed learning:

- the democratic ideal;
- ideology of individualism;
- egalitarianism;
- subjective or relativist epistemology;
- humanistic education;
- the construct of adulthood and adult education's search for identity.

It is significant that both Tough and Candy were writing at a time before learning in the workplace became popular and none of their reasons are work-based. But in the UK *National Adult Learning Survey* of 1997, Beinart and Smith (1998: 79) used the concept of non-taught learning and they suggested that there are four types, all of which are much more work-oriented:

- studying for qualifications without enrolling on a course;
- supervised training in the workplace;
- time spent keeping up to date about work by reading or attending seminars;
- trying to improve knowledge and skill without taking part in a taught course.

Of their respondents, 57 per cent claimed to have participated in non-taught learning in the three years prior to the survey and 41 per cent said that they had been involved in both taught and untaught learning. By the 2001 national survey (LaValle and Blake 2001), non-taught learning had become self-directed learning and 60 per cent of the respondents had claimed to have undertaken it in the previous three years. Once again the emphasis is on work-based learning apart from the older respondents, although there is a category of other forms of self-direction in their report.

While self-directed learning is not a new phenomenon, its orientation to work and the fact that it is included in surveys on adult learning are both indicative of the effects of advanced capitalism on society. The extent to which this is the main driving force for self-directed learning is harder to determine, although most respondents (82 per cent) were undertaking their learning in order to improve their knowledge or skills. Significantly, this is one of the implications of the change in terminology from lifelong education to lifelong learning: education is a social institution provided by others, such as the State or the workplace, but learning is individual and so it is the individual learners' responsibility to direct their own learning.

However, our life-world is more than just ourselves and our own individuality; we live and work in families, communities and organisations and so our learning has a social dimension.

Learning in communities of practice

We are all born into families and learn the sub-culture of our immediate environment through interaction with significant and generalised others and, increasingly, through the media and our early years at school. While this is clearly an aspect of lifelong learning, it is one that I do not wish to explore here since we would be looking at the intricacies of primary socialisation, family life and early schooling. For the sake of this study I want to take childhood development as a given and I want to focus on secondary socialisation and learning in adulthood generally.

Most of us live our lives in communities which form part of our life-world. Each community has its own norms, values and language. We are members of families, schools, colleges, universities, clubs, leisure organisations, churches and work communities. During the process of social living, we might join some of these organisations and learn to become members, and as members we might continue to learn in order to remain an active participant in the organisation or, eventually, we may have to, or decide to, leave the organisation and move on. All three processes involve learning and, as yet, only the first two have actually been studied in any depth from a learning perspective (Lave and Wenger 1991; Wenger 1998) and we will examine briefly both of these studies in order to highlight the sociological issues that they raise.

In both of these studies we are introduced to the term 'community of practice' which Wenger (1998: 45) regards as 'the sustained pursuit of a shared enterprise'. While Wenger's own research was conducted in a work-based situation neither he nor Lave restrict the use of the term to work-based organisations. We will discuss these in the next section. Basically, the Lave and Wenger (1991) study is about the process of learning during socialisation and so we will first of all focus upon this and we will show how their understanding of learning is both behaviouristic and functionalistic, and that the process which they examine assumes only certain forms of learning. In addition, we will argue that any sociological approach to learning must be consistent with sociological theory itself.

Lave and Wenger (1991) trace the way in which individuals become members of one of five different groups: four occupations – midwives, tailors, quartermasters, butchers; one NGO – Alcoholics Anonymous. They (p. 54) claim that there is an absence of theorising about the social world in terms of learning, which is rather sweeping since there had been a great deal of research in both Europe and America that pointed in this direction – from studies of the life-world (Schutz and Luckmann 1974), studies of work (Argyris and Schön 1974, 1978; Schön 1983, 1987) and sociology of learning (Jarvis 1987). Nevertheless, they insightfully trace the learning trajectory of someone moving from the periphery of an organisation centrifugally, although they do not look at any people who are not successfully socialised and seek to understand their learning even though they make reference to such persons (p. 36). They view legitimate peripheral participation as 'a way to speak about the relations between newcomers and old-timers, and about activities, identities, artefacts, and communities of knowledge and practice' (p. 29) and, while they are conscious of the idea of negotiation here, they do not look at disagreement between the two nor the power inherent in the position of the old-timer.

They are rightly concerned about the whole person and about the way that the learner relates to others within the organisation and how the organisation maintains its own culture and transmits it through learning in different situations within the organisation – hence their study raises important points about the way that we learn in organisations. They (1991: 34) see situated learning as:

> a transitory concept, a bridge, between a view according to which cognitive processes (and thus learning) are primary and a view according to which social practice is primary, generative phenomenon, and learning is one of its characteristics.

They (p. 35) go on to claim that 'learning is an integral part of generative social practice in the lived-in world'. This is a clear statement of lifelong learning within this specific context and one with which it would be difficult to disagree, although their understanding of learning is restricted. They (p. 53), for instance, point out that as 'an aspect of social practice, learning involves the whole person' and they conclude that learning implies that learners become different persons (p. 53), but nowhere do they discuss the concept of the person nor discuss how the whole person is affected by the learning, and neither do they include in their own definition of learning anything other than action and knowledge. Indeed, they define learning as 'a dimension of social practice' (p. 47). This, then, is a behaviouristic definition of learning, which is a restricted understanding of human learning (see Jarvis 2006). They go on to narrow their approach even further:

> The practice of the community creates the potential 'curriculum' in the broadest sense, that which may be learned by newcomers with legitimate peripheral access. Learning activity seems to have a characteristic pattern. There are strong goals for learning because learners, as peripheral participants, can develop a view of what the whole enterprise is about, and what there is to be learned. Learning itself is an improvised practice.
> (Lave and Wenger 1991: 92–3)

The socialisation process as they describe it is rather as if the sub-culture of the organisation, internalised by old-timers, is static and that in passing from periphery to centre newcomers pass through a static sub-culture which they internalise. However, since the communities of practice which they describe are themselves recipients of the social forces exerted by globalisation and advanced capitalism, there is not a static sub-culture and even the old-timers are forced to learn new things. This sense of change and the way that the old-timers negotiate global change and the potential of conflict between the old-timers are not discussed. Lave and Wenger could claim that for the purposes of their study they placed parameters around the communities of practice but this artificialises the process that they researched.

Fundamentally, this is an insightful study of successful socialisation processes in which behaviouristic learning and a functionalistic approach to organisations are utilised. It is concerned to show how this learning process contributes to the maintenance of the organisation as a whole, but it does not discuss conflict, change or individual meaning and motivation. Neither does it account for the type of learning that leads some people not to join an organisation or others to leave it – but these are also lifelong learning in the community. Indeed, their conception of learning, limited as it is to behaviour and meaning is very restricted. Herein lie some of its weaknesses. We can also see here the fundamental relationship between behaviouristic approaches to learning and functionalistic interpretations of society or social groups – both of which have severe limitations. This is a point to which we have already referred in Chapters 1 and 6, and one to which we will return below.

Nevertheless, this study laid the foundations for Wenger's (1998) excellent study of *Communities of Practice*. Wenger's approach overcame many of the problems that were raised in the previous paragraphs, but not all of them. He used a similar approach to the previous book, but this time he used just two case studies rather than five short vignettes and these are based on a claims processing office. He focused upon one person, Ariel, in the first study and one procedure taught in a training class in the second. At the heart of this study is a social theory of learning in which he (1998: 3–17) suggests that in order to devise such a theory it is necessary to look at eight different sets of theory:

- social structure
- power
- identity
- subjectivity
- situated experience
- meaning
- practice
- collectivity.

Wenger illustrates how the office functions, how newcomers enter it and acquire its culture and how they respond to the pressures generated by the changes introduced from above. In this sense, this is a significant study of the way that the office functions. However, he (1998: 14) makes a most important point in understanding his work when he suggests that while the social structure-situated experience axis is an important backdrop of his work he neither concentrates on 'structure in the abstract or the minute choreography of interactions'. While this makes his study manageable, it does raise some questions about learning as specific processes that occur in situated experience. Indeed, he suggests that situated experience is one of the contributory factors to learning in the same way as is the social structure and power, and so on, whereas I would argue that social structure, power and the practice itself are contributory factors of experience which is the start of the learning process. This is because I see experience as the start of the learning process and that the process happens within the person, who is in a social situation. Wenger (1998: 89) would certainly accept that the person is changed as a result of learning but he (p. 86) defines learning as a characteristic of practice. In this sense Wenger has a behaviourist approach to learning and for him it is something that happens as a result of acting in social situations rather than as a result of living itself, and while in many situations they occur simultaneously they are not actually precisely the same phenomenon: I cannot act without being alive but I can be alive and conscious without practising. However, Wenger's work is so insightful because we all live in a number of different communities of practice during the process of daily living; for instance, I am a member of my work organisation, of leisure organisations, of family, and so on. In all of these his approach appears to be perfectly valid but if I undertake self-directed learning to suit my own interests when I am alone then I learn because I am consciously aware not because I am doing anything. Similarly, isolates learn, partly they learn that they are excluded but they also learn about themselves and about their life-world.

Wenger would claim, I think, that his is an organisational theory of learning but, like other organisational theories, as we pointed out earlier (see also Jarvis 2006), it neglects the person of the learner. Indeed, he has an over-socialised conception of the person (Wrong 1963) – one of the major criticisms of certain forms of functionalist and structuralist theory. From the position adopted here, it is the experience that we have in a social context that is the basis of learning and of the ensuing actions, and the insightful research that Wenger has undertaken here point to an enriched understanding about experiencing social situations from which we learn. Nevertheless, from a management perspective, neither individual persons nor their learning processes might be as significant as the smooth and efficient functioning of the organisation itself, so that Wenger's excellent study has been widely acclaimed in management circles. It certainly raises important issues for a sociological approach to learning.

The alternative to this critique would, I think, be that we would need to redefine learning and move away from the person of the learner to activities or organisational procedures in which the learning occurs – but then we are actually discussing totally different phenomena and if we adopted such an approach to learning we would still be faced with the individual process that we have defined as learning. Consequently, the philosophical–psychological approach adopted in the first volume of the study (Jarvis 2006) still appears to be fundamental to human learning, but we do need to expand our understanding of human experience in the social context so that we can have an even richer understanding of human learning.

The experiences we have will affect not only our learning but perhaps also the way that we learn. For instance, in an authoritarian regime I might learn to learn non-reflectively but in an open and democratic regime I might learn to learn in a critical, creative and reflective manner – this might well depend upon the experience we have, our will power and the biography (how we have been moulded by previous learning) that we bring to the situation. These factors contribute to the experience that we subsequently have and from which we learn. Lippitt and White's (1958) well-known study of different leadership styles producing different behavioural outcomes points the way in this respect.

It is also necessary to study the way that we learn when we leave a community of practice but I do not know of any studies that examine this process apart from those in primitive societies studied by anthropologists as referred to earlier in this volume – see Turner (1969) but it does seem important to look at reference group theory and revisiting the idea of the influence of significant others on our learning. During our lifetime we all go though the process of joining and leaving organisations, as well as being members of them, so that our life-wide learning does need research.

Learning in the workplace

The workplace is one of the communities of practice, perhaps the most significant in many people's lives, so that it is not surprising that Wenger's (1998) study has become such a popular piece of work. Indeed, when we return to our understanding of globalisation, it is hardly surprising that the workplace features so prominently in contemporary studies of learning, nor is it surprising that employability features most prominently in the European Union policy statements about lifelong learning. More significantly, it is a world within which knowledge is not only changing rapidly, it is the world in which most new knowledge is being produced through research – much of which is conducted in the workplace. We will recall Stehr's (1994) point that the knowledge society only employs certain forms of knowledge and they are the ones that change the most rapidly. In addition, Lyotard (1984) argued performative knowledge – pragmatic knowledge – will be legitimated in this current age – one of advanced capitalism and globalisation. Capitalism is after all an instrumental phenomenon. Consequently, it is not the learning process in the workplace that is important but the learning outcomes. Forms of behaviouristic learning theory dominate, despite their weaknesses (Jarvis 2006), and the accredited learning becomes the currency in the job market. Learning opportunities are commodities to be sold and educational organisations are being forced to adapt to a global capitalist learning market.

Indeed, the first studies of learning in the workplace only really emerged in the same period that we have been tracing the effects of globalisation and most of them came from the USA (e.g. Argyris and Schön 1974, 1978; Schön 1983; Casner-Lotto *et al.* 1988; Willis and Dubin 1990) and an American who published in the UK (Marsick 1987). America has traditionally emphasised pragmatism much more than Western Europe and with it has been a focus on practical knowledge. These ideas have spread from the USA. Indeed, globalisation has spread out from the centre – rather like the ripples of water that occur when a stone is thrown into a pond. The nodal point of globalisation has been the USA, so that the process has been referred to as Americanisation. However, Western Europe became a subsidiary nodal point (Westernisation) and, perhaps, South-east Asia has become a third. Almost certainly South-east Asia is now the most rapidly developing one, with parts of India also changing nearly as rapidly.

In the USA, there was little distinction drawn between workplace learning and other forms of adult education, but in the UK, there was a much more strict separation between education and training, as the work of R. S. Peters (1967: 14–16), amongst others, illustrates. Education was considered to be much more theoretical while training was practical and skills-based, although this distinction was queried by a number of other philosophers. Consequently, adult education was seen as a continuation of the school-based education about which Peters wrote. Training was rather regarded as being of lower status than education and it was only in the latter part of the twentieth century that considerable effort was placed upon equating the two, reflecting the emphasis on practical knowledge and pragmatism. Taylor (1980: 338), for instance, equated personal growth and professional development and even then prime minister, John Major, frequently reiterated the belief that there was no difference between education and training. Gradually, the distinction was blurred, aided by the fact that the knowledge economy demanded a much more practical orientation to professional development. Consequently, lifelong education had to become lifelong learning in order, amongst other things, to hide the perceived difference between education and training. This was the point at which vocational education colonised liberal adult education conceptually and the distinction that I have drawn between the two ways of viewing lifelong learning reflects this process: we also traced the merging of the two concepts earlier in this study.

Paradoxically, in more recent years it was scholars in America that led a new division in adult education – now not education and training but adult education and human resource development. This is not a knowledge and skills division but it is one which focuses on the purposes of learning and reflects the advanced capitalist society and the covert power that it exercises over people. Now people are resources: they are means, and not an end in themselves, which is a debatable moral position. They are resources that are to be developed but they are to be developed for the sake of the organisation and ultimately for the sake of capital itself rather than for their own enrichment. Indeed, Hargreaves (Hargreaves and Jarvis 2000) showed that human resource developers spend much of their time communicating management's expectations and designing training needs that respond to their expectations, so that they are themselves important resources in the development of management strategy. While management education has necessarily utilised a lot of the research into learning in the workplace, management is itself being forced to change as managers can no longer be administrators of bureaucratic organisations but they are forced to become leaders in the new and more dynamic workplace (Argyris 1983).

With the neo-liberal emphasis on work there has been considerable research on learning in the workplace and many advances in our understanding of human learning have been highlighted. This is hardly surprising since, for the first time, research on adult learning focused on a site for learning other than the classroom, neither is it surprising that some of the theorists of learning in the social context have failed to take into consideration all the sociological research into organisations, as we demonstrated above with Lave and Wenger's work.

Amongst the advances that have occurred are the emphasis on practice, so that action learning, action research and practitioner researcher have all emerged. From the outset Argyris and Schön, together and separately, developed our understanding of learning in practice. They questioned the traditional relationship between theory and practice, reflecting the pragmatic basis from which their work emanated. For them practitioners did not only have a theory in use, they had an espoused theory and it was the latter that led to action. Much later, I (Jarvis 1987, 1999), amongst others, argued that theory was learned in practice rather than in the classroom. However, Argyris and Schön (1974), recognising the problem of theory and practice, distinguished between two forms of learning stemming from two forms of behaviour – Model 1 and Model 2 and with them single-loop and double-loop learning. Model 1 behaviour is a matter of conforming to established practices without otherwise testing the validity of the learning outcomes. They (1974: 19) define single-loop learning as that form which occurs that designs 'actions that satisfy existing governing variables', whereas double-loop learning is that which questions the taken for granted and enables us 'to change the field of constancy itself'. The focus on learning in practice led Schön (1983) to focus on the reflective practitioner. Since that work there have been many studies that have focused on reflection in the workplace, including Boud whose focus was not initially the workplace but experience and learning (Boud et al. 1985) but who also recognised that experiences began with disjuncture – although he did not use the word – rather he called it problem-based learning (Boud 1985; Boud and Feletti 1991) and then he did emphasise learning in the workplace.

At the same time another approach to learning was being developed which also reflected the pragmatism of contemporary society and was to prove useful to management in introducing innovation into the workplace – action learning. Developed by Revans (1980), it has been further elaborated upon by McGill and Beaty (1992), amongst others. Basically, this is a technique which starts from an experiential learning base and uses action as the mode of learning, but each actor is supported by a group – all the members being action learners and all supporting each other. This support is necessary for innovators frequently need support from like-minded individuals as they try to change established procedural patterns. In my own doctoral research (Jarvis 1977) I discovered that professionally oriented practitioners experienced low job satisfaction in bureaucratic organisations.

In a similar fashion, mentoring has been developed in the workplace. Here it is not the group who might all be peers, but one or two senior colleagues who act as teachers, coaches, guides or even counsellors in workplace learning. Some of the early work on mentoring had no specific relationship to the world of work (Daloz 1986) and even some later work (Herman and Mandell 2004), but many more recent publications have focused on work (Murray with Owen 1991; Glover and Mardle 1995; Megginson and

Clutterbuck 1995). In these instances, the mentor is one who assists the learning process but less frequently one who specifically teaches.

Research is also a form of learning and so in recent years we have seen the development of two similar approaches to research: action research (Carr and Kemmis 1986; McNiff 1992) and practitioner research (Jarvis 1999). In both of these, practice, usually that which occurs in the workplace, is the site for the research, the practitioner is the researcher, the research is practical and the research is usually small scale. In action research, the researchers reflect upon their practice and seek to improve it. In practitioner research, the researchers merely seek to understand the events and processes rather than try to change them.

Since learning is experiential and taking place in the practice site, it both questions the traditional formulation that theory should be applied to practice and that the accreditation for learning should only occur in the educational setting where theory was traditionally taught. In the traditional approach to theory, learning was assumed to happen in the classroom when the theory was taught and little or no important learning occurred in the practice. All that happened was that the practitioners applied their learning to the practice situation and one who had high theoretical qualifications (and therefore often entitled to a higher salary) was almost bound to be the better practitioner. But once it was recognised that learning occurred in the practice setting, the formulation of the relationship between theory and practice was called into question. Had the fact that we had moved into a pragmatic society been recognised, we would have recognised that practical knowledge is based upon experience and that the theory-in-use was one actually learned in practice – that there is no fundamental divide between the theory and the practice and, if there is, then practice precedes theory and through reflective learning we formulate our own theory.

Once this is recognised, then the accreditation of learning in the classroom is insufficient and new means of assessment have to be devised. Consequently, the accreditation of prior and experiential learning has become significant. Nevertheless, as late as 2000, Storan (2000: 13) could rightly claim that prior experiential learning 'still cannot be considered as an integral part of Higher Education sector in the UK'. Indeed, he claims that the development of this process in higher education has actually slowed down, illustrating how the universities had resisted the changes that are occurring. However, it may not only be the universities that resist accreditation of learning in the workplace, some employing organisations might do the same since accreditation gives employees exchange currency in the workplace and additional accreditation makes them more employable elsewhere. Consequently, employing organisations offer a lot of in-service learning opportunities that carry no qualifications and it is the responsibility of the learners to complete their own portfolio of learning in order for it to be accepted in the wider learning market. Indeed, as we will show in the next chapter, many employees attend further education in order to gain qualifications that make them more employable. Indeed, this is necessary in a mobile society, although Europe is far from the mobile society that many European politicians envisaged, with less than 1 per cent of the workforce being mobile in this way, although this can be partially accounted for by the existence of the different languages of practice throughout the continent.

It could be argued, however, that it is not only globalisation that is the immediate cause of this process of accreditation but the mobility that it engenders. Within Europe, for instance, it is increasingly important for the European job market not only to have accreditation of experiential learning but to have an agreed set of standards that facilitate mobility – hence we have had the development of EUROPASS and more significantly of a European Qualifications Framework. In many ways this framework is similar to the National Vocational Qualifications Framework developed in the UK. The framework seeks to be broad enough to cover the whole range of learning from basic competencies to doctoral research and the European Framework currently has eight levels. Having an educational qualification is, therefore, also a key to social inclusion whereas social exclusion often coincides with the lack of qualifications – work, rather than property, has become the key to the door of citizenship.

However, life is more than work and so the relationship between work-life learning and the remainder of life has also become a subject for study. This idea was reflected in a study of learning in the workplace entitled *Learning, Working and Living* (Antonacopoulou *et al.* 2006) but perhaps even more significantly in Merriam and Clark's (1991) study in which they looked at the patterns of work, love and learning in adult life; they showed the diverse patterns of relationship between the three and recognised that personal identity is to be found within this relationship.

Social and personal identity

When I used to be invited to speak at pre-retirement courses, one of the exercises that I asked the participants to undertake was that well-known psychological one on identity. I would put on the flip chart the question, 'Who am I?' and the response which began 'I am (a) . . .'. Then I asked the participants to complete the answer ten times. We took feedback and on many occasions the respondents placed their occupation high on the list – usually in the top three. I would then ask them a simple question, 'Who will you be when you retire?' The point is that we do identify with our work and the process of identification seems to move from performing a role to a sense of belonging to one of identifying with either the role or the organisation, or both. At the same time, since the respondents were able to put down several answers, if not all ten, indicates that there are a number of other social identities – indicating that they belonged to a number of communities of practice, some of which were more important than work, such as the nation, the ethnic people, the family, the faith community and even leisure communities

Wenger (1998: 188) suggests that identity formation is a dual process: identification and negotiation. We identify with the job or the organisation and feel part of it, but we have to negotiate with those with whom we interact since we do have some control over the meanings of our identification process. Wenger rightly recognises that at this point the power of the external world operates in the process of negotiation. In this sense, we can understand that when we are faced with retirement we may also be faced with an identity problem, but since not all my respondents placed occupational identity as one of their top three identities, it illustrates that the nature of belonging also affects an individual's identity. Moreover, the fact that Wenger highlights the process of negotiation illustrates a much more fundamental process – that there is an identity behind the identities. There is a personal identity which might be described as: 'I am Me' or 'I am whom I perceive myself to be'. In this sense, our personal identity relates to our own experiences of ourselves and this we learn as we go through our lives, and yet it is a paradoxical phenomenon. From early on in our lives we develop a sense of self and, despite all the experiences of social life, we still regard ourselves as the same person. Each of these different experiences happens to the same person: it is 'I' who have these experiences, so that there is a sense in which personal identity reflects my being and all the other phenomena with which I identify and which provide me with a social identity are subsidiary to it. However, in this rapidly changing and globalising world, many of these phenomena are no longer stable but are transient – changed or destroyed through the ravages of time. The stronger that we identify with these phenomena, the greater the loss – identity crisis – we experience when the changes occur.

This distinction we have drawn between personal and social identity relates to the two processes of primary and secondary socialisation which have been discussed earlier in this study, although it is impossible to draw a clear distinction between them since it is the same person who has all the experiences. Nevertheless, primary socialisation does result, for most young people, in a sense of self. As Mead (Strauss 1964) showed, this is formed in relationship to significant others as a result of social behaviour. The social act is the precondition of consciousness and children develop a sense of awareness through social experience. Communication underlies the emergence of mind, through language children develop the ability to think and through interaction with significant others they gain a sense of self. In the formation of the mind itself lies the basis of personal identity. For the majority of children there are stable relationships with the significant others and within the security of this stability both mind and self emerge.[1] Only when this initial relationship is unstable are there problems with the formation of the self, but in mobile, global society, this stability is sometimes threatened and individuals grow up 'scared'. There is a sense that with the formation of the self, we develop our personal identity, but the self not only is, it is always becoming, until the day of death, and so the individual self continues to have experiences throughout conscious life – and, therefore, to learn. But the personal identity, the sense of self, does not change a great deal, especially after we have reached maturity. Part of that personal identity, that self, may include our nationality or our ethnicity since these reflect the environment of our initial relationships and our own initial life-world.

Nevertheless, we live in an inter-subjective world. As Jenkins (2004: 49) suggests, as embodied selves:

- We realise ourselves in relationship to others.
- This process continues throughout our lives as our individual identities adapt and change.
- The presentation and elaboration of self-identification draws upon a wide palette of accessories.
- The self is both individual and interactional.

However, as members of a wide variety of communities of practice as we grow and develop, so we learn to play roles within them, identify with them and develop a sense of belonging, so that we have multiple social identities depending on the roles we play and the groups to which we belong – these are, in a sense, secondary identities. Hence, we may identify with our jobs and, like the respondents in the pre-retirement courses that I referred to above, their occupational identity may be the dominant one within the context of the work environment. Nevertheless, these secondary identities tend to be more transient, although related to the primary identity. Certainly, in the many times I have conducted that identity exercise on pre-retirement courses, very few people ever wrote that they were themselves. As individuals move on from communities of practice, so their identity lapses and disappears. The greater their identification with that social identity, the greater the sense of meaning that it gives, the greater the trauma when it is lost.

However, identity is learned during our lifetime – there are the primary and the secondary identities. The primary one is developed early in our life, with the formation of the self – self-identity – and mind. It is maintained, retained and developed through lifelong learning – in the sense of learning throughout our lifespan and through all the stages of our development. Since we live with this identity and through our learning we usually gently develop our personal identity to the situations of our life-world – rarely are there major identity crises from the time that this identity is established. Consequently, we learn to take it for granted. In contrast, the secondary identities relate to our membership of varieties of communities of practice and, therefore, they relate to our life-wide learning. We are more conscious of the activities that relate to these communities of practice and, therefore, we are perhaps more conscious of our secondary identities. Nevertheless, the primary identity – the self-identity – is still at the heart of our actions and it is this which assists us in the negotiation about which Wenger writes, but he is writing about secondary identities.[2]

Since we use the term 'lifelong learning' to include both lifelong and lifetime learning, we lose this important distinction in our discussion of identity. It is the self-identity – the identity of the person, the Me, which is private and fundamental to our being. Self-identity is ontological – it is about our being and becoming. It is for this reason that we emphasise that it is the person who learns and why we regard learning as an existential phenomenon. It is the self, the primary identity, which reflects our being and which is always becoming until the day that we die.

Secondary identities change as we move through life, but primary identity is much more stable. However, in brainwashing it is the primary identity that is attacked since the process often seeks to create a new, often artificial world in which we learn to doubt our self-identity (Lifton 1961) and eventually replace it. In brainwashing, we can see how those who control the external world shape our self-identity, our sense of self. But culture is never value-free, so that our primary identities are always shaped by those who control culture and, clearly, our primary and secondary identities rarely contradict each other – except in times of mental illness. Consequently, we can understand how our identities are always shaped by the external world in which we live and why we seek to live in harmony with it, so that there is always a strong tendency to accept the values and meanings of the world into which we are born and develop – we tend to be conservative and traditional, even when the world in which we live is neo-liberal. We are growing up to accept this world and its values – to identify ourselves with it, both through our primary and our secondary identities – and to take it for granted.

Conclusion

In lifelong learning, we can recognise the ontological basis of learning – it lies in being and becoming, whereas in life-wide learning, this process still continues but has added to it, a secondary process whereby we play and identify with different roles and so we develop secondary identities. Both are influenced by the social world and in both we reflect that world, so that it is not surprising that traditional Marxist scholars in a state-based society, such as Althusser (1972), were able to regard the various social institutions as state ideological apparatuses. Consequently, we can see that lifelong learning is not value-free either – it is occurring in a globalised capitalist world and it is acting as a socialising agent within it. We can see that many of the institutions, communities of practice, in which we learn to play roles and identify with them are in harmony with the global world of advanced capitalism. Even so, there are some few social groups in the West who are anti-globalisation and they seek to undermine its culture. More significantly, those parts of the world that do not accept the values of advanced capitalism, such as Muslim societies, generate people with different values and different identities – often ones which conflict with the dominant West. Individuals learn to be themselves in whatever society they are born into and identify with it and its values.

Chapter 9

Participants in lifelong learning

Teachers and students

As the previous pages have demonstrated there have been significant changes in the education of adults, stemming either directly or indirectly from the processes of globalisation. These changes have, obviously, affected both students and teachers. We have already shown that there has been a significant increase in the amount of education offered to adults throughout the world and later in this chapter we will offer a more thorough analysis of this in respect of the UK. But before that it is necessary to examine the occupation of teachers of adults and it will be asked whether there is a single occupation, let alone single profession, of adult educator. The chapter, therefore, is divided into two sections: the first examining the occupational structures of teaching adults and the second looking at student participation and the barriers to that participation.

Teachers of adults

It is not that long ago that it was possible to assume that adult education was a single occupational group, discuss whether it was a profession and compare how adult educators were prepared for their work throughout Europe (Jarvis and Chadwick 1991) but this would now be a harder, probably almost impossible, task. The reasons for this are manifold, although many stem from the processes of globalisation that constitute the focus of this book and governments' reaction to what is occurring.

In the first instance, it is not necessary to define the concept of a profession although it is necessary to look at the structures of occupations which regard themselves as professions. Few of them are actually a unity; they nearly all have different specialisms within them, so that many years ago Bucher and Strauss (1966: 193), in their studies of medicine, could write 'that professions consist of loose amalgamations of segments which are in movement'. This certainly reflected the occupation of university teacher at that time: there were three or four segments – teaching, research or administration in the UK, and teaching, research and service in the USA. Practitioners could perform three or four different roles. This was also true in other branches of adult education – full-time teachers were both teachers and administrators while part-time teachers concentrated only on teaching. But society has changed with tremendous rapidity and so have these loose amalgamations of segments. By the time that I wrote the third edition of *Adult Education and Lifelong Learning* (Jarvis 2004: 141) I was able to delineate 17 different roles for a teacher:

Group 1 (in direct contact with learners):
- teacher/facilitator
- teaching assistant
- supervisor
- trainer/coach
- mentor
- counsellor/adviser
- administrator
- assessor.

Group 2 (one stage removed from learners):
- researcher
- trainer of teachers/trainer
- author of learning and teaching materials
- programme/curriculum planners
- educational policy makers
- programme administrators
- programme technical staff
- consultants and evaluators
- retailers/marketers.

No doubt it would be possible to specify others now, including recognising that even the teaching/lecturing role occurs over the Internet, or to suggest that some of these are themselves actually loose amalgamations of segments. The number of segments has altered and while it would be possible to argue that some of these have never been seen as the roles of a teacher of adults, many teachers of adults have performed these at different times. Indeed, some of them were also performed within the context of the three different segments mentioned above. But with the development of information technology and distance education, many new roles emerged. Now with the subsequent developments making education into a commodity which is produced for the knowledge market, other roles have also emerged. What is significant about this process is that as some of these roles have become specialisms in their own right, they have become separate occupations, and because of their separation into new occupations some are not now regarded as necessarily being part of the teacher's role.

It might still be argued that this does not mean that there is not an occupation of adult educator. However, this is much more complicated with the development of continuing professional education. It will be recalled that the knowledge economy has one of its bases in knowledge itself – the rapidly changing knowledge that Scheler (1980 [1926]) called artificial since it changes before it has time to get embedded within the culture of a society. This means that those occupations based upon these different forms of knowledge have been forced to develop continuing education programmes for their own professionals and it has taken specialists in each specific occupation to develop their own programmes, so that there is now a continuing education segment in most of the major occupations and professions. Indeed, in many of them continuing professional education is mandatory if they are to retain their licence to practise. Each profession has, therefore, developed its own cadre of adult educators. An example of this might be university teaching in the UK.

In the 1990s, the Dearing Committee (1997) investigated university teaching in the UK and it recognised that it was not a profession in the context of teaching – indeed, it was not professional in its training and further training of university teachers. Amongst its recommendations were:

> We recommend that, with immediate effect, all institutions of higher education give high priority to developing and implementing learning and teaching strategies which focus on the promotion of students' learning.
>
> (Recommendation 8)

And,

> We recommend that institutions of higher education begin immediately to develop or seek access to programmes for teacher training for their staff, if they do not have them, and that all institutions seek national accreditation of such programmes from the Institute for Learning and Teaching in Higher Education.
>
> (Recommendation 13)

Now there are centres for learning and teaching in many universities in the UK both preparing new recruits into university teachers and teaching them how to teach, but also offering continuing professional development for university teachers. It is significant that this is happening with only the teaching segment of the traditional roles of the university teacher, although the administration roles have also been developed, but much less formally, with more senior academics studying for diplomas and degrees in educational management and administration. All the members of the university academic staff are generally expected to have a research degree so that they have also served a research apprenticeship. Similar innovations have happened in many of the professions essential to the development of the knowledge economy.

There are at least four observations that we might make on these events in the development of teaching. First, there have traditionally been criticisms of university teaching and, to some extent there still are. But the universities did little or nothing about it in the past. I recall writing to a vice-chancellor about this in the 1980s, recounting how an American university that I had visited honoured its best teachers each academic year and suggesting that we might do likewise – but that vice-chancellor did not even deign to reply. As the knowledge economy and lifelong learning has placed more stress on the production of employable graduates and the universities have needed to recruit sufficient students to ensure their own funding, so the emphases have changed. Indeed, the preparation of employable graduates might itself be seen as a production process in the learning economy. Universities have been responsive to the demands of the global society although the rhetoric of the universities is that they are improving their standards rather than that there are major social forces that have almost removed the choice from them. The point is that now university teachers are regarded as producers of the new employable workforce – as educators, and even educators of adults; but, and more significantly, universities are employing adult educators under a differ-ent name to do their staff development. Regrettably, some universities over-looked the fact that they already had experienced adult educators whose expertise has been overlooked in the process of change. Consequently, there has been a tendency to 'reinvent the wheel'.

The second point is similar to this in as much as these demands have been made on every occupational group – each occupation has, therefore, had to produce its own educators, both for professional preparation and for lifelong learning. Consequently, each profession has generated its own adult educa-tors and, like the universities, not all of them have actually utilised trad-itional adult educators to undertake this work. Lifelong learning, or even adult vocational education, is central to contemporary globalised, advanced capitalist society but Kett (1994: xviii) has made the very shrewd observa-tion that: 'Today no one can plausibly describe adult education as a marginal activity, but professional adult educators have become increasingly marginal to the education of adults.'

In my own study of professional education (Jarvis 1983) I made the point that educators of adults straddle two professions – their own and education and I raised the difficulty then about the extent to which this was possible. Naturally, with the ways that social borders, such as between professional groups, have been bridged, we are seeing a new phenomenon – the need for practitioners to specialise might well mean that a new type of adult educator is appearing, but in each of the different professions, and the one thing that they have in common is the education of adults. However, there is even another form of adult educator appearing – the teacher-practitioner or lecturer-practitioner (Jarvis and Gibson 1997) – in which the practitioner plays both roles either simultaneously both teaching and working in the workplace, or sequentially by practising in the workplace for some of the time and teaching in an educational institution for some of the time.

Fourth, we might see, therefore, that the education of adults as an occupation, if it is one, crosses all the other occupations and professions. It is common to all of them but at the moment there is a tendency for each group to be separated by their occupational boundaries. Educators of adults have become role players in many of the other occupations, and while some are employed within the further and higher education sections others are independent consultants or involved in human resource development within the profession or employing organisation. Consequently, it can be asked whether the education of adults is an occupation, let alone a profession.

An occupation is a person's work or principal activity and so some educators of adults might actually regard themselves primarily as educators rather than doctors, nurses or engineers, although they may actually see themselves as straddling two professions. Consequently, the question of each practitioner's own secondary identity arises – whether they see themselves as educators or members of their original occupation, or both. It may be an irrelevant question to ask whether the education of adults is an occupation but it is certainly a role, and so we can usefully employ a similar distinction to the one made by Elliott in 1972, between occupational professions and status professions. However, the distinction that I want to make is between role professionals and occupational professionals. Certain the educators of adults are role professionals even though they are not necessarily occupational professionals.

Traditionally, a profession has been a full-time occupation and using this criterion in its most obvious sense, the education of adults is not a full-time occupation for all its practitioners and so it cannot be a profession – except in the role-professional sense which we will discuss below. Professionalisation, according to Vollmer and Mills (1966: vii–viii) 'refers to the dynamic process whereby many occupations can be observed to change crucial characteristics in the direction of a "profession" even though some of these may not move very far in this direction'. Many commentators have commented on this process of structural change, but since there is not a single structure it is not possible to describe a process of professionalisation for educators of adults. However, the idea of role professional does lend itself to understanding professional from an attitudinal and practice perspective and in order to do this two other terms lend themselves to analysis: professional and professionalism (Jarvis 1983).

A professional, as opposed to amateur, is one who receives emoluments for practice and is expected to perform in a competent, if not an expert, manner. The first of these two meanings is self-evident but the second assumes that practitioners are masters in the performance of their role and this is to be expected of professionals. Consequently, we can see that being a reflective practitioner, seeking to keep abreast with new developments in the education of adults, and so on are not just things that practitioners do – they become moral duties for a professional.

In a similar manner, professionalism has two meanings: commitment to the occupational and employing organisation and a dedication, even a moral commitment, to the competent or expert performance of the role. The first of these two is contentious since it assumes that commitment to the occu-pational or employing organisation is always a moral duty and if a member is forced to denounce an occupational or employer practice one is disloyal and a 'whistle-blower'. However, neither all employment or occupational prac-tices operate for the good of the wider community, often they act only for the good of the occupation or the financial benefit of the employing organ-isation – this is almost inherent in the nature of capitalism, especially in such a competitive environment as today's global society. But if the practice is not beneficial to the wider community, then it can be argued that it is moral to denounce it publicly if private protestations are ineffective. In these instances, professionalism may be regarded as an immoral practice. Indeed, it might be seen to be diametrically opposed to the second meaning of the term – when the professionalism of the practitioners can be seen in the know-ledge, attitudes, skills, beliefs and values that they exhibit. In this sense, professionalism is a moral position which should take the role-professional beyond the stage of competence to that of expert. It could be argued, therefore, that professionalism demands expertise rather than competence and that it is a moral duty, so that the professionalism of role-professional educators of adults demands expertise.

Paradoxically, as this demand becomes more apparent, it should foster a greater understanding of adult learning and of lifelong learning in particular across the occupations and professions and, in this sense, it should regener-ate research, practice and study of this area of practice, and maybe a sense of unity amongst adult educators. Globalisation has certainly resulted in fundamental changes in adult education as an occupation and so it is now necessary to see how the process has affected the learners.

Learners and lifelong learning

Earlier in the book we saw how the knowledge economy, a result of the globalisation process, has resulted in the increase in the amount of post-school education being offered. Indeed, Campbell (1984: 14) records that 'in 1974–5, adult learners in credit and non-credit courses in Canada became the new majority within the university's clientele'. He actually goes on to give statistics on this phenomenon, but the major point is that adult learners had become a 'new majority'. Indeed, he (1984: 90) says that:

Continuing education divisions have been so busy responding to increasing public demand that few have had time to examine the implications of their growth or the underlying philosophy of the university in continuing education provision or the structure most appropriate to the task which, it is conceded, the heterogeneity of the adult student body makes the more difficult.

Structural changes generated a situation throughout North America and Western Europe where there were more opportunities for adult learners to continue their learning than ever before, although in the 1980s in the UK the Conservative government endeavoured to curtail the provision of liberal adult education. The structures of the education system changed during this period and lifelong education, in the forms of continuing and recurrent education, emerged.

However, these opportunities were not evenly spread across the whole adult population. The knowledge economy, as we have seen, only required certain types of worker and so one of the major variables was related to the demands of the labour market. But, even if this factor were not so predominant, people have different orientations towards education and so they are most unlikely to respond to the opportunities in the same way. Indeed, Cross (1981: 124) incorporated both opportunities and barriers into her model and she (p. 99) highlighted the different types of barriers – situational, institutional and dispositional. Since its publication this distinction has been adopted in a wide variety of studies on adult participation.

From the 2001 *National Adult Learning Survey* (LaValle and Blake 2001) we know that amongst those who continued their learning, 51 per cent focused entirely on vocational learning (an increase of 7 per cent from 1997), while a further 17 per cent (a decrease in 6 per cent) combined the vocational and the non-vocational; 24 per cent (a decrease of 2 per cent) undertook no additional learning and 8 per cent (a change of 1 per cent) restricted their learning to the non-vocational (p. 13). Moreover, a greater proportion of the higher socio-economic classes have continued their education and training. In fact there is a consistent pattern of the AB socio-economic class (56 per cent in 2005) having a higher percentage than the C1 (51 per cent), who in turn have a higher percentage than C2 (40 per cent) who have a higher percentage participation rate than DE (26 per cent) (McGivney 2006: 67). This pattern is consistent for all the statistics about socio-economic class and participation over the preceding decade. Significantly, 39 per cent of all those unemployed in 2005 had not engaged in any learning since they left school (McGivney 2006: 68, citing Aldridge and Tuckett 2005) and 90 per cent of those who were unemployed in 2003 in Scotland had not participated in education and training since they left school (McGivney 2006: 62). Indeed, there is a consistent pattern between the higher the educational qualifications the greater the likelihood of continuing to study (LaValle and Blake 2001: 25). And so the question might be asked, What type of skills do the employers want from their employees and where does the skills gap lie?

The Learning and Skills Council conducted a survey into this and discovered the following skills gaps (*Social Trends 2006*: 45). Over 40 per cent of the employers specified one or more of the following in decreasing percentages: skills in communication, customer handling, team working, problem solving and technical and practical; between 40 per cent and 20 per cent specified management, IT, literacy and numeracy; the other two were professional IT and foreign languages. When asked why staff lacked these skills, 73 per cent suggested that it was a lack of experience while 34 per cent also discussed the lack of motivation, whilst failure to train staff, staff not keeping abreast with changes and recruitment and rapid turnover also featured in their responses.

Nevertheless, between 40 per cent and 42 per cent of the respondents to the NIACE surveys have participated in current or recent learning and while the younger age groups are still the most likely to do so – 47 per cent and over of all respondents under the age of 54 years, 32 per cent of the 55–64 age group, 17 per cent of 65–74 and 10 per cent of 75 plus still participate. McGivney (2006: 64) notes that over half of the respondents 65 plus had undertaken no learning since they left school – clearly 'learning' here must refer to formal learning. The older age groups are less likely to enrol in learning for vocational reasons, so that the UK government's policy of supporting mainly vocational education is another indicator that third and fourth age citizens are discriminated against in advanced capitalist societies.

It is significant that:

> women are more likely to engage in organised learning than men. Women are more likely than men to be learning in their own time and they are more likely than men to have workplace opportunities to learn at work. LSC [Learning and Skills Council] figures for LSC-funded provision show that women of all ethnic backgrounds predominate in all forms of post-compulsory provision except work-based learning.
>
> (McGivney 2006: 65)

Without pursuing this analysis any further at this point, we can see that all these forms of lifelong learning are going to be culturally and socially reproductive. Lifelong learning is going to reproduce the advanced capitalist system of contemporary societies. In the terminology of Botkin *et al.* (1979), lifelong learning is more likely to be maintenance learning than innovative, despite the emphasis on entrepreneurship and change.

Since there is so much emphasis on lifelong learning in contemporary society and so many opportunities to continue to learn, the fact that so many people have not continued their education beyond schooling is an important factor; so it is necessary to investigate the barriers to learning which, as we've mentioned, Cross (1981) distinguished as situational, institutional and dispositional. In a similar manner the *National Adult Learning Survey 2001* (LaValle and Blake 2001) distinguished between societal and peer pressure; practical obstacles and personal difficulties. The reasons that the surveys discovered are summarised in Table 9.1 for the years 1997 and 2001 under the sub-heads of situational, institutional and dispositional – Cross's figures for 1981 are in brackets and all figures are percentages of potential learners in the different surveys. In the UK studies, LaValle and Blake (2001: 39) make the point that men are more likely to say that they are more interested in other things or give work-related reasons why they do not wish to study whilst women are more likely to focus on family responsibilities.

Table 9.1 Perceived barriers to learning

	1997	2001
Situational		
Cost (53)	21	26
Benefits would be cut	5	4
Nobody paying the cost	11	14
Not enough time (46)		
Due to work	29	29
Due to family	24	22
Due to children	N/A	13
Due to adult	N/A	4
Home responsibilities (32)	24	22
Job responsibilities (28)	18	19
No child care (11)	N/A	13
No transport (8)	N/A	9
No place to study (7)	N/A	N/A
Peers do not encourage (3)	N/A	N/A
Institutional		
No wish to return full-time (35)	N/A	N/A
Course requires too much time (21)		
Course not at right time (16)	N/A	N/A
Cannot get information (16)		
Do not know about courses	20	24
Cannot find out about courses	11	11
Do not know how to find out	N/A	10
Attendance requirements (15)	N/A	N/A

Suitable courses not available (12)	N/A	N/A
Too much red tape at enrolment (10)	N/A	N/A
Do not have necessary qualifications (6)	15	15
Literacy difficulties	5	6
English difficulties	4	4
Numeracy	N/A	4
No way to get credit (5)	N/A	N/A
Poor health/disability	7	4
Dispositional		
Too old (17)	13	11
No confidence (12)	N/A	17
Worried about keeping up	13	15
No energy (9)	N/A	N/A
Do not enjoy it (9)		
Prefer to do other things	39	24
No interest	16	12
Tired of school (6)	17	N/A
Do not know what to learn (5)	N/A	N/A
Do not want to appear ambitious (3)	N/A	N/A

Sources: Beinart and Smith (1998); LaValle and Blake (2001).

Note
Figures in brackets are Cross's for 1982.
All figures are percentages of potential learners in the different surveys.

Since these are different surveys conducted at different times and using different instruments, it is not legitimate to try to draw precise comparisons. Nevertheless, it is possible to make a few general observations, such as the barriers to learning have not changed a great deal despite the changes in the social structures, with society becoming more open and placing a greater emphasis on learning. The issues of time, cost and gender still predominate and the after-effects of those who were not successful at school are still very relevant in later life.

However, times have moved on since the work that Cross reports and in the later UK surveys, a new and very significant variable enters the debate – the Internet, since we do live in an information society. LaValle and Blake (2001: 94) record the different reasons why respondents use the Internet and amongst the reasons that they give are:

- Get information about leisure/hobbies   53%
- Get information about work   52%
- Get information about learning   44%

- Get health information   29%
- Get information to help children with their learning   26%

Sargant and Aldridge (2002, vol. 1: 106) also report that, amongst other things, the Internet is used for:

- Finding information for learning/training   38%
- Finding information relating to children's schoolwork   23%
- Learning on/offline   22%

Aldridge and Tuckett (2005: 23) note that 53 per cent of their respondents with access to the Internet say that they are learning, whereas that figure declines to 21 per cent for those who have no access. In addition, projects are being established that seek to encourage young people, especially, to use the mobile telephone for learning.

However, Aldridge and Tuckett (2005: 1) make a number of significant points about the statistics up to 2004:

> Older learners have fared particularly badly, with participation in the three years leading up to the survey among 65–74 year olds down from 19 per cent in 1996 to 14 per cent in 2004; and participation amongst the over 75s plummeted from 15 per cent to 10 per cent over the same period. These figures contrast with the modest rises for 45–64 year olds.
>
> Over the same time-frame, the higher-paid workers – in professional and managerial or white-collar occupations – showed a quite marked increase in participation in the late 1990s, which has now tailed off. Between 1996 and 2004 the learning divide widened, with participation falling among all but the highest socio-economic groups, and participation among the poorest (DEs) declining from 26 per cent to 23 per cent.

That there has been an increase in participation amongst the 45–64 year olds might indicate that in future years older people will be more engaged in learning activities, perhaps through such institutions as the University of the Third Age. Even so, the decline in participation of the higher-paid groups might indicate that their initial education has better equipped them for their employment or it may be just a blip in the current trends of the learning society. The following year, they (Tuckett and Aldridge 2006: 14–15) noted that there was a considerable increase in those who expressed the intention to learn and they pose the question: is this the beginning of the learning society? But they also recognise that 'one swallow does not make a summer' and intentions might not be implemented.

What is clear, however, is that lifelong learning still reinforces the cultural and social divisions in capitalist society although the more open structures do allow some highly motivated people – or those few in specific occupations which do not always require a lot of learning, such as the so-called celebrities – to move through the system and to accumulate consider-able wealth while they do so.

Conclusion

The whole ethos of education itself has become a teaching and learning market – new approaches to teaching and to learning are being introduced all the time. Pressure is being placed on educational institutions to respond to the market pressures and teach new courses at different levels and in new ways. The preparation and introduction of these courses has been speeded up. Clearly, teaching has become more stressful. In the same way, more emphasis is being put on learners to get more education and qualifications so that they can play their role in the labour market.

While the social structures in the UK have changed over the period of globalisation since the late 1960s, there was certainly an increase in 'white collar' occupations as the advanced capitalist economy emerged. Now there is a great deal more openness in society, but the above statistics suggest that there is less rapid social structural change. Education is certainly not only the 'handmaiden of industry' as Kerr et al. (1973) suggested, but in the insti-tutionalised form of lifelong learning it is a subservient servant of advanced capitalism in many ways, even to the extent of being incorporated into it.

One of the major roles of the university teacher was as researcher and so it is now necessary to examine how research has been affected by the contemporary conditions, and this will constitute the focus of the next chapter.

Chapter 10

The changing nature
of research

It will have become quite clear from the previous chapters that the interconnectedness of the whole world means that things initiated at the centre spread through the remainder of the globe. At the same time, there is a less powerful movement in the opposite direction, where the local seeks to retain its distinctiveness, resists the pressures from the centre, and so on. We have seen how the market competitiveness and efforts to improve profitability in the global core have been the cause of many changes in the nature and transmission of knowledge and also in the place of education and training in some people's lives. The changes have affected all people in a wide variety of ways. Amongst the changes has been the nature of research itself and this brief chapter traces some of these changes, and it will have three sections: research and policy; research and learning; research and practice.

Research and policy

Since the year 2000, the European Union has been committed to the Lisbon ideal that by 2010 Europe will have the most dynamic economy on earth, an aim that it recognised in 2004 (Kok 2004) that it would not achieve. It was this type of perspective that led the EU to publish policy documents about lifelong learning and the learning society (EC 1995, 2000a, 2001b) and to institute the European Year of Lifelong Learning in 2006. It also published a research paper (EC 2000b) indicating that Europe should become a research area and spelling out aspects that needed consideration. In the UK, this led to a number of policy statements about lifelong learning (Fryer 1997) instituted by the newly constituted Department of Education and Employment. This meant that both the EU and some national governments funded research into lifelong learning and employment.

In the UK, for instance, the ESRC (Economic and Social Research Council) – a national government-funded research council[1] – instituted a research programme entitled the Learning Society: knowledge and skills for employment. Funding of £2.5 million was committed to this programme and 13 projects were selected – a fourteenth project was later added. Coffield (2000) suggests that while the EU policy documents emphasise knowledge, the UK programme was more concerned with learning, although by 1995 the EU had also issued a policy document on *Teaching and Learning* (EC 1995). Coffield (2000: 6) points out that lifelong learning 'was driven up the political agenda in most industrialised countries by pressure from powerful groups'. In a sense he was correct but the political agenda was driven by the power of the substructure. The pressure groups were not only national groups but were ones that exercised pressures from the substructures of global society.

The ESRC programme was one of many initiatives sponsored by the new Labour government when it came to power and Coffield (2000: 1) indicates that the government expected all research to be governed by three principles; the research must be:

- central and relevant to central government policy debate;
- realistic to people's lives;
- engage open-mindedly with policy rather than be driven by ideology paraded as intellectual enquiry.

The language of the third one indicates the in-built bias of language itself, since government policy is also ideological but ideology clothed with power can be labelled as policy. The fact that not all the findings were in accord with government policy indicates a relationship between research and policy – that the topic of the programme can be dictated by government but it cannot control honest research findings although some governments do make it hard for researchers whose findings are contrary to their policy to publish their results.

However, the significance of this programme lies in the fact that a whole raft of research and other political initiatives came from the government, developing the demands that came from the global core. A great deal of funding was given to a research programme aimed specifically at responding to these demands. In this sense, the future direction of research and curricula for teaching about the learning society were being given by this programme. At the same time, the extent to which the research findings were to affect society as a whole is much more debatable. Coffield (2000: 6) makes the point that 'too often lifelong learning has been used simply to re-brand existing centres, courses and students, without any new thinking, new kinds of students or any new pedagogy'.

At the same time, work-based learning initiatives have sprung up in a number of different situations, some sponsored by new universities free from the traditions that inhibit change, that also reflect this change in the research agenda, with many research projects being undertaken by a wide variety of teams (see, for example, Armsby et al. 2006), some of which are challenging the more traditional university approaches. Change, therefore, is gradually happening but it takes a lot longer to generate institutional and cultural change than the type of timespan that is reflected in Coffield's comments. The demands of the substructure supported by government initiatives do change the global super-structure and that pace is to a large extent controlled by the power of the forces that emanate from the global core.

The pressures from the substructure were not instituted without some opposition from educators more generally. For instance, in the *Memorandum on Lifelong Learning* (EC 2000a) the two aims of lifelong learning were employability and active citizenship. However, the EC put the memorandum out for public discussion and invited responses. Three thousand responses, many of which criticised the narrowness of the document, meant that the next document had to add two more aims: social inclusion and personal development (see Chapter 4). In fact, it was forced to elaborate on this:

> Lifelong learning, however, is much more than economics. It also promotes the goals and ambitions of European countries to become more inclusive, tolerant and democratic. And it promises a Europe in which citizens have the opportunity and ability to realise their ambitions and to participate in building a better society.
>
> (EC 2001b: 7)

The general acceptance of the economic aims of Lisbon, reflecting the wishes of the core to produce a completely neo-liberal global society, was not acceptable to all the people in Europe, as was reflected in this statement. In the UK, government policy on the learning society was also broadened. The UK government made money available for a research programme on the wider benefits of learning. The newly named Department of Education and Skills (DfES) funded a research centre in the University of London (Institute of Education and Birkbeck College) to investigate the relationships between learning, health, well-being and civic engagement. From its inauguration, this unit was more concerned with non-employment outcomes of learning and produced six research reports. Preston and Hammond (2002) report that amongst the wider benefits are:

- esteem and efficiency;
- independence of thought, problem solving and improved IT skills;
- social integration;
- the college as a community resource.

Feinstein (2002a: 33) reports that 'the wider crime benefits of learning are substantial and approachable statistically'. Feinstein (2002b: iv) suggests that 'there are substantial health returns' from learning, which is also important to public finance. Brassett-Grundy (2002: 41) concludes that those who participated in family learning could see many gains for their families as a whole and for individual members. Blackwell and Bynner (2002) recognise both the benefits of lifelong learning and the possibilities of social exclusion for certain families, especially mothers, who were not able to access learning opportunities. Schuller *et al.* (2002: iii) conclude that: 'A very general but crucial conclusion is that the sustaining effect of education is pervasive, operates at many different levels and is critical to the lives of countless individuals and communities.' It highlights how education 'underpins the maintenance of personal well-being and social cohesion'.

Consequently, we can see that there has been a movement away from exclusive discussions about lifelong learning and employability but it took a government initiative to fund such a broad-ranging programme. Other studies (Duke *et al.* 2005) have also sought to address the matter of balance between the economic and the social, but it is significant that none of the examples illustrate that transnational corporations recognise and promote the wider benefits of learning. Indeed, the whole movement of learning cities and regions might also be seen as an endeavour to counterbalance the emphasis placed on lifelong learning by corporations. There is a sense in which we can see that research into the social benefits of lifelong learning followed the social pressures exerted by the substructure and that many of these came from national governments rather than international agencies although, it would be true to say, that throughout this period the EU has funded the Grundtvig programme of the European Commission on adult education which it has endeavoured to keep separate from the more vocational programmes.

Research and learning

Among the changes that we have traced in this study include the way that perceptions of knowledge have changed and what types of knowledge are now regarded as relevant to contemporary society. For instance, the emphasis on practical rather than theoretical knowledge and the speed at which certain forms of knowledge change are certainly related to changes in research in the knowledge economy.

Traditionally, knowledge was accepted as true if it could be empirically demonstrated, rationally argued or shown to work in practical situations. Research was conducted or cases argued and reports constructed, published and disseminated so that, if they were accepted, they found their way into the body of knowledge of an academic discipline or professional group and were eventually included in curricula and taught to future generations of scholars or practitioners. But the global processes have speeded up the rate of change. It will be recalled that Scheler (1980 [1926]) regarded scientific and technological knowledge as being artificial because it changed too rapidly to be incorporated into a society's culture before it changed. He even suggested then that knowledge changed 'hour by hour'. While his typology of knowledge was not accepted in the earlier discussion, his awareness of the varying speeds of change of knowledge was recognised. Consequently, knowledge essential to the knowledge economy is recognised to change exceedingly rapidly and this has two consequences for traditional research reports: first, that by the time they are published, they are often already history and, second, that the situation they report may probably have changed as well. Therefore, the traditional idea that theory could be taught and then applied to practice was itself outdated. Significantly, any idea of teaching a topic in one situation and applying it unthinkingly in another one both dehumanises the practitioner and fails to understand how human beings learn. Therefore the relationship between theory and practice had to be reconceptualised.

In the first instance, this meant that certain approaches to 'truth' had to be rethought, especially in relation to technological knowledge, which had to be regarded as relative to the situation.[2] If this is the case, then the practice situation may be different from the situation in which earlier research was conducted and, therefore, the theoretical knowledge is out of date and cannot be applied, although it might be used as guidelines for practice. However, the practice situation being a new one requires new learning and new knowledge – practical knowledge learned though practical experience. Significantly, in pragmatism there is no divide between theory and practice, so that a new emphasis has been placed on the need to learn in practice situations and also new forms of research in practice situations have arisen. Hence we saw the introduction of action learning (Revans 1980).

A renewed emphasis on experiential learning occurred in the early1980s when Schön (1983) published *The Reflective Practitioner* and Kolb (1984) published *Experiential Learning*. Both of these books captured the spirit of the times and gave rise to a great deal of research about human learning – research that included the work of Boud, Brookfield, Jarvis and others. Schön's study captured the fact that practitioners needed to learn in the practice situation and that their learning was of a different kind from that which occurred in the classroom – in a sense, it broke away from the behaviourist and cognitivist learning theories that predominated at that time. Kolb's work contextualised experiential learning, drawing on thinkers from the past, and his well-known learning cycle captured, in an oversimplified manner, the essence of experiential learning. However, learning in different sites from the classroom, especially the workplace, now became crucial to the development of our understanding of human learning.

Boud (Boud *et al.* 1985) also focused on the nature of both reflection and on the nature of the problem that initiated reflection (Boud 1985; Boud and Feletti 1991). Since he was also interested in adult and student learning, he has subsequently extended his studies by looking at adult learning (Boud and Griffin 1987) and self-assessment (1995), amongst other topics. At the same time, Brookfield (1986), whose work has focused primarily on teaching, wrote *Understanding and Facilitating Adult Learning* and in the following year Jarvis (1987) examined experiential adult learning from a sociological perspective. What has been lacking throughout the whole of this period is a recognition of the person of the learner and a philosophical understanding of human learning (Jarvis 2006).

From this period onwards, there has been a growing recognition that learning takes place at work and that it is not merely the application of old theories to new situations. But because of the way that situations change so rapidly, it has been argued (Lyotard 1984) that grand theory is finished. This is a view that has become quite popular, mainly, I think, because there has been a general view that all knowledge changes rapidly – which is not entirely true. Consequently, it may be correct to argue that certain situations and forms of knowledge, such as technological knowledge in advanced capitalist societies, do not lend themselves to grand theory, other situations change less rapidly and the knowledge associated with them sometimes appears almost static, and grand theory is more appropriate in these situations.

One of the other responses to the idea of relativity of knowledge has been reductionism, especially in respect to the human being where many theories seeking permanence have been reduced to a biological and genetic baseline. While the human being's body does play a significant part in growth and development, reductionism produces oversimple arguments and, for instance, we do have to recognise that human attributes, such as intelligence, have both a biological and an experiential foundation, as Horn and Cattell (Cattell 1963) demonstrated many years ago.

We can see, therefore, how the global pressures created situations which led to unexpected consequences for our understanding of learning in the learning society. As a result of the situations that were created, a whole raft of new research has begun and our understanding of human learning enriched considerably, but these situations have also led to new approaches to research itself.

The practice of research

Rapid change and action learning also led to changes in research emphases. For instance, action research (McNiff 1992), using some of the same thinkers as Kolb (1984), e.g. Kurt Lewin, combines the thinking of Schön with a more formalised approach to research. McNiff (1988: 2) suggests that action research is 'a way of characterising a loose set of activities that are designed to improve the quality of education'. Basically, in education, this involves teachers reflecting on their practice, identifying ways in which the quality might be improved and trying to initiate changes that produce improved performance. But it is more than just practice that is researched; it is the recognition that the social conditions in which the actions are performed are inextricably intertwined with and affect the performance itself. Consequently, the change in actions also involves changing the social conditions. It might be objected that this is not a very rigorous approach to research and so it might be dismissed as no more than individual performers seeking to do better under a grandiose title of research. In fact, McNiff's book does not really specifically answer criticisms of this nature although it recognises them, but they can be answered since this is a legitimate form of research because it is conducted under rigorous and controlled conditions.

One thing that we have to recognise about action research, as we do about practitioner research, is that it cannot have external validity because it recognises that all situations are unique and changing rapidly. Therefore, there are no previous examples or research into the same topic by which to test current research. Consequently, it demands rigorous internal validation by carefully examining each stage of the research, usually in a small team whereby the subjectivity can be minimised, whilst at the same time recognising that subjectivity is part of the process. New performances need to be carefully considered and tested. Action research, as its name implies, is future oriented which has profound implications in our understanding of knowledge itself.

An action planned for the future is always interdisciplinary. It is impossible to consider an action in which the actor decides to incorporate, say, 50 per cent sociological, 25 per cent philosophical and 25 per cent psychological knowledge in the action. Action is of necessity interdisciplinary and this creates a problem for action research since its research reports can result, with inexperienced researchers, in a mere discussion of what has occurred rather than a more profound critical discussion of the process. As will be argued below, the first part of action research can be multidisciplinary but the action must be interdisciplinary. Nevertheless, such profound analyses of action and of improved performance do occur and, like pragmatism itself, the findings are validated by the fact that they fulfil their claims in the practice situation; in other words, they work. Consequently, action research finds its main validation with peers and practitioners and the change in performance does not have the time-lag that the traditional theory–practice perspective built into the system.

In a similar manner, practitioner research (Jarvis 1999) uses the practitioners' own experience as the base for research but it differs from action research in as much as it is a carefully controlled research on practices that have been performed, but improving the practice thereafter does not feature on the immediate agenda. Practitioner research is a reflection back on the action, but the action is a case study and it can be that of a whole department or even a small unit. Like action research it uses qualitative methods and seeks to understand both the performance and reasons for it – so that it takes into consideration the social situation within which the performance has occurred. Since it is an analysis of an event, or events, that have already occurred it can be single disciplinary or multidisciplinary. If it is interdisciplinary, it runs the same risks that action research does in becoming a mere discussion. Like action research, practitioner research needs the same rigorous peer validation.

In a sense, both of these approaches to research are, themselves, learning exercises. This underlies the fact that research itself is always a learning exercise, although the learning is conducted under controlled conditions and what is learned is only valid if the control mechanisms enable the researcher to uncover the 'truth' of an event, situation, and so on. But, these forms of research, because they are learning under rigorous conditions controlled by the learners themselves, democratise research. Research no longer seems far removed from ordinary practitioners and this has led to a greater emphasis on practitioners continuing to gain additional qualifications through higher degrees – even practitioner doctorates.

Like learning itself, the site for research has been extended and now practitioners can own their own practice and their research about it, whereas in traditional research into practice the researchers would be removed from the practice, research it and report upon it, thereby owning the research about the others' practice. In this sense, research has been democratised but the flip side of this is that large research projects with full-time professional researchers have higher status in the same way that quantitative has traditionally had a higher status than qualitative research.

Clearly there has been some good and necessary quantitative research conducted about lifelong learning, as the NIACE reports discussed in the previous chapter highlight. Here statistics point to 'facts' – events that occurred in previous years and because they have happened they cannot be changed. It is this search for unchanging 'truth' that appears to give quantitative research high status, coupled with the fact that numerical descriptions appear to be more exact that qualitative ones. But quantitative research methods are notoriously difficult to enact with the type of precision that the statistician would like and unchanging truths almost inevitably relate either to inanimate objects, unchanging physical conditions and past events. They cannot capture people's experiences nor can they capture the unique 'now' of contemporary situations and so their validity has its own limitations.

Research in this learning society is necessarily more situated, experiential and qualitative. The rapidly changing conditions have led to the changes in the way that research is viewed by practitioners although it takes longer for policy makers to accept the changes, since 'science' is still regarded as one sure route to 'truth'. But neither education nor learning is a 'pure' science and so this type of rapidly changing society demands more emphasis on the human and social sciences. It is almost paradoxical that the knowledge economy with its focus upon technological innovation should result in more qualitative research.

Conclusion

Whilst we have traced the changes that stem from the global substructure we can see that some are more planned than others. However, the global core is not overtly political, although it would be false to claim that it does not play a political role or that the pressures that it exerts do not have political implications, so that it is necessary in the next chapter to examine the policies that have been initiated, partly as a result of the global substructure, to create a learning society.

Chapter 11

Policies, practices and functions

In this study we have traced the effects of the global pressures on society, on knowledge, on education and, ultimately, on the learners themselves. We have recognised that the global substructure exercises a covert power throughout the whole world but as yet we have not looked at this in policy terms and so in this penultimate chapter, we return to our original model in Chapter 3 and trace the effects of the global pressures on the policies of the various layers of society.

It must be pointed out that since the global core is neither a country nor even a single entity it cannot frame and implement policies at a global level: each constituent corporation can have its own internal policies and we will discuss these at the national and local levels. The global core consists of a number of very large corporations and many small and medium-sized companies all vying to produce commodities which can be sold in the global market, so that they have the same aims, similar knowledge and labour force demands, and so on. In order to produce these, they control a great deal of the advanced technology in the world and, therefore, use much of the most sophisticated scientific knowledge. These companies lie at the heart of advanced capitalism and it is this core that exerts pressure on all layers of each society – although this pressure is not exerted equally on all countries, neither do the countries all respond in precisely the same way. Nevertheless, the global pressures have exerted considerable pressure at international, national and local levels which have resulted in the formation of policies which have led to changes in education and lifelong learning which, in their turn, perform certain functions in society. Consequently, this chapter falls into three main sections: policies, practices and functions.

Policies of lifelong learning and the learning society

In Figure 3.2, we noted that each society comprises a number of layers around and below the core – international, national, regional/local and finally organisational and individual. In this section we will briefly look at the international and the national levels, and we will examine each in turn,

although it is acknowledged that through political activism and the democratic processes the local levels can affect national policy and so on. Indeed,
these pressures can act in such a way as to initiate national and international
policy, so that there is always pressure acting in both directions.

International level

The first layer around the global core is the international one and in Europe,
we have seen the European Union seeking to respond to the pressures eman-
ating from the centre. Enshrined in the Maastricht Treaty are Articles 149
and 150: the first seeks to develop a European dimension of education and
the second focuses on the need for a vocational training policy. Thereafter,
the EU has developed its three dimensions of education and training, higher
education and lifelong learning. The use of these terms illustrates that there
is no tight conceptual definition of lifelong learning since it would otherwise
have embraced the other two. Without analysing the vast array of policy
documents that have appeared since then, we can see that the Bologna
Declaration of 19 June 1999 indicates how European higher education
should develop in order to make it compatible across the whole of Europe –
this is part of the Europeanisation process but education and training and
lifelong learning have focused on the demands of both the global core
(globalisation) and Europeanisation. For instance, in 1995 a White Paper
appeared on *Teaching and Learning: Towards the Learning Society* (EC 1995) in
which three aims for education and training were postulated:

- social integration;
- enhancement of employability;
- personal fulfilment.

The paper recognised the impact of: the information society, internationalisation, scientific and technological knowledge. It also recognised that as part
of the process of developing a learning society, continuing education and
training must become an essential ingredient. Two years later, a European
Study Group on education and training concluded that there were four
significant aims for education and training (EC 1997: 1):

- constructing European citizenship through education and training;
- reinforcing European competitiveness and preserving employment
  through education and training;
- maintaining social cohesion through education and training;
- education and training in an information society.

Consequently, there have been two policy strands running through the
European Commission's policy documents – globalisation and Europeanisa-

tion. By 2001, these four aims had taken the form of 13 more specific objectives and employability had become more dominant since the Lisbon objectives of making Europe 'the most competitive and dynamic knowledge-based economy in the world' (EC 2001c, Annex: 4). But the EC was careful to recognise the significance of the good life as well as democracy and employability that could stem from education and training (Annex: 4).

At the same time, policy documents began to appear on lifelong learning (EC 2000a, 2001b). In the first – A Memorandum on Lifelong Learning – lifelong learning was seen as a way of achieving the three aims of citizenship, social cohesion and employment. The memorandum had six key messages (EC 2000a: 10–20):

- new basic skills for all;
- more investment in human resources;
- innovation in teaching and learning;
- valuing learning;
- rethinking guidance and counselling;
- bringing learning closer to home.

This document was put out for public consultation and over 3,000 replies were received and a little over a year later another document was published (EC 2001b) in which there were now four specified aims of lifelong learning:

- active citizenship;
- personal fulfilment;
- social inclusion;
- employment related aspects.

Running through all of the European policy documents, therefore, we see the forces of globalisation and Europeanisation operating on the member states of the EU, and those aspiring to join it. In a sense, therefore, there are two projects being embodied in lifelong learning in Europe – the response to the dynamic forces of advanced capitalism and the need to create a European citizenship. In this sense, it is hardly surprising that Europe has been less able to respond to the forces of globalisation than some other societies such as South-east Asia – but it does also mean that the social situation in Europe has resulted in a vision of lifelong learning and the learning society that has also encouraged traditional adult education through Grundtvig projects as well as more vocational ones through other schemes, such as Leonardo.[1]

However, we can see that two sets of forces operate on all the European countries in respect of lifelong learning and that the European project is educationally wider than that demanded by the forces of globalisation. More significantly, the two are not always completely compatible since, for instance, capitalism's success depends entirely on its being lean, efficient and effective.

The corporations need to produce commodities as cheap and as efficiently as possible, which means that production costs have to be reduced, which in turn means that unproductive and unnecessary labour has to be shed. In this sense, a form of social exclusion (unemployment) is a necessary condition for the health of the capitalist system, but the EU has consistently supported projects that seek social inclusion and even personal fulfilment, so that the neo-liberal economics of the knowledge economy have been played down in European policy on lifelong learning – but this does not mean that every member state has to adopt a similar balance to that which the European Commission has tried to achieve. At the same time, we have seen how not only does the learning society have learning organisations, it also has learning cities and learning regions – but the fact that these are occurring does not deny the covert power, the very significant covert global economic and technological power, of the substructure of the globe.

Not all countries are in such an active politico-economic community as the European Union but this does not mean that they are not exposed to international pressures. In fact, institutions like the World Bank and the International Monetary Fund exercise a tremendous amount of power on the poorer countries to which they lend money on behalf of the richer nations. Through policies such as the structural adjustment policy these poorer countries are even more exposed to the neo-liberal economic policies of Western capitalism without the protection of more powerful governments trying to modify the demands in the way that both the European Union and the UK government have done. It is in this competitive situation that the rich in the underdeveloped world get richer because they gain more power and wealth, whilst the poor get poorer. There is then a tendency to blame the poor for their own poverty on their laziness or lack of education and they are told that through lifelong learning they can gain employment and earn a living. The effects of the structural adjustment policies are hidden within the claims of how lifelong learning, amongst other things, can improve their lot. Even if they could, there are underdeveloped countries where lifelong learning policies have hardly been implemented for a variety of reasons – despite Western aid.[2]

National level

In response to both the economic global pressures of the neo-liberal core and the socio-economic and political pressures from the European Union, countries within the EU have introduced national policies for lifelong learning. In the UK, for instance, a National Advisory Group for Continuing Education and Lifelong Learning was established and it made its first report in 1997 (Fryer 1997). This report argued for a culture of lifelong learning for all and suggested a ten-point agenda in order to create this change (Fryer 1997: 3–10):

- a strategic framework;
- a revolution in attitudes;
- widening participation and achievement;
- home community and workplace;
- simplification and integration;
- partnership, planning and collaboration;
- information, advice and guidance;
- new date, targets and standards;
- new technologies of broadcasting and communication;
- funding and finance.

While it is clear that the impetus for this report is economic and work-oriented, it also makes considerable reference to the social needs of the nation, which is in accord with the European reference to social inclusion and some reference to citizenship, although there is little in the report about personal fulfilment. This report led to a UK government policy document, *The Learning Age* (DfEE 1998a) which was even more oriented to the economic needs of the nation and proposed such innovations as the University for Industry and Learn Direct – a national information service. This report certainly reflected the neo-liberal principles of the New Labour government and with it its desire to introduce lifelong learning, although in the first instance it made little reference to those other specified aims of lifelong learning, although there is the one reference in the Minister's Foreword that says 'learning offers excitement and the opportunity for discovery. It stimulates enquiring minds and nourishes our souls' (DfEE 1998a: 10). A neo-liberal agenda had been set and the UK became a leading country in Europe in implementing an agenda that was much in accord with the demands of the global substructure. Significantly, citizenship does not play quite such a leading role in the UK as it does in the European documents, but the UK has been less concerned with Europeanisation than the Commission, although British citizenship – and the learning required from it – has become an issue as a result of the problems of migration which itself, in many cases, can be traced back to the globalising forces and the wealth of the West. Economic migration is perfectly understandable in an unequal world.

Many initiatives in the UK followed this Green Paper, which have led to almost continuous change within the educational system ever since. Indeed, there has been an ever-increasing focus on education for employability and continuing professional development in the UK to the extent that liberal adult education funding is being cut and the provision of life-wide education is being restricted yet again, as we have noted earlier in this study.[3]

In contrast to the emphasis of the UK government, it is interesting to look briefly at similar documents from two other industrialised societies: one inside the EU – Finland, and the other in South-east Asia – Hong Kong. The Finnish government's policy document had its own vision:

By the year 2004 Finland will be one of the leading knowledge and interaction societies. Success will be based on citizens' equal opportunities to study and develop their own knowledge and extensively utilise information resources and educational opportunities. A high-quality, ethically and economically sustainable mode of operation in network-based teaching and research will have been established.

(Ministry of Education 1999: 29)

As the Finnish vision is based on the citizens' opportunities, so Hong Kong's vision is based on the student's all-round development and the aims of education in the twenty-first century are three-fold: enabling students to enjoy learning; enhancing student's effectiveness in communication and developing a sense of creativity and commitment (Education Commission 2000: 30). This will be achieved through the following principles: student focused, 'no-losers'; quality; life-wide learning; society-wide mobilisation (Education Commission 2000: 36–42).

While the UK vision has been driven much more by neo-liberal economic policies from both the global substructure and the political ideology of New Labour, we can see more humanistic approaches from both Finland and Hong Kong. Yet it is the rapid changes in global society, driven by the global substructure, which have necessitated these educational reforms. Whether the policies are actually put into practice in more humanistic ways or whether the policy statements are mere rhetoric is another matter – but the wording of the statements illustrates the different ways that the governments think they can win support for their changes and this alone illustrates profound cultural differences between the countries.

Of course government policy statements do not appear without consultation at all levels of society. Consequently, there are less powerful forces acting upwards and back towards the centre in most social situations. In the UK, for instance, the policy statement followed an advisory group's report and several non-governmental organisations (NGOs) were represented on that group so that they had an opportunity to influence policy. In this sense, the NGOs are interest groups and they play significant roles in policy formation. Pressure or interest groups in lifelong education have not been the subject of a great deal of research – indeed, it may be that their influence has waned considerably since we in the UK, for example, enjoy such a high standard of living and people equate their needs with the products that the corporations are producing and selling. Advertising creates these 'needs' which demonstrates the covert power of the substructure in information societies. Bauman (1988: 76–7) warned us that even the advertising is not experienced as oppressive:

These pressures [of advertising], however, are not experienced as an oppression. The surrender they demand promises nothing but joy; not just the joy of submitting to something greater than myself ... but straightforward, sensual joy of tasty eating, pleasant smelling, soothing drinking, relaxing driving, or the joy of being surrounded with smart, glistening, eye-caressing objects. With such duties, who needs rights?

And a number of years later he (1999: 156) noted:

Once the state recognizes the priority and superiority of the laws of the market over the laws of the *polis*, the citizen is transmuted into the consumer, and a 'consumer demands more and more protection while accepting less and less the need to participate' in the running of the state.

Even the EU was forced to recognise that there had been a decline in citizens' participation:

Civil society plays an important role in giving voice to the concerns of citizens and delivering services that meet people's needs. Churches and religious communities have a particular contribution to make. The organisations that make up civil society mobilise people and support, for instance, those suffering from exclusion or discrimination. The Union has encouraged the development of civil society in the applicant countries, as part of their preparation for membership. Nongovernmental organisations play an important role at global level in the development of policy. They often act as a warning system for the direction of political debate.

(European Commission 2001a: 10)

In the UK, the National Institute of Adult Continuing Education (NIACE) has been a leading interest group during the whole of this period. In the early years it seemed to have supported the UK government's policies in a very friendly manner whereas in the more recent rounds of cuts in liberal adult education it seems to have distanced itself a little more from them. Interest group activity is a very delicate activity if it is to be effective since governments are less inclined to listen to advice if the group or the adviser is perceived to be hostile to its policies in the first instance and even when the government listens it may not always accept what it hears. It is also likely to exclude from the consultation process those pressure groups perceived to be critical of its approach – often claiming that since it is democratically elected it has a mandate to govern without interference from anybody, let alone pressure groups. It is no wonder that Bauman (1999) could write a book entitled *In Search of Politics*.[4]

Apart from the government, most professional groups have mandatory continuing professional development and in many cases retaining a licence to practise depends upon the extent to which continuing professional

education is undertaken. The introduction of professional continuing education has not been a matter of government policy but of professional policy
in response to the rapidly changing knowledge that contemporary society is
generating. Indeed, in some ways the professional response has been a factor
in making government aware of the need to introduce national policies. Some
professions stipulate the number of days per annum that members must
undergo professional development courses and, as we pointed out earlier,
not all professionals are happy about being forced to undertake professional
continuing education at inconvenient times, etc. At the same time, many
practitioners are undertaking development courses in universities and colleges – often at their own expense. Additional qualifications are currency in
the job market or added evidence that the holders should be promoted.

Not only the professions but the large corporations also have their own
expectations and training policies – we have already alluded to this in respect
of the corporate universities. However, this professional development has
already moved beyond the confines of mere skills or competencies: the dir-
ector of the University of Chicago Hospital (UCH), for instance, says this
about the hospital programme:

> Our vision in creating the orientation program for UCH was to develop
> a program where our employees could learn to be good citizens. To us, a
> good citizen moves beyond performing just the job tasks. Rather a good
> citizen acts like he/she is the owner of the business, desires to satisfy
> customers, understands that customer satisfaction comes from how
> the job is done, and takes responsibility for continually striving to do a
> better job.
>
> (Cited from Meister 2000: 93)

Here then we see that for the corporations lifelong learning is also about active
citizenship, but in this case the citizenship is of the corporation. Corporate
citizenship might well become more important for the employees than the
active citizenship that the State seeks, and corporations are actively seeking
to cultivate this element of professional training. Loyalty to the company can
impinge on active citizenship in the State since many employees do not have
the security to live without the income from their employment and so they
are more dependent on the company than on the State. When the ideals of
active citizenship were formulated in the Greek city states, citizens had to be
property owners which gave them independence to speak freely without fear
or favour since their wealth, and therefore their standard of living, would be
unaffected by their actions. In today's world, the only property many citizens
have is their home, often supported by a mortgage, payment of which depends
upon their employment, so that people do not feel free to be active citizens
of the State, especially if it means that they need to speak out about their
employers' practices.

One of the strengths of Marshall's (1950) work was the insight that he had that there must always be a tension between citizenship and capitalism. This is a point upon which Turner (1990: 193) elaborated:

> It is clear however that political rights are of a very different order from economic rights, since in many respects the development in capitalist societies stopped, as it were, at the factory gates. Democracy did not develop fully into economic democracy.

Indeed, the battles for workers' rights occupies many a page in the history of most societies of the world as the public has sought to exercise power over the private domain of capital – and we might also add to economic rights those of the consumer. Our understanding of globalisation emphasises the need for civil action since the power of the State is itself being undermined but not destroyed by these processes, but we have already seen how historical processes have helped generate a sense of passivity amongst the people.

Policies about lifelong learning then have been initiated throughout the world as a result of the forces for rapid social change that have emanated from the globalisation process and from the demands of the knowledge economy. These policy statements have been formulated at the international and national levels of societies throughout the world: they are always wider than the very specific demands of the global substructure, although employ-ability is always the dominant aim of lifelong policy documents, but at national level they seek to include more about citizenship, welfare and human potential. At the local level we are seeing a new form of community education or, using the contemporary vocabulary, community learning.

Local level

The learning cities and learning regions are a response to the pressures of change that have occurred and have been created through local policy decisions in the regions where they operate. The European Union has sup-ported international projects and in the UK the government has offered considerable support to establish them locally. In some countries, the learn-ing cities and regions are extremely extensive, like in some parts of Germany, whereas in others they are much less frequent. As an example, in the Basque country in northern Spain, a White Paper was prepared by the regional government which argued the case formally for the whole region becoming a learning region and had, as its basic aim, that all residents should have 'a real opportunity to learn, in a different, more flexible way adapted to their needs' (Jaurlaritza and Vasco n.d.: 32). Despite the official nature of this White Paper, Longworth (2006), correctly in my experience, makes it clear that learning cities will only appear when local government and the people together across the whole region combine to make it happen.

We live in a globalised and network society. Since the formation of learning towns and learning cities they have networked; learning city networks exist around the world with opportunities for regions to exchange ideas and grow and develop.

Practices of lifelong learning in the learning society

Many of the practices of lifelong learning have been discussed in this book and as we trace the policies through the system we can see that there have been quite specific outcomes at the international, national and regional levels, some of which we will discuss below.

International level

In many ways UNESCO has taken a lead in having a decade of literacy and similar awareness-raising activities. Within the European Union there have also been a number of specific practices developed to further Europeanisation, such as joint research projects within the Framework programme, joint adult education programmes through Grundtvig, other joint higher education teaching programmes through ERASMUS, SOCRATES and LINGUA, and so on. In all of these, co-operation between educational institutions has been a major goal. This is also true for lifelong learning which was commemorated through the European Year of Lifelong Learning in 1996, the aims and themes (EC n.d., Annex 1) of which may be interpreted as being both in response to the demands of advanced capitalism and to further Europeanisation:

- high-quality general education;
- promotion of vocational training;
- promotion of continuing education and training;
- motivating individuals for lifelong learning;
- co-operation on education and training;
- raising awareness of the importance of creating new opportunities for lifelong learning;
- raising parents' awareness of the importance of education and training;
- developing the European dimension

In precisely the same way 2005 was declared the European Year for Education for Democratic Citizenship. However, the European Association for Education for Adults recognised that although there has been a lot of rhetoric on social capital, continuous cutbacks in the provision of adult education have also occurred – a point to which we have referred above in relation to the UK.

National level

At the national level, the creation of adult learners' weeks throughout Europe and beyond is another approach to raising people's awareness of the need for continuing learning and this might be seen as a response to global sub-structural pressures and those of international and national government to increase adult participation.

With the decline in welfare provision in advanced capitalist societies, something which is necessary if taxes are to be kept sufficiently low so as to ensure that industrial and commercial corporations remain located in the country, there has been a growing emphasis on adult literacy so that the unemployed can gain sufficient basic skills to get them into employment. It is interesting to compare the literacy campaigns in the developed world with those in the third world. In the latter there is a sense of giving people dignity and improving their own human condition whereas in the West adult literacy is regarded much more as a means of 'welfare to work' and equipping individuals to be independent of the State and earn their own livelihood. These campaigns are probably best seen in the West as a response to the lifelong learning aim of making people employable and, second, as a concern for social inclusion contained within the European policy documents. Work with other groups, such as the Roma people, is more directly related to social inclusion and some of this is actually funded by the European Social Fund.

Local level

In order to further lifelong learning, learning partnerships and learning region and city networks are being developed, all of which are seeking to engage all the providers of learning in collaborative networks. These partnerships and learning regions have endeavoured to popularise lifelong learning through fairs, festivals and a wide variety of local events. At the same time, it is at the local level that there have been considerable cutbacks in the provision of liberal adult education – which provides opportunities for individual fulfilment. These have occurred, often because of the cost, and this raises a major debate about issues about economic rationality. Clearly every society has to have a labour force and has to be productive in order to survive and provide opportunities to all its citizens, so that the relationship between vocation and leisure education is not an either/or one but a 'both/and' one. Even in countries where there has been cultural revolution, this debate is just as realistic and Mayo (2004: 63–4) notes that economic rationality has sometimes taken precedence over liberating education, even in countries that have sought to adopt Freirian approaches to education such as Tanzania.

As we have also seen, there has been an expansion of the higher and further education sectors in response to the global pressures, with government funding being targeted at the vocational rather than the liberal sector. In this sense it could be argued that the government has not only embraced the neo-liberal ideology that emanates from advanced capitalism but is furthering its cause through the use of the state provision of education. At the same time, the policies that have been generated by government are much broader than they need to be if they were merely to further the demands of the substructures of the world, so that the forces of neo-liberalism are being tempered by more humanistic policies at each layer of society.

Some functions of lifelong learning

The term 'function' has traditionally been associated with the sociological theory known as 'structural functionalism' and we have illustrated some of the weaknesses of structural functionalism in the discussion about learning organisations and communities of practice. At one level, however, 'function' means the contribution that the existence of a phenomenon makes to the coherence of the social system as a whole. It may be seen that this approach apparently has conservative overtones and so another broad approach is to regard the functions of a phenomenon as the consequences of its existence. This is certainly less biased than the former approach although it assumes that there are consequences and that there is a phenomenon that is the cause. By contrast to aim or policy, a function occurs as a result of the phenomenon's existence even though the outcomes might not have been the intention of the initiator or the provider. However, it must be recognised that in this sense function is used here in as value-free manner as is possible, although it is clear that although this analysis seeks to be objective it is almost impossible to be totally objective. It is perhaps significant to note at this point that while one of the aims of lifelong learning in all the European policy statements has been active citizenship, it is hard to find any evidence that active citizenship has become a function of lifelong learning, except in the sense that corporations are beginning to regard their employees as 'citizens' of the corporation.

In this case, the phenomenon under discussion is not static nor is it homogeneous and the nature of social change is to be seen in the way that the social system has adapted to the global pressures that emanate from the core of society and to the political pressures that are introduced as part of the process of adaptation to the changes that are occurring. We will return to the nature of social change in the brief concluding chapter. In this section we will examine some of the major functions of lifelong learning in these rapidly changing circumstances.

Throughout this study we have maintained that there are broadly two quite distinct manifestations of lifelong learning – one which is private, lifelong, non-vocational and often non-formal and even individual, while the other is social/public, work-life long, vocational, often formal. In order to discuss the functions of these two manifestations, I want to return to an approach I used in a previous study (Jarvis 1987: 133–50) where six pairs of functions were employed. This will provide a baseline whereby we can compare the way that we looked at education two decades ago with the way that it is viewed today. The six pairs are: maintenance of the social system and the reproduction of social relations; the transmission of knowledge and the reproduction of the cultural system; individual advancement and selection; second chance education and legitimation; leisure time pursuit and institutional expansion; development and liberation.

Maintenance of the social system and the reproduction of social relations

Each society needs certain institutions that serve to hold it together: Talcott Parsons (1951) called these functional prerequisites although Althusser (1972) regarded them as state ideological apparatuses. Education has traditionally served to socialise young children into the life of the society so that they learn to take their place within it; higher education and vocational training has done the same, and we noted how the large corporations are now actually referring to this socialisation process as corporate citizenship education. However, lifelong learning is wider than this but we can see that in its social/ public form it acts to produce and maintain an up-to-date workforce and to ensure that everybody learns the values of the advanced capitalist system. Kerr *et al.* (1973: 57) were not wrong when they suggested that education is the handmaid of industry although in today's language we could say that lifelong learning – work-life learning – maintains and sustains the global socio-economic system of neo-liberalism.

Society, however, is much more open than it was two decades ago and yet there is a sense in which the learning divide both reflects the social relations of contemporary society and reproduces them. We have seen (Chapter 9) how fewer people from the lower social classes than from higher ones participate in lifelong learning and so they have fewer opportunities of employment whereby they might be able to move through the social hierarchy. For those who have these opportunities, there is a greater opportunity to be socially mobile. So there is only a degree of openness and the learning divide also reflects a social class divide and, at this point, lifelong learning helps reproduce the social class system. But it must be recognised that those who framed the European Union policies did see lifelong learning as a method of social inclusion and those who seek to offer adult literacy still work to bring people into the system through lifelong learning. From the Althusserian perspective, however, it would be true to say that lifelong learning – especially in its work-life manifestation – still acts as an ideological apparatus but that apparatus is as much one in the service of advanced capitalism as it is of the State. Indeed, the power of the State may have declined, but it certainly has not withered away, and lifelong learning is a major ideological apparatus supporting advanced capitalism.

Transmission of knowledge and the reproduction of the cultural system

Whilst formal education might be seen to serve a function of transmitting knowledge, it is important to recognise that the driving forces of the global world demand that certain forms of knowledge take precedence over others. As we argued earlier, the knowledge society (Chapter 5) only utilises certain forms of knowledge, so that non-utilitarian knowledge has a lower status and so we have seen the decline in some of the humanities. Consequently, knowledge cannot be treated in a simple manner any longer – certain forms of knowledge are transmitted and researched to a greater degree than others. Indeed, lifelong learning, in its social/public form, may function in such a way as to marginalise those forms of knowledge that are not considered useful to the pragmatic global capitalist society. Moreover, it would be false now to concentrate on theoretical knowledge – a function of work-life lifelong learning is to transmit practical knowledge which is legitimated pragmatically. Lifelong learning, within the work-life understanding of the term, provides opportunities to learn certain forms of knowledge and one of its functions is to transmit certain forms of practical and theoretical knowledge. Consequently, lifelong learning may be dysfunctional to the maintenance of the broader knowledge base.

Nevertheless, we need more research to know the extent to which certain academic disciplines have been marginalised and the extent to which they are taken up in non-formal learning situations. We know, however, that with non-formal learning organisations, such as the University of the Third Age, opportunities to pursue the humanities still exist, as they do in liberal adult education, and so it might be claimed that in lifelong learning there are still opportunities to reproduce what has traditionally been regarded as culture.

Education traditionally reproduced culture and the philosophers of school education in the 1960s, such as Richard Peters (1967), argued for a broad curriculum enabling young people to appreciate the breadth of culture. Indeed, Peters (1966: 45) also advocated that education should be concerned to transmit 'worthwhile knowledge', but no knowledge has intrinsic value; as a culture changes so does the concept of 'worthwhileness'. As Marx pointed out, the dominant ideas of any society are the ideas of the ruling classes and so worthwhile knowledge is that knowledge that those who are dominant in contemporary society deem to be worthwhile. Indeed, leaders in business and industry often claim that schooling is not equipping young people for the world of work and increasingly their voices are being heard within the educational system. However, it could be argued that the school system needs to be protected against the demands of business and industry, giving children the opportunity to develop more broadly. Nevertheless, schooling itself has traditionally had a middle-class bias as Bourdieu (1973: 73) pointed out when he claimed that 'the inheritance of cultural wealth which has been accumulated and bequeathed by previous generations only really belongs . . . to those endowed with the means of appropriating it for themselves'. Consequently lifelong learning might be dysfunctional to the reproduction of high culture.

Individual advancement and selection

Clearly among the aims of lifelong learning it is anticipated that learners will be employable and that they will remain so throughout their working lives. The emphasis placed on qualifications in job interviews, and so on, points to the fact that one of the functions of lifelong education in the knowledge economy is to provide a basis for selection for employment and for individual advancement thereafter. Indeed, academic qualifications have become a major currency in the labour market. As Baudrillard (1988: 22) suggested:

> In order to become an object of consumption, the object must become a sign; that is, in some way it must become external to a relation that it now signifies, a-signed arbitrarily and non-coherently to this concrete relation, yet obtaining its coherence, and consequently, its meaning, from an abstract and systematic relation to all other object-signs.
>
> (italics in original)

The qualification is the sign that enables individual selection rather than the learning itself and lifelong learning sustains the learning market.

Second chance education and legitimation

Traditionally, adult education was regarded as providing an opportunity for those who had failed in their schooling to have a second chance of entering the system, although even by the time that this term was being used it was widely recognised that there were many who had never had a first chance, and so adult education actually provided opportunities to some who had never had them previously. When the British Open University was founded, it was regarded as 'the university of the second chance' by many although for many it was the first chance to gain a university education. Birkbeck College, the University of London external degree system, and the adult colleges in the UK such as Ruskin, Hillcroft and Fircroft were also regarded as institutions offering a second chance, or a first chance to those who had been deprived of such previously.

It was also recognised in the 1970s that schooling was not being successful with everybody and so adult basic education courses in literacy and numeracy were started. From the outset these schemes were introduced to provide the underprivileged with an opportunity beyond school to gain an education. However, as the knowledge economy has developed and educational social welfare is downplayed, adult basic education has become regarded as a possible way into employment and attending adult basic education courses has been coupled with unemployment, so that government policy has led to making certain forms of education compulsory and failure to attend such courses has meant that unemployment benefits would be curtailed. We have a 'welfare to work' policy. Indeed, Kumar (1978: 255) insightfully commented that: 'Keeping them [young people] off the streets, and attached to their allotted tasks, seems to be another, perhaps more important function [of education].' Consequently we see lifelong learning absorbing surplus labour force by giving unemployed people something to do and a second function is legitimating their unemployment – had they had the learning then they would not have been unemployed!

Legitimation is also one of the wider functions of lifelong learning. The more learning and the better the qualifications, then the better the job and the job holders' position is in a sense legitimated by their education. Bourdieu (1973: 84) reminded us of this function many years ago:

> By making social hierarchies and the reproduction of these hierarchies appear to be based upon the hierarchy of 'gifts', merits, or skills established and ratified by its sanctions, or, in a word, by converting social hierarchies in academic hierarchies, the educational system fulfils a system of legitimation which is more and more necessary to the perpetuation of the 'social order' as the evolution of the power relationship between classes tend more completely to exclude the imposition of a hierarchy based upon the crude and ruthless affirmation of the power relationship.

In today's more open society, this same function is still relevant. Indeed, it is even more relevant because learning is seen to be fundamental to the perpetuation of the knowledge economy and as society is more open there is always the feeling that people can rise up that ladder through hard work, endless studying, and so on. This is perhaps enhanced because there are more educational institutions, more educational opportunities and lifelong learning does not carry with it the overtones of elitist education through the 'better' universities.

Leisure time pursuit and institutional expansion

Traditionally adult education has been a middle-class leisure time pursuit since they have the cultural capital to appreciate it, but it might now be that learning is more associated with work than with leisure time – learning (work-life learning) is either part of the work life or an extension of it, so that for many, lifelong learning might not be equated with leisure at all. And yet, for those many who still attend liberal adult education classes and the many involved in non-formal education through universities of the third age and similar institutions, lifelong learning is still a leisure time pursuit.

Clearly the educational institution has expanded since the global core demands an increasing number of educated workforce and we have seen in an earlier chapter the extent to which work-life lifelong learning has contributed to this growth, but we have also seen how lifelong learning (liberal adult education) has been curtailed as a result of the same global forces. The expansion has meant that an increasing percentage of school leavers and adults requiring continuing professional development have returned to education – this has led some to claim that the inevitable outcome of this expansion has been a decline in standards (Furedi 2004) which leads one to draw the rather controversial conclusion that among the functions of learning for work in the formal system are to expand the system and to lower its quality. But, then, Lyotard (1984) made the point that higher education no longer trained the elite of society so much as the professionals to perform their work role in the knowledge economy.

Development and liberation

I (Jarvis 2006) argued in the first volume of this series that learning is fundamental to our humanity and that it is a major driving force for human growth and development, and so one of the functions of both forms of lifelong learning is human development. This claim is in accord with the work of Dewey (1916: 51) who wrote:

> Since life means growth, a living creature lives as truly and positively at one stage as another, with the same intrinsic fullness and the same absolute claims. Hence education means the enterprise of supplying the conditions which ensure growth or adequacy of life, irrespective of age.

Dewey used the term education but it is the sense of 'being educated' – that is, in the process of learning. In research into the hidden benefits of learning, Schuller and his colleagues (2002) showed that learning resulted in many benefits in human living including better health, and they showed that learning results in human development. Consequently, all learning, perhaps with the exceptions of some forms of brainwashing and indoctrination, provides growth. However, it could be argued that many people in the West are being indoctrinated into the advanced capitalist system since their lifestyles are of such a high level of affluence that they do not feel that they need to change it in anyway – whether it be for ecological reasons or because of the poverty and hardship the global system generates for the unfortunate people of the underdeveloped world. Whether they are any happier for their high standard of living is, however, a more debatable question. Consequently, we might argue that one of the functions of work-life lifelong learning, even though reflective and Freirian methods of teaching and learning are apparently employed in many lifelong learning projects, is still to domesticate people within the advanced capitalist system. In this sense, lifelong learning is far from the practice of freedom and in this it can be contrasted to lifelong learning in which it might be – although it does not always function this way. Nevertheless, lifelong learning in less affluent contexts might actually function as cultural action for freedom.

Moreover, the need to be liberated, to be free to think and criticise and to act in and against the current global situation is rarely discussed within the context of lifelong learning – in this sense learning itself has been domesticated and those who are satisfied with their high standard of living have been entrapped within the affluent outcomes of global capitalism. In short, while learning itself can be liberating, within the social contexts which we have discussed, such liberating and empowering ideas might sound as rhetoric and lifelong learning, in its social form, domesticating.

Conclusion

Throughout this book we have argued that social change is being driven by the global core and that this has resulted in the learning society and lifelong learning. In drawing the study to a close, the final brief chapter returns to the model of globalisation and argues that in the first instance the changing social conditions are the major cause of change and that human learning is a response to change. Thereafter, that learning might be an agency for change. At the same time, the learning society that we now know is a product of these social pressures generated by the substructures. As we pointed out in the opening chapters, citing the work of Lukes (2005), power does not have to be exercised in a crude manner, there are other dimensions to it which are much more covert. The power and the forces of these social pressures are tempered by the policies and practices that are created at the international, national and local levels of each society. Even so at this point in history, resistance to these changes is not well organised within the education sector.

Chapter 12

The need for the learning society and lifelong learning

This book has endeavoured to analyse the emergence of lifelong learning and the learning society. It has sought to show that lifelong learning and the learning society that we currently have are to a great extent the creation of advanced capitalism. But the sub-structural forces are not the only causes of this situation; the argument being presented here is not a determinist one and we have argued that there are international, national and regional forces seeking to modify these sub-structural forces, as policies have been formulated at the different political levels. Indeed, these policies have endeavoured to broaden the concerns of lifelong learning and the learning society; they have added citizenship, social inclusion and personal fulfilment to the aim of employability demanded by the core. Nevertheless, the dominant driving force behind this type of society has been, and still is, advanced capitalism – this is the driving force of globalisation.

The nature and speed of change has been controlled to a very great extent by the structure of the global substructure. Because it is not a single entity but many corporations, large and small, all endeavouring to create new commodities to sell in the global market, the competition engenders rapid change. New commodities, cheaper prices and greater efficiency mean that new forms of knowledge, new methods of production and greater control of retailing and advertising techniques mean that change is rapid and endemic. The types of knowledge needed are those which Scheler (1980 [1926]) called 'artificial': these are the practical, technological and some science and social science knowledge. It is necessary to translate the new knowledge into production as fast as possible – often at such a speed that the effects of the product are not always tested before they are marketed, so that the risk society (Beck 1992) is generated by the need to be at the forefront of new marketable commodities. It is also acknowledged that other risks are generated by the complexity of some of the new products which mean that it would take considerable time to test them before that could be utilised – if, indeed, they can be tested.

The knowledge is legitimated by its usefulness and so research into new knowledge focuses upon those forms that will continue to enhance the productive process; 'blue skies' research takes second place because business and industry wants to commission its own specific research projects. Governments have to some extent followed suit. Pragmatism is the philosophy underlying advanced capitalism and the market and so it is unsurprising that it also legitimates knowledge that leads to the production of commodities that sell to make profit! Profits are the endgame in this type of society and vast wealth is generated each year. In the basic mechanics of the production cycle, as shown in Figure 12.1, we see how this form of society functions economically and where the wealth is generated.

This very simple cycle demonstrates how capital works – in each cycle of production resources, capital and knowledge are inputted and the production process leads to the creation and sale of a commodity – from the returns generated from the sale of the commodity, some capital is ploughed back in to production process through the purchase of new resources (raw materials, plant, etc.) and in the wages paid to staff. The cheaper the raw materials can be purchased, the lower the wages, and so on, the lower will be the financial cost of producing the goods, so that corporations locate their production where costs are lowest. If there is excess labour, then the excess has to be shed; if the ecological costs need not be calculated or can be avoided, then these enhance the financial returns. Therefore, we can see that unemployment in the countries or regions where the production is occurring is a sign that the production process is lean and efficient; if countries whose resources can be used have an underdeveloped economy, then the resources cost less, and if production can be located where wages are low, then the system is even more profitable. This then is the basis of the knowledge economy. The lower the costs, the more capital can be extracted in each cycle in the form of profits.

The more technological the commodity or the production process, the

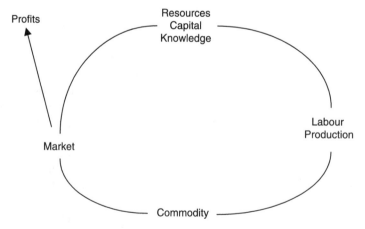

Figure 12.1 The cycle of production.

greater part knowledge plays in the production process. Knowledge, therefore, has market value. But the higher the price that the commodity is marketed for, the greater the financial returns to the company and, therefore, again the more capital can be extracted from the production process in the form of profits, which are then returned to the owners of the means of production, or the shareholders.

The rationale for the whole process is profit, not the betterment of human life for all, and the returns to those who control the process are in many cases inordinate. However, the pension funds are large shareholders in many of these corporations, so that almost everybody who is a member of a private or occupational pension scheme is dependent on this cycle of production. It is only those who have no private pension scheme who do not benefit and so we can see that even within a wealthy country, the rich get richer and the poor get poorer.

But there is another group who also get similar types of return for their activities – the celebrities and sportspeople, since they function to keep the people occupied and satisfied. It is no wonder that sports, especially globalised sports, are funded to a tremendous extent by the substructure – the advertising serves to market their products but it also functions to keep the people occupied! Whether the people are actually happier as a result of the labours of the celebrities is a different matter – indeed, it may be that the people are pacified rather than satisfied – and research is just beginning to raise questions about the levels of people's happiness in contemporary wealthy societies. But we have come to believe that 'there is no alternative' to the knowledge economy and this might be a manifestation of a form of false consciousness – but not false class consciousness in Marx's sense. Indeed, it might be argued that this form of 'being occupied, entertained and satisfied' is a form of inauthenticity – in Nietzsche's sense of the word, or even another manifestation of Bloom's (1987) closing of the mind. It has certainly produced a sense of complacency in our society in respect to the wider issues of the world.

Nevertheless, no society can survive without work and employment in one form or another, so that it is not work or employment that are questioned in this analysis – but the reasons why the forces of change are generated and the way that the receipts from the production processes are distributed. Basically, we can conclude that the globalised system that we now have needs a learning society and lifelong learning and it would be unrealistic to deny these needs but the way that the returns are distributed certainly needs more discussion.

Lifelong learning for employment is vital to the success of the process for that part of the workforce whose work demands knowledge, but for the remainder of the workforce, they are the unskilled and routine service workers who do not need a great deal of knowledge – they are the flexible workforce that can be moved from one employment to another, or dispensed with, as their services are no longer required by one corporation, and so on. It is these who learn basic skills and gain the lower qualifications that can equip them for their work. Knowledge workers are, however, important employees and replacing them is much harder unless there is also a highly educated but unemployed reserve army of labour – as we see in such countries as India and may well see in the West. The remaining group of workers, those who provide services, also need to have the latest skills, computer skills, interpersonal skills, and so on – so that there is also a demand for lifelong learning amongst the service workers. We have seen, however, that for the most part the type of learning to which lifelong learning refers is what I have called a social/public understanding of learning – work-lifelong learning, but in the final few paragraphs of this book I want to argue that we all need a learning society and lifelong learning, but we need one that emphasises the private lifelong learning which is a driving force of our own humanity (Jarvis 2006) rather than one which exists to sustain the current type of society.

When we talk about the private and individual form of learning, this does not mean that we favour individualism. Learning is a private matter but we are never outside of human relationships until the point of death. We live in relationship, we learn to be in relationship and we must also learn to live together (Delors 1996). The point is that our individualism is only realisable in relationship (see Appendix). Perhaps it is Delors that began to set an alternative agenda for the learning society and so in concluding this study we want to return to the four pillars of learning that he suggested – learning to know, to do, to be and to live together. However, we want to suggest six reasons why we need a learning society. We need a learning society so that we can learn:

- to be – persons not just employees;
- to do – to work not only to labour;
- to know – or have opportunities to learn a broader spectrum of knowledge;
- to live together, respecting each other and as active citizens seeking to create a better world – even the good society;
- to respect the world and not just use its resources for the benefit of the minority;
- to keep striving towards the type of society that lifelong learning and the learning society actually offer.

We will deal with each of these very briefly in turn since we will return to these in the final volume of this trilogy.

To be – persons

As we have seen above in the cycle of production people are resources – they can be employed when necessary and removed if their jobs are no longer necessary. When people are declared redundant, it is clear that we mean that their occupational role is no long necessary to the production process. However, when people are resources, it is not a big step to move from saying that the people's jobs are redundant to saying that the people themselves are redundant. It is easier not to say that but to treat people that way and that is a danger that primitive peoples, poor peoples in undeveloped societies and even those who are socially excluded in more advanced countries face. Such people may be regarded as inferior and unnecessary to the dynamic progress of the world. The colonisation of language can easily result in the colonisation of the mind and we live in a world where these things are perfectly possible, as the history of the last century reminds us.

Human beings are not resources, they are people. There is no such thing as social capital but we have accepted the colonisation of our language passively – even actively: there are people relating with each other and offering to enter relationships with others in order to respond to each other's needs and together enrich each other's lives.

To do – work or labour

In the modern world, the classical concept of work (the worker as producer and creator) has begun to disappear although there are still some crafts and professions that are based on work but work has been transformed to labour. Work and the production of our own efforts underlay the rise of capitalism since the endproduct of work is the market and a product only has value if it has either exchange value or use-value. However, a significant outcome of work is the self-fulfilment and self-achievement of the worker, the creator. But now, the aim of contemporary globalised society is labour. People have to be labourers – even flexible ones as the system's demands change – but, unlike work, labour has little intrinsic satisfaction or opportunity of self-fulfilment. Even the caring professions are moving in this direction so that the end-product for the organisations that employ carers is either profit (if private) or not making a loss (if State controlled). In order to be active citizens people have to be labourers contributing to the common good. Employability is now the key to active citizenship and what we do is how society judges us, values us and identifies us. But we need to rediscover work and learn to do work that is intrinsically satisfying and fulfilling to the human being.

To know

'This type of learning is less a matter of acquiring itemized, codified information than of mastering the instruments of knowledge themselves, and it can be regarded as both a means and an end in life' (Delors 1996: 86). As an end, knowing is not only pleasurable but it is life-enriching and gives us all the facility to live a more sustained and fulfilling life and so we need to keep on learning – learning skills, knowledge and emotions whereby the whole of our lives is enriched – this form of enrichment knows no monetary value.

To live together

Traditionally, we have learned knowledge and skills and the idea of learning to live together is something that has become more urgent as we examine both our history of destruction and the difficulties that migrants face in coming to a new country, and yet we live in a mobile world. Migration is not a new phenomenon but it is one which offers us tremendous opportunities of meeting people from different cultures and enriching our understanding of humanity but it also lies at the heart of active citizenship – that we need to work to produce a world in which people do learn to live together. Consequently, we might expect the European Union with its concerns to integrate the peoples of Europe to enrich our discussion on this matter. Indeed, it has published many policy documents in which active citizenship features but the White Paper on governance (EC 2001a: 7) recognises the fact that not only do people feel alienated from the EU's work but that they have disappointed expectations. Indeed, it could have gone on to say that people no longer trust the politicians who seek to govern. While the White Paper defends the European Union and its achievements (rightly, in many ways), its only solutions are system solutions: the EU must conduct its business openly, in a participative manner, be accountable, be effective and be coherent. And so active citizens should be informed, knowledgeable and able to participate in public debate, and they should also understand the way that the European system functions

Active citizens then should be involved in the process of governance and through democratic means, as civil society, the voices of the citizens should be heard expressing citizens' needs and warning those in government if its direction is wrong. This is hardly the public service role of active citizens in the city states of Greece when they ruled their cities and through their involvement they achieved both esteem and a sense of personal achievement and fulfilment. But then the citizens were free to play that role since they owned sufficient property to give them security. Now today's citizens' only property is their skill which can keep them in a job for a period of time, and few jobs are lifelong and unchanging and even fewer people have tenure in their occupation that enables them to be secure if they speak out in the common good. Indeed, just look at the negative connotations of the word 'whistle-blower' and look how often whistle-blowers are forced to leave their employment.

We live in an apparently open society having a form of representative democracy, but there are opportunities for the few to engage in the process of governing and even for the few, the powers of the economic sub-system of the knowledge economy means that even the power of the State, even the multi-State, is circumscribed to some degree. It may be that human potentiality might be achieved through being actively involved trying to bring about that better future through public service but the type of citizenship described here fails to recognise the human condition since it is framed within a totalising system. The opportunity to achieve and the honour and esteem that come from this form of active citizenship might best be captured with the phrase 'public service' – but this is not the way that active citizenship is commonly considered today.

We have to learn to live together and to work to produce a world in which this is possible: to live together in harmony is perhaps the ideal of all communitarian and utopian thinking.

To respect the world

We live in a world where we talk of another form of globalisation – global warming. A world in which the ozone layer is being destroyed, where deforestation is a daily feature, where the world's resources are used wastefully in consumer society – but we have to learn to respect the world. Perhaps the message to respect the world is made most clear by O'Sullivan (1999: 2):

> At the outset of this work, I would like to dramatize my position of the current forces of transnational economic globalization. I believe that in their present form they represent the most destructive and malignant forces of modernism. They are hydra-headed hierarchies gone wild.

Clearly we have to learn to respect the world but, as O'Sullivan argues, education has not got a comprehensive cosmology – neither have the corporations upon which we have focused in this book. But if the scientists are to be believed, then the situation is urgent and we do need to learn to respect the world quickly and also to get the corporations to do the same.

To keep striving towards the type of society that lifelong learning and the learning society actually offer

Throughout this book we have been critical of those who have been evangelical about lifelong learning and the learning society and the reason has not been because we do not believe in lifelong learning and do not want to see a learning society emerge – it is precisely because we do! Lifelong learning is fundamental to conscious living, it is the driving force of humanity (Jarvis 2006), but – and as Levinas (1991 [1969]) reminds us – in relationship with others we can actually transcend the totality of the system and reach towards infinity (see Appendix). Indeed, Freire reminded us many years ago that education should be utopian and one of his last books was entitled *Pedagogy of Hope* (1996) when he revisited his classic *Pedagogy of the Oppressed* (1972b). Fundamentally, in the idea of the learning society and with it lifelong learning, there is an ideal that transcends the present society and offers hope, but this has been a sociological study of what we now call lifelong learning and the learning society and the argument of this chapter is that now we need to transcend the current situation and discover the type of society that is implicit in the ideas of the present society – but we have to reach beyond it.

Conclusion

The period that we have traced in this book in the emergence of lifelong learning and the learning society is but a short one in the history of the world – probably less than half a century. In this brief period, the ecology has been put at risk like never before, humanity is divided between those who have and those who have not – those who have not exist in the first world as well as the third and there are people in the third world whose lifestyle is first world – so that it is not now a simple society-based[1] social class situation. We do need a learning society – one in which the agenda and curriculum are wider than we have at present and in which learning really is for active citizenship, social inclusion and personal fulfilment and in which employability takes its right place. We do need lifelong learning that asks questions about the future of humanity and the future of the planet and these should be seen as important as employability and more important than corporate profit.

At the heart of the human being is learning and humanity is in but a stage in the human project. As we argued in Volume 1, learning is inextricably intertwined with human consciousness – but our perceptions of the world and the experiences from which we learn are never free of the social context within which we learn. But we need to have a wider perspective, even more knowledge and understanding – we need a broader agenda – even broader than the ones that the politicians are proposing, so that our consciousness of the world will be different. With the rapidity of change, we need to keep on learning and we need a changed learning society with a more humanistic understanding of learning. But the learning society, as a concept, is utopian – but the society that it has produced is far from that. Yet a function of utopian thinking is to point us beyond the mirage to yet another that stands beyond it – to a perhaps better society than we now have – certainly a fairer one. Education and learning have a major part to play in this – but this must also be a learning society with new priorities and new concerns, where people matter more than profit or, in Kant's words, people are ends not means.

Appendix[1]

Infinite dreams, infinite growth, infinite learning – the challenges of globalisation in a finite world

The theme of this paper is unashamedly utopian, reaching beyond any single academic discipline and looking at the hopes and the fears generated by this rapidly changing world. But it is one that reflects some of the current concerns in global politics, partly initiated by the UK government and partly expressed as a response to the tsunami disaster. This is a world of globalisation and, perhaps, it is the effects of these global processes, especially disasters, that have made us aware that we live in a global village and that we are all one people, with all our similarities and our differences – glocalisation as well as globalisation. Beck (1992), for instance, argued that globalisation has a standardising effect on the world and I think that he is to some extent correct, but it was long before the effects of globalisation that we first became aware that we are a world of nations that should be united, and even before then religious thinkers and other idealists looked upon humankind as a whole. We are all one people, united in our humanity and, perhaps, in our ideals although certainly not always in our cultures, aspirations or practices. We live in a world in which we seek to understand and to give meaning to our lives. But, despite the efforts of science over many centuries, it is a world that we do not and cannot understand. Science examines facts and empirical evidence but no fact has intrinsic meaning. It is us who give facts meaning; it is us who have dreams and visions of a world where empirical realities may be put to different uses as we, the people, seek to discover our humanity and our unity.

Consequently, this paper has a utopian theme running through it – it looks to the future but it also challenges the present. It looks at a world that is about questions and not answers, that is about learning not education, that is transformed (or at least in a permanent state of transformation) without prescribed ends. I want to argue that we need visions of the infinite rather than an infinite number of visions and I will do this in three short sections: infinite dreams – religious, political and economic utopias; infinite growth – the challenges of globalisation in a finite world; infinite learning – but not an organised learning society, despite the fact that a utopian strain underlies some educational theory. My conclusion is that we do not need answers but a willingness to keep on learning and acting in relationship with the others who always impinge upon our freedom creating moral demands on us all and that our responses, actions, should be founded upon one universal value of concern for the Other rather than a multitude of cultural ones (Jarvis 1997). At the same time, I have to acknowledge that since I come from one culture – Western, which is itself a combination of Judeo-Christian and Greek thought – this paper must reflect that culture and so I acknowledge from the outset that this is a fundamental weakness in my presentation.

Infinite dreams – religious, political and economic utopias

Utopia is itself difficult to define. Nozick (1974: 294), for instance, suggests that 'it must be, in some restricted sense, the best for all of us; the best world imaginable', while Levitas (1990: 1) claims that 'Utopia is about how we would live and what kind of world we would live in if we could. . . . [It is the] construction of imaginary worlds, free from the difficulties that beset us in reality.' She suggests that it embodies form, function and content and she (1990: 191) indicates that utopianism 'has as a precondition a disparity between socially constructed need and socially prescribed and actually available means of satisfaction'. It is what is desired and it is 'desire for a better way of being. It involves imagining a state of being in which the problems that actually confront us are removed or resolved' (p. 191). Mannheim (1936: 184–90) thought that utopianism is associated with wish-fulfilment. These hopes and aspirations have generated religious, political and economic responses in which visions of a better world, a republic, an ideal city or even a paradise from which humankind emerged and will rediscover are to be found throughout the literature.

Religious utopias

It is here that I am forced to acknowledge my cultural limitations for I can only write of those from my own religious culture. Judeo-Christian thought has always had prophets who denounced the evils of the present world and announced the coming of a better one – a kingdom that God would create. Such pronouncements often appeared at times when the Hebrew faith, in the first instance, was under attack. When Christianity was also suffering the same fate, it responded in the same manner. Indeed, during one of the early persecutions the writer of the Revelation of St John the Divine 'saw a new heaven and a new earth' (Revelation 21:1) which reflects the writings of the Old Testament prophet (known by Old Testament scholars as trito-Isaiah), 'For behold, new heavens and a new earth' (Isaiah 65:17). Immediately one reads these passages, there is a sense of a timeless dream – as if utopia is created and will be unchanging for ever. Time has been stopped!

Throughout the history of the Christian Church there has always been a utopian, even an eschatological, future in which there would be a new heaven and a new earth – the Kingdom of God would come. In similar ways throughout that period, Christian sects have established their ideal communities seeking to establish their own perfect world in an imperfect society, and there have been many studies of these movements (see, for instance, Wilson 1967). But the ideal community seeks structures, and often languages, that are perfect and unchanging, since the ideal cannot change. Other utopian ideals to be found within religious utopias lie within the framework of millenarianism – when the present world will end with the coming of the Messiah who will establish a new reign on earth.

Without probing more deeply into these interesting religious movements, we can see that they emerge out of a sense of desire for a better world and when they are created they seek a form of perfection, stability that is unchanging, but this must lie outside of the realms of time and, therefore, beyond practicality. Nevertheless, we find underlying these religious ideals ones which are both political and economic.

Political utopias

Kumar (1991) claimed that utopia as a political concept began with Sir Thomas More's famous study in 1516, *Utopia*. Levitas (1992) disagrees and in a sense Kumar is himself inconsistent because he recognised Plato's *Republic* as a late development in Greek utopian thought. He (1987: 3) suggested that:

> Utopian themes reach back to the earliest Greek writings. From Hesiod's *Works and Days*, of the early seventh century bc, came to canonical depiction of the Golden Age, the bitterly lamented age of Kronos's reign when men 'lived as if they were gods, their hearts free from sorrow, and without hard work or pain'.

In precisely the same way Plato pictured an ideal city state in *The Republic*, with a carefully thought-out system of governance. In the nineteenth century in England two political utopian classics were produced: Marx's *The Communist Manifesto* and William Morris's *News from Nowhere*. Marx argued that the proletariat would rise up against the ruling classes and the ensuing revolution would result in a dictatorship of the proletariat who would abdicate when the time was right for a stable classless society to be introduced – perhaps a timeless one! But one of Marx's weaknesses lies at this point since his theory of change is that thesis produces its own antithesis and results in a synthesis. But unless we stop time, classlessness becomes its own thesis which produces its own antithesis, and so on. In contrast, Morris pictured himself in the twenty-second century when there is no need of government, money, or private property since everybody lived in harmony as a result of the workers' revolution. Once again, in both visions, it is necessary to step outside of time in order to realise them since they postulate an unchanging world where government and even money itself seems to be redundant.

In a sense, the right met the left in the middle of the twentieth century when the right-wing theorists postulated a world where the state was rolled back (Hayek 1944; Nozick 1974) and there was minimal government; private property and the free market constituted the basis of their way to a better society. Only in this situation, they argued, could the people be free and achieve self-fulfilment. In one sense they were right, people need freedom to be creative and to achieve their potential. But, in another they were wrong since the market is neither equal nor free and, as we shall argue below, it generates inequality and poverty, so that their vision is also flawed.

Economic utopias

In fourteenth-century England, visions of economic utopias began to appear and these were far less sophisticated than the visions of Hayek and Nozick. For instance, in the poem mocking the monasteries and their indulgent lifestyle we read:

> There are rivers broad and fine
> Of oil, milk, honey and of wine
> (*The Land of Cokaygne*)

Kumar (1987: 9) also notes the *Big Rock Candy Mountain*. But, O'Neill (1993) points to another more contemporary food manifestation – McTopia, which seeks to relate fast food to some aspects of utopian thinking, although it may also be dystopian since it lowers the levels of aspiration of the 'milk and honey' for all to consuming the food that the poor, in the West at least, can afford – in this sense there is a democratisation of eating. But here time plays a significant part since fast food cannot be slow because the space occupied by the consumer must constantly be filled by another paying customer or else that occupation eats into the profits of the industry. Yet, the food and the processes are universal for wherever one goes one discovers precisely the same timeless process and taste. From the sophisticated economic analyses to the more critical and polemical, we find economic visions of a better world, but they are impracticable or even offer a distorted perfection.

Adult educators have also been fascinated with these utopian visions. In the dialogue between Myles Horton and Paulo Freire (Bell *et al.* 1990: 52–3), we hear Horton saying:

> I thought maybe that's the answer, these utopian colonies, these communes, getting away from life, and kind of separating yourself and living

your own life. I was attracted to it but I was very sceptical from the very beginning. It seemed to be too precious, too 'getting away' from things. I ended up visiting all the remains of the communes in the United States – Oneida, Amana, New Harmony in Ohio . . . I ended up concluding that they were just like I had already concluded – that a person shouldn't live within himself. . . . And I discarded utopian communes. Finally, it just became very clear that I would never find what I was looking for. I was trying the wrong approach. The thing to do was just find a place, move in and start, and let it grow.

Grow it did – it became Highlander, a place that helped to foster the civil rights movement in the southern states of the USA. Yet neither he, nor Freire, regarded education as anything other than utopian. Elsewhere, Freire (1972a: 40) actually wrote: 'When education is no longer utopian . . . when it no longer embodies the dramatic unity of denunciation and annunciation, it is either that the future has no meaning, or because men are afraid to risk living the future as creative overcoming of the present, which has become old.'

There have been many visions of utopia, religious, political and economic. We can have an infinite number of dreams but they may not be attainable. Indeed, their major function may well be to remind us that we do not live in a perfect world and to help mould our desire for a better one since there are different worlds to which we can aspire even if some of them remain unrealistic and unrealisable. In this way, utopian thought breaks the bonds of the social order, as Mannheim (1936: 184–90) argued, whereas ideologies do not. But embedded in utopian thinking are ideologies. This is clearly true of Hayek's analysis in which the market and the economic system – the capitalist system – can create freedom and perhaps infinite growth. Certainly by the time of late capitalist ideas, we constantly hear politicians claiming that their policies will produce more growth – infinite growth – rather than the slowing down of economic growth, and so on.

Infinite growth and the challenges of globalisation

One of the constant claims of capitalism is that of growth – constant growth, almost unrestrained growth, and so in advanced capitalism we discover a covert ideology of infinite growth that will produce a utopian world of consumption in which to live. The reference above to McTopia points to the global nature of this phenomenon of advanced capitalism, but globalisation is not really utopian.

Globalisation might best be understood as a socio-economic phenomenon that has profound political and cultural implications. From an oversimplistic perspective, it can be understood by thinking of the *world* as having a sub-structure and a superstructure, whereas the simple Marxist model of society was that each *society* had a substructure and a superstructure. For Marx, the substructure was the economic institution and the superstructure everything else in social and cultural life – including the state, culture, and so on. Those who owned the capital, and therefore the means of production, were able to exercise power throughout the whole of their society. But over the years ownership has changed to control, and the capital has become intellectual as well as financial. But the other major change has been that this substructure has become global rather than societal and comprises two main driving forces: the first is the way that those who have control of the economic and technological substructure in the countries of the dominant West have been enabled to extend their control over the substructures of all the other countries in the world; the second is the standardising effects that these substructural changes are having on the superstructures of each society since the common substructure means that similar forces are being exerted on each people and society despite each having different histories, cultures, languages, and so on. Consequently we can see why the forces of globalisation exercise standardising pressures while a variety of peoples and societies resist this by endeavouring, to differing extents, to retain their own cultures and values – the glocal.

The process of globalisation, as we know it today, began in the West (USA followed by Western Europe) in the early 1970s. There were a number of contributory factors at this time that exacerbated this process, such as:

- the oil crisis, which dented the confidence of the West;
- the demise of the Bretton Woods Agreement, that eventually enabled both free trade and the flow of financial capital to develop throughout the world;
- the development of sophisticated information technology through the Star Wars programme, through which the information technology revolution took off, with one development leading to another, as Castells (1996: 51f.) demonstrates. He (1996: 52) makes the point that 'to some extent, the availability of new technologies constituted as a system in the 1970s was a fundamental basis for the process of socio-economic restructuring in the 1980s';
- the economic competition from Japan, that challenged the West;
- using scientific knowledge in the production of commodities in the global market;
- the fall of the Berlin Wall – the democratisation of the Eastern Bloc – for, from the time it occurred, there has literally been 'no alternative' (Bauman 1992) to global capitalism and so it reinforced the process.

While this is a brief outline of the globalisation process, we want to focus on three aspects here in order to develop our argument: power, inequality and social exclusion and natural resources (see Held *et al.* 1999 for a full discussion of global transformations).

Power

The driving force of advanced capitalism are the transnational corporations and their law is the law of the global market, whereas the laws of the states are still apparently controlled by the democratic (or not so democratic) governments, although the extent to which the national governments are sovereign is much more questionable (see Korten 1995; Monbiot 2000). Certainly the laws of the market have simply bypassed the laws of the states and the corporations are now able to exert tremendous pressures on national and local governments in order to pursue their own policies. These processes have made the nation states far less powerful than ever before in their history, so that politicians now call for partnerships between the public and private sector. But they are only willing to do this and to co-operate with these powerful institutions because they are realists and recognise where the power lies – it is at least shared, if not lost! But as Bauman (1999: 156) noted:

> Once the state recognizes the priority and superiority of the laws of the market over the laws of the *polis*, the citizen is transmuted into the consumer, and a 'consumer demands more and more protection while accepting less and less the need to participate' in the running of the state.
> (italics in original)

In other words, the consumer becomes a less active citizen and the political dimension of citizenship becomes little more than electing those who will manage the state; political power is subsumed within economic power and democracy suffers.

Inequality and social exclusion

The global market always favours the rich – since the market is never free. Very few people who have had power have not used it in some way to become rich – even very rich (fat cats). Those countries that have developed a knowledge economy have continued in their growth, others like much of sub-Saharan Africa are virtually excluded from the market. Bauman (1999: 175–6) summarises a United Nations Development report which illustrates these points:

- consumption has multiplied by a factor of six since 1950, but one billion people cannot even satisfy their most elementary needs;
- 60 per cent of residents in developing countries have no basic social infrastructures, 33 per cent no access to drinking water, 25 per cent no accommodation worthy of the name and 20 per cent no sanitary or medical services;
- the average income of 120 million people is less than $1 per day;

- in the world's richest country (USA), 16.5 per cent live in poverty, 20 per cent of the adult population are illiterate; 13 per cent have a life expectancy of shorter than 60 years;
- the world's three richest men have private assets greater than the combined national products of the 48 poorest countries;
- the fortunes of the 15 richest men exceeds the total produce of the whole of sub-Saharan Africa;
- 4 per cent of the wealth of the world's richest 225 men would offer the poor of the world access to elementary medical and educational amenities as well as adequate nutrition.

This is the other side of Hayek's vision of economic utopia – the creation of a new serfdom. What is being described here is a situation within which there is no global welfare and the poor of the world have no social rights as such by virtue of their humanity – but need care and concern. Moreover, while the lack of welfare provision is not a precondition of globalisation, it certainly helps global capitalism expand its profitability with greater ease since the people are merely human resources and the greater their need the easier it is to exploit them.

Natural resources

But it is not only human resources who are used and impoverished in the process, it is natural resources. We constantly hear that the world's oil stocks are running out, the forests are being destroyed in Brazil, the 'greenhouse gases' are destroying the ozone layer, and so on. The global market has made infinite demands on the globe and its people in order to produce finite growth – let alone infinite growth. The vision of infinite growth is an ecological nightmare. This is a world which exploits the many and their environments in order to satisfy the demands and wants of the minority.

The vision of economic growth has produced corporate power, the decline of democracy, impoverishment of people and potential ecological disaster. The challenge is to halt the destructive processes of globalisation and to facilitate an equal distribution of the world's resources. Religious visions are idealistic and unrealisable; political and economic ones are not only not universal, they are unrealistic, wrong and even dystopian. And so we turn to learning – to infinite learning.

Infinite learning

The present age has made people realise the reality and potentiality of life-long learning – now this is being taken for granted as we recognise that schooling is not the end of education nor of learning and that some forms of intelligence still continue to expand with learning experiences throughout the lifetime. Adult educators have always recognised this and there has always been an emphasis on self-directed learning in adulthood (Houle 1961; Tough 1979). Learning, then, has always been recognised as something that individuals undertake and, to some extent, it is something that they choose to do. But, more recently, the focus has been on the actual learning experience. This has produced a very wide variety of theories of experiential learning (Kolb 1984; Jarvis 1987, *inter alia*). Over the past twenty years the writing on experiential learning has been voluminous, but that on existential learning less so. Yet it is important to recognise that by virtue of our existence, we learn. Learning is the driving force of our human-ness itself. It is the foundation of the process of our being and our becoming throughout the duration of our finitude (Jarvis 1992).

But globalisation has brought another challenge to learning, since this rapidly changing economic system of production is demanding a more knowledgeable workforce. So lifelong learning has gained prominence – not because of the efforts or writings of adult educators but because of the needs of the economic system. This has also produced theories of the learning organisation, learning society, and so on. Everyone learning! Infinite learning! And so, Ranson (1994: 101–29) conceived of this learning society as a new order – one which would, or should, produce a more democratic way of living: 'The challenge for the time is to create a new moral and political order that responds to the needs of a society undergoing historic transition' (Ranson 1994: 105).

Here then, once again, we look forward to that utopian society – in this case a political democracy created by rational thought and debate and a clear understanding of education. Three conditions for the learning society are suggested: presuppositions – learning is valued and with it openness to new ideas; principles – active citizenship and practical reason; purposes, values and conditions – at the levels of self, society and polity. Ranson goes on to map these out in considerable detail, which includes a discussion on reforming government at national and local level and locating education within it. He recognises that this is a vision, one which will not be realised, if society does not change to enable this to happen. He concludes with the rather lame plea that teachers and educational managers can help spread this vision throughout society. In other words, this utopian vision merely fulfils the functions of other utopian thought – to remind us that our present system is not perfect and to educate our desire for a better world.

A wider educational vision is adopted by O'Sullivan (1999) whose utopian vision of learning embeds 'the human community within the earth community and ultimately within the universe' (p. 30). His vision is not of the learning society that Ranson sees, it is far less prosaic for his is a vision of learning, transformative learning. Of course his vision is attractive, of course his vision of the universe kindles within us that desire for a better world and in this sense he is both educating our desire and pointing to the fact that all the apparent advances in the world have not produced that perfect world. And so, we need to keep on learning, to keep on being transformed and yet the paradox of this transformative learning is that even when we produce transformations in the world, the vision still seems as far away as it is ever was – and so we just have to keep on learning. Infinite learning, infinite transformations, but like the mirage in the desert that utopia still lies in front of us and beyond us – beyond time itself. But then so it should for these dreams of different worlds serve both to show us that we have not yet travelled far along the road to the perfect society and also educate our thinking so that we too can desire that which lies beyond – beyond time, even beyond our dreams. Herein lies one of the greatest paradoxes of human existence: we who are (finite being in time) desire a world that can only lie beyond time – in infinitude itself.

Utopianism is more than just a motivating factor however significant it has been in the lives of many great thinkers. E.P. Thompson (1977: 790–1) wrote:

> And in such an adventure two things happen: our habitual values (the 'commonsense' of bourgeois society) are thrown into disarray. As we enter Utopia's proper and new found space: *the education of desire*. This is not the same as 'a moral education' towards a given end: it is rather, to open a way of aspiration, to 'teach desire to desire better, to desire more, and above all to desire in a different way'.
>
> (italics in original)

But, as we shall argue, perhaps teaching and learning does not lie in the realms of education itself – but in relationship with the Other. Indeed, it is not infinite learning to which we point now but learning the infinite.

Conclusions

So then, it is not only transformation that we desire but transcendence. We have to transcend that which is – transcend the boundaries, even those of visionary worlds. For many of these who draw boundaries limit freedom and offer a world of control; they are totalizers (Levinas 1991 [1969]). And so these have to be transcended but what more is there to transcend? Perhaps we need to learn to transcend even ourselves without destroying our own integrity. It was Emmanuel Levinas (1991 [1969]) who pointed us in this direction. For him, there is a clear distinction between 'need' and 'desire': the former seeks to fill something that is lacking, which is like many of the visions that we have described above, where a desire is what transcends the self – the me and myself self-centred categories, as John Wild puts it in his Introduction (Levinas 1991 [1969]: 16). For him this desire is never satisfied – it is infinite – and Being is a journey into the infinite. A perfectly disinterested desire is goodness. But it is not a journey undertaken alone but with the Other, with whom I might establish a bond without seeking control. This is what Levinas (1991 [1969]: 40) calls religion. It is in the endeavour to discover perfect relationship that points to infinity – it is people not place. For it is the society of the I-with-the-Other, when freedom itself is maintained and when it is recognised that when my spontaneity (freedom) is impinged upon, there is the beginning of ethics. Herein, concern for the Other, within impinging upon that freedom, lies at the heart of the infinite – it is seeking a quality of life.

> To approach the other in conversation is to welcome his expression, in which at each instance he overflows the idea a thought would carry away with it. It is therefore to *receive* from the Other beyond the capacity of the I which means exactly: to have the idea of infinity. But this also means: to be taught. The relation with the Other, or Conversation, is a non-allergic relation; but in as much as it is welcomed this conversation is teaching (enseignment). Teaching is not reducible to maieutics; it comes from the exterior and brings me more than I contain. In it non-violent transitivity the very epiphany of the face is produced.
>
> (Levinas 1991 [1969]: 51, italics in original)

So then in relationship itself lies the idea of infinitude. In a world of perfect relationship we can begin to explore infinity and so in exploring the face to face, the vision of the infinite is caught and learned and offers us something that lies beyond time in Being itself. So then, it is not infinite visions, even of the learning society, that we need but the vision of the infinite that produces different worlds – and the others interact with us as we seek to transcend the finitude of our being in this journey of life.

Notes

1 Lifelong learning in the social context

1   While I do not want to separate children's learning from adult learning as if they are different processes, I do want to emphasise that Figure 1.1. depicts the form of learning most frequently regarded as children's learning, although we all follow it throughout our lives when we have novel primary experiences.
2   Subsequent to completing this book, I realised that Figure 1.1 could be repeated almost precisely for cognitions as well, so that we could draw a cognitive learning diagram with box 2 reading 'has cognitive disjuncture' and so on – so that there are parallel processes – learning from the sense and learning from cognitions – that go to make up Figure 1.2.
3   For instance, when we learn a person's name for the first time, we should keep using the name when we address the person so that we learn to associate the image of the person with the name that we have learned.
4   This is a phrase I think originally came from one of Peter Berger's writings.
5   If I could find a really clear way of combining the diagrams, I would – but at present I feel that the two separate diagrams together communicate most clearly the learning process.
6   Issues of morality and the learning society will be discussed in the third volume of this trilogy.
7   We will return to this diagram when we discuss socialisation in the next chapter.

2 Human learning within a structural context

1   This section comprises a major part of the opening two sections of Chapter 3 of Volume 1.
2   We shall discuss this fully below.
3   This different approach to learning has led many in the West sometimes wrongly to accuse students from Confucian heritage countries of plagiarism.
4   The debate on individualism and individual human rights has tended to neglect the fact that we, as individual selves, are only selves in relation to others.

3 Human learning within a global context

1   I have dealt with this more fully in Jarvis and Parker (2005), chapter 8.
2   It is significant and paradoxical that in the European Union there has been a deliberate weakening of the power of the nation states as they cede power to Brussels, although a strong state may be the only power that can ultimately

contain the globalisation process. However, it would take a united world political system to control globalisation.

3   The Christian values referred to here are certainly not the same as those embraced by the fundamentalist American Right – most of which would not be accepted by those within the churches that do not accept a fundamentalist approach to the Bible. These values will become more apparent in the third volume of this trilogy.

4   Multilayered governance is a concept first utilised by Held *et al.* (1999: 62–77) although I have adopted it in a more simple manner here.

5   Helena Streijffert from Jonkoping University suggested that I should include organisations in the construction of this diagram, for which I thank her.

6   We will return to the ethical issues in the final chapters of this study and even more so in the final volume of this trilogy.

4 Outcomes of the globalisation process

1   I have traced this process much more thoroughly in *Adult Education and Lifelong Learning: Theory and Practice* (Jarvis 2004: 39–66).

2   I think, but I cannot find, that there was a specific statement in a University Grants Commission report about 1984 in which this was specifically stated.

3   Perhaps we might add a fifth pillar – learning to live in harmony with the living planet.

5 The information and the knowledge society

1   This is a point to which we will return in the third volume of this trilogy.

2   After having completed this book I came into contact with the United Nations Economic and Social Commission for Asia and the Pacific (UNESCAP), especially its Transport and Tourist Division. It became clear to me that in tourism there is a special emphasis on those forms of knowledge that are not regarded as undergirding the knowledge society, such as cultural and religious knowledge, and so on. People involved in the tourist industries are learning the traditional forms of knowledge and tourism depends to a great extent on these forms of knowledge. International and national agencies, therefore, are not only preserving these forms of knowledge but promulgating them. However, there is a danger that these forms of knowledge cease to be 'living' cultural knowledge and become historicised.

6 The learning society

1   This topic will be covered more thoroughly in the third volume of this trilogy.

7 Lifelong learning

1   *Social Trends* now employs the National Statistics Socio-economic Classification rather than the more traditional social-economic class breakdowns. The top four classifications are nearly all traditional white collar-type occupations and approximately 50 per cent of the population between 16 and 59 years fall into these categories.

2   It might be argued that it will not be long before some of the private universities become public corporations.

3   The ageist nature of these statistics is evident since statistics are not collected for the older age groups.

8 Life-wide learning

1   It is no accident that Buber (1958) sees the I–Thou relationship as a primary word with which the world of relation is established. A primary word signifies relationship.
2   Having formulated this distinction, I was reminded (Hull 2002) that it is similar to Arendt's distinction between 'who-ness' and 'what-ness' but I do not think that it takes political activity, as Arendt does, to generate 'who-ness' – merely being in the world and interacting throughout our lives both gives and confirms that primary identity. Nevertheless, I do agree that this distinction illustrates both our individuality and our togetherness in social living.

10 The changing nature of research

1   It is significant that a great deal of research is now being funded by the government and this makes the research field answerable not only to the education departments in government but also to the Treasury and, while I have not researched this, it does appear to be a tenet of government policy to take control of research in this manner.
2   It should be noted that the arguments about the relativity of knowledge do differ in respect to certain forms of knowledge: for instance, certain scientific truths are always true, e.g. light always travels at the same speed, but our understanding of the nature of light has changed. Cultural forms of knowledge change less rapidly and may reflect changing phenomena.

11 Policies, practices and functions

1   At the time of proof-reading this text there is a new policy statement from the EU – *Adult Learning: It is never too late to learn*. Unfortunately it was published too late to include in this analysis but it will be included in Volume 3.
2   For a study of a poorer nation see Laksamba's (2005) study of Nepal.
3   It might be argued that the conditions for liberal adult education in the UK in 2006 under the New Labour government are similar to what they were during the period of Mrs Thatcher's premiership.
4   A political study of lifelong learning and the learning society would enrich our understanding of education at this present time.

12 The need for the learning society and lifeling learning

1   The third volume of this trilogy will address some of these concerns.

Appendix

1   This paper was originally prepared for a conference in Uganda in 2004 but which I was unable to attend through illness. Subsequently, it was published in *Lifelong Learning in Europe*, vol. 10, no. 3, pp. 148–155 (2005c).

References

Abercrombie, N., Hill, S. and Turner, B. (2000) *Dictionary of Sociology* (fourth edition). Harmondsworth: Penguin.

Aldridge, F. and Tuckett, A. (2004) *Business as Usual . . .?* Leicester: NIACE.

Aldridge, F. and Tuckett, A. (2005) *Better News This Time?* Leicester: NIACE.

Allee, V. (1997) *The Knowledge Evolution.* Boston, MA: Butterworth-Heinemann.

Allen, K. (2006) 'Today, our chance to fight a new hi-tech tyranny', *The Observer*, 28 May, p. 8.

Allman, P. (1982) 'New perspectives on the adult: an argument for lifelong education', *International Journal of Lifelong Education*, 1 (1): 41–51.

Althusser, L. (1972) 'Ideology and ideological state apparatuses', in Cosin, B. (ed.) *Education, Structure and Society.* Harmondsworth: Penguin.

Antonacopoulou, E. Jarvis, P. Andersen, V., Elkjaer, B. and Høyrup, S. (eds) (2006) *Learning, Working and Living.* Basingstoke: Palgrave Macmillan.

Archer, M. (2000) *Human Being: The Problem of Agency.* Cambridge: Cambridge University Press.

Arendt, H. (1958) *The Human Condition.* Chicago, IL: University of Chicago Press.

Arendt, H. (1977) *The Life of the Mind, Book 2: Willing.* San Diego, CA: Harcourt.

Argyris, C. (1983) *Increasing Leadership Effectiveness.* Malabar, FL: Krieger.

Argyris, C. and Schön, D. (1974) *Theory in Practice: Increasing Professional Effectiveness.* San Francisco, CA: Jossey-Bass.

Argyris, C. and Schön, D. (1978) *Organizational Learning: A Theory of Action Perspective.* Reading, MA: Addison-Wesley.

Aristotle (1925 edition) *The Nicomachean Ethics.* Oxford: Oxford University Press.

Armsby, P., Costley, C. and Garnett, J. (2006) 'The legitimation of knowledge: a work-based perspective of APEL', *International Journal of Lifelong Education*, 25 (4): 369–83.

Aronowitz, S. (2000) *The Knowledge Factory.* Boston, MA: Beacon Press.

Baile, S. and O'Hagan, C. (2000) *APEL and Lifelong Learning.* Belfast: University of Ulster.

Ball, C. (1998) 'Learning pays', in Ranson, S. (ed) *Inside the Learning Society.* London: Cassell, pp. 36–41.

Barber, B. (2003 edition) *Jihad versus McWorld.* London: Corgi Books.

Baron, S., Field, J. and Schuller, T. (eds) (2000) *Social Capital.* Oxford: Oxford University Press.

Bateson, G. (1972) *Steps of an Ecology of Mind*. New York: Ballantine.

Baudrillard, J. (1988) 'The system of objects and consumer society', reprinted in *Jean Baudrillard: Selected Writings* (ed.) Poster, M. Cambridge: Polity, pp. 10–56.

Bauman, Z. (1988) *Freedom*. Milton Keynes: Open University Press.

Bauman, Z. (1992) *Intimations of Post Modernity*. London: Routledge.

Bauman, Z. (1998) *Work, Consumerism and the New Poor*. Buckingham: Open University Press.

Bauman, Z. (1999) *In Search of Politics*. Cambridge: Polity.

Bauman, Z. (2000) *Liquid Modernity*. Cambridge: Polity.

Bauman, Z. (2003) *Liquid Love*. Cambridge: Polity.

Bauman, Z. (2005a) *Liquid Life*. Cambridge: Polity.

Bauman, Z. (2005b) *Europe: An Unfinished Adventure*. Cambridge: Polity.

Beck, U. (1992) *Risk Society*. London: Sage.

Beck, U. (1994) 'The reinvention of politics', in Beck, U., Giddens, A. and Lash, S., *Reflexive Modernization*. Cambridge: Polity.

Beck, U. (2000) *What is Globalization?* Cambridge: Polity.

Beck, U. and Beck-Gernsheim, E. (2002) *Individualization*. London: Sage.

Beck, U., Giddens, A. and Lash, S. (1994) *Reflexive Modernization*. Cambridge: Polity.

Beinhart, S. and Smith, P. (1998) *National Adult Learning Survey 1997*. London: DfEE.

Belenky, M., Clinchy, B., Goldberger, N. and Tarule, J. (1986) *Women's Ways of Knowing*. New York: Basic Books.

Bell, B., Gaventa, J. and Peters, J. (eds) (1990) *We Make the Road by Walking: Conversations on Education and Social Change – Myles Horton and Paulo Freire*. Philadelphia, PA: Temple University Press.

Bell, D. (1973) *The Coming of Post-Industrial Society*. New York: Basic Books.

Bell, D. (1980) 'The social framework of the information society', in Forester, T. (ed.) *The Microelectronics Revolution*. Oxford: Blackwell.

Benner, P. (1984) *From Novice to Expert*. Menlo Park, CA: Addison-Wesley.

Berger, P.L. and Luckmann, T. (1966) *The Social Construction of Reality*. London: Allen Lane/Penguin.

Bergson, H. (1998 [1911]) *Creative Evolution*. New York: Dover Publications.

Bergson, H. (1999 [1965]) *Duration and Simultaneity*. Manchester: Clinamen Press.

Bergson, H. (2004 [1912]) *Matter and Memory*. New York: Dover Publications.

Bernauer, J. and Rasmussen, J. (eds) *The Final Foucault*. Cambridge, MA: MIT Press.

Beynon, H. (1975) *Working for Ford*. Wakefield: EP Publishing (first published by Penguin, 1973).

Blackwell, L. and Bynner, J. (2002) *Learning, Family Formation and Dissolution*. University of London: Centre for Research on the Wider Benefits of Learning, Report No. 4.

Bloom, A. (1987) *The Closing of the American Mind*. New York: Touchstone.

Bok, D. (2003) *Universities in the Market Place*. Princeton, NJ: Princeton University Press.

Bologna Declaration (1999) http://www.hefce.ac.uk/Partners/world/bol/

Bologna Process (2005) *Towards A European Area of Higher Education*, BFUGB8 5 Final, 27 April.

Bornschier, V. (1980) 'Multinational corporations and economic growth', *Journal of Development Economics*, 7: 191–210.

Boshier, R. (1980) *Towards a Learning Society*. Vancouver: Learningpress Ltd.

Botkin, J., Elmandjra, M. and Malitza, M. (1979) *No Limits to Learning*. Oxford: Pergamon.

Bottomore, T. and Rubel, M. (eds) (1963) *Karl Marx: Selected Writings in Sociology and Social Philosophy*. Harmondsworth: Penguin.

Boud, D. (ed.) (1985) *Problem-Based Learning in Education for the Professions*. Sydney: HERDSA.

Boud, D. (ed.) (1995) *Enhancing Learning through Self-Assessment*. London: Kogan Page.

Boud, D. and Griffin, V. (eds) (1987) *Appreciating Adults Learning*. London: Kogan Page.

Boud, D. and Feletti, G. (eds) (1991) *The Challenge of Problem-Based Learning*. London: Kogan Page.

Boud, D., Keogh, R. and Walker, D. (eds) (1985) *Reflection: Turning Experience into Learning*. London: Croom Helm.

Bourdieu, P. (1973) 'Cultural reproduction and social reproduction', in Brown, M. (ed.) *Reproduction in Education, Society and Culture*. London: Sage.

Bourdieu, P. (1992) 'The purpose of reflexive sociology', in Bourdieu, P. and Wacquant L., *An Invitation to Reflexive Sociology*. Cambridge: Polity.

Bourdieu, P. and Passeron, J.-C. (1977) *Reproduction in Education, Society and Culture*. London: Sage.

Bourdieu, P. and Wacquant, L. (1992) *An Invitation to Reflexive Sociology*. Cambridge: Polity.

Brasset-Grundy, A. (2002) *Parental Perspectives of Family Learning*. University of London: Centre for Research on the Wider Benefits of Learning, Report No.2.

Brookfield, S. (1986) *Understanding and Facilitating Adult Learning*. San Francisco, CA: Jossey-Bass.

Buber, M. (1958) *I and Thou*. Edinburgh: Clarke.

Bucher, R. and Strauss, A. (1966) 'Professional association and the process of segmentation', in Vollmer, H. and Mills, D. (eds) *Professionalization*. Englewood Cliffs, NJ: Prentice-Hall.

Campano, R., Pascu, C. and Burgelman, J.-C. (2004) *Key Factors Driving the Future Information Society in the European Area of Research*. European Commission Technical Report EUR 21310 EN.

Campbell, D. (1984) *The New Majority*. Edmonton: University of Alberta Press.

Candy, P. (1991) *Self-Direction for Lifelong Learning*. San Francisco, CA: Jossey-Bass.

Carnevale, A., Gainer, L. and Schulz, E. (1990) *Training the Technical Work Force*. San Francisco, CA: Jossey-Bass.

Carr, W. and Kemmis, S. (1986) *Becoming Critical: Education, Knowledge and Action Research*. Brighton: Falmer.

Casner-Lotto, J. and Associates (1988) *Successful Training Strategies*. San Francisco, CA: Jossey-Bass.

Castells, M. (1996) *The Rise of the Network Society*, Vol. 1 of *The Information Age: Economy, Society and Culture*. Oxford: Blackwell.

Cattell, J. (1963) 'The theory of fluid and crystallised intelligence', *Journal of Educational Psychology*, 54 (1): 1–22.

Chene, A. (1994) 'Community-based older learners: being with others', *Educational Gerontology*, 20 (8): 65–78.

Clarke, A. (2001) *Learning Organisations*. Leicester: NIACE.

Coffield, F. (ed.) (2000) *Differing Visions of a Learning Society* (2 vols). Bristol: Policy Press.

Coleman, J. (1990) *Foundations of Social Theory*. Cambridge, MA: Belknap Press.

Collins English Dictionary (1979) Glasgow: Collins.

Cooper, D. (1983) *Authenticity and Learning*. London: Routledge and Kegan Paul.

Cosin, B. (ed.) (1972) *Education, Structure and Society*. Harmondsworth: Penguin.

Crawford, J. (2005) *Spiritually Engaged Knowledge*. Aldershot: Ashgate.

Cross, K.P. (1981) *Adults as Learners*. San Francisco, CA: Jossey-Bass.

Crossley, M. (2006) *Bridging Cultures and Traditions: Perspectives from Comparative and International Research in Education* Bristol: University of Bristol, Graduate School of Education.

Crowther, J. (2006) 'Social movements, praxis and the profane side of lifelong learning', in Sutherland, P. and Crowther, J. (eds) *Lifelong Learning*. London: Routledge, pp. 171–81.

Csikszentmihalyi, M. (1990) *Flow: The Psychology of Optimal Experience*. New York: Harper and Row.

Cussack, S. and Thompson, W. (1998) 'Mental fitness: developing a vital aging society', *International Journal of Lifelong Education*, 17 (5): 307–17.

Daloz, L. (1986) *Effective Teaching and Mentoring*. San Francisco, CA: Jossey-Bass.

Dearing, R. (Chair) (1997) *Higher Education in the Learning Society*. Norwich: HMSO.

Delors, J. (Chair) (1996) *Learning: The Treasure Within*. Paris: UNESCO.

Department for Education and Employment (1998) *Learning City Network: Practice, Progress and Value*. London: Department for Education and Employment.

Department for Education and Employment (1998a) *The Learning Age*. London: Department for Education and Employment, Cm 3790.

Department for Education and Skills (downloaded 2006) *The Future of Higher Education* http://www.dfes.gov.uk/hegateway/strategy/hestrategy/exec.shtml

Department for Education and Skills (downloaded 2006) *Trends in Education and Skills* http://www.dfes.gov.uk/trends/index.cfm?fuseaction= home.showChart&cid.

Dewey, J. (1916) *Democracy and Education*. New York: Free Press.

Dominice, P. (2000) *Learning from our Lives*. San Francisco, CA: Jossey-Bass.

Dreyfus, S. and Dreyfus, H. (1980) 'A five-stage model of mental activities involved in directed skill acquisition', unpublished report.

Drucker, P. (1994) 'Knowledge, work and the knowledge society: the social transformations of this century', Edwin L Godkin Lecture, Harvard University http://www.ksg.harvard.edu/ifactory/ksgpress/www_news/transcripts/druclec.htm (downloaded Dec. 2005).

Dubin, S. (1990) 'Maintaining competence through updating', in Willis, S. and Dubin, S. (eds) *Maintaining Professional Competence*. San Francisco, CA: Jossey-Bass.

Duke, C., Osborne, M. and Wilson, B. (eds) (2005) *Balancing the Social and the Economic*. Leicester: NIACE.

Durkheim, E. (1915) *The Elementary Forms of Religious Life*. London: George Allen and Unwin.

Durkheim, E. (1964 [1933]) *The Division of Labor in Society*. New York: Free Press.

Education Commission (2000) *Learning for Life Learning through Life*. Hong Kong Education Commission.

Edwards, R. (2000) 'Lifelong learning, lifelong learning, lifelong learning: recurrent education', in Field, J. and Leicester, M. (eds) *Lifelong Learning*. London: Routledge, pp. 3–11.

Edwards, R. and Usher, R. (1994) 'Disciplining the subject: the power of competence', *Studies in the Education of Adults*, 26 (1): 1–14.

Edwards, R., Miller, N., Small, N. and Tait, A. (eds) (2002) *Making Knowledge Work: Supporting Lifelong Learning*, Vol. 3. London: RoutledgeFalmer.

Elliott, P. (1972) *The Sociology of Professions*. London: Macmillan.

Erikson, E. (1963) *Childhood and Society*. New York: Norton.

Eurich, N. (1984) *Corporate Classrooms*. Princeton, NJ: Carnegie Foundation for the Advancement of Teaching.

European Commission (n.d.) *Report from the Commission on the Implementation, Results and Overall Assessment of the European Year of Lifelong Learning (1996)*. Brussels: Directorate General XXII.

European Commission (1995) *Teaching and Learning: Towards the Learning Society* (White Paper on Education and Training). Brussels: European Commission.

European Commission (1997) *Accomplishing Europe through Education and Training Executive Summary* http://europa.eu.int/comm/education/reflex/en/res-en.html

European Commission (2000a) *A Memorandum on Lifelong Learning*. Brussels: European Commission, SEC (2000) 1832.

European Commission (2000b) *Towards a European Research Area*. Brussels: Communication from the Commission to the Council, COM (2000) 6.

European Commission (2001a) *European Governance: A White Paper*. Brussels: European Commission, COM (2001) 428 final.

European Commission (2001b) *Making a European Area of Lifelong Learning a Reality*. Brussels: European Commission, COM (2001) 678 final.

European Commission (2001c) *The Concrete Future Objectives of Education and Training*. Brussels: Council of the European Union, EDUC 23 5980/01.

European Commission (2003) *Compendium: European Networks to Promote the Local and Regional Dimension of Lifelong Learning*. Brussels: European Commission – Education and Culture.

Falzon, C. (1998) *Foucault and Social Dialogue*. London: Routledge.

Faure, E. (Chair) (1972) *Learning to Be*. Paris: UNESCO.

Featherstone, M. (1995) *Undoing Culture: Globalization, Postmodernism and Identity*. London: Sage.

Feinstein, L. (2002a) *Quantitative Estimates of the Social Benefits of Learning, 1 Crime*. University of London: Centre for Research on the Wider Benefits of Learning, Report No. 5.

Feinstein, L. (2002b) *Quantitative Estimates of the Social Benefits of Learning, 2 Health (Depression and Obesity)*. University of London: Centre for Research on the Wider Benefits of Learning, Report No. 6.

Fetherstone, N., Lash, S. and Bobertson, R. (eds) (1995) *Global Modernities*. London: Sage.

Field, J. (1999) 'Participation under the magnifying glass', *Adults Learning*, November, pp. 10–13.

Field, J. (2000) *Lifelong Learning and the New Educational Order*. Stoke-on-Trent: Trentham.

Field, J. and Leicester, M. (2000a) 'Lifelong learning or permanent schooling', in

Field, J. and Leicester, M. (eds) *Lifelong Learning: Education Across the Lifespan.* London: Routledge.

Field, J. and Leicester, M. (eds) (2000b) *Lifelong Learning: Education Across the Lifespan.* London: Routledge.

Flecha, R. (2000) *Sharing Words.* Lanham, MD: Rowman and Littlefield.

Foster, A. (Chair) (2005) *Realising the Potential.* London: Department for Education and Skills.

Foucault, M. (1979) *Discipline and Punish.* Harmondsworth: Penguin.

Foucault, M. (1987) 'The ethic of care for the self as a practice of freedom: an interview with Michael Foucault on January 20, 1984', in Bernauer, J. and Rasmussen, D. (eds) *The Final Foucault.* Cambridge, MA: MIT Press.

Freire, P. (1972a) *Cultural Action for Freedom.* Harmondsworth: Penguin.

Freire, P. (1972b) *Pedagogy of the Oppressed.* Harmondsworth: Penguin.

Freire, P. (1996) *Pedagogy of Hope.* New York: Continuum.

Freire, P. and Macedo, D. (1987) *Literacy: Reading the Word and the World.* London: Routledge and Kegan Paul.

Friedman, T. (1999) *The Lexus and the Olive Tree.* New York: Farrar Straus Giroux.

Fryer, R. (Chair) (1997) *Learning for the Twenty-First Century.* London: Department for Education and Employment.

Furedi, F. (2004) *Where Have All the Intellectuals Gone?* London: Continuum.

Galtung, I. (1971) 'A structural theory of imperialism', *Journal of Peace Studies*, 8: 81–117.

Gehlen, A. (1988) *Man: His Nature and Place in the World.* New York: Columbia University Press.

Gennep, A. van (1960 [1908]) *The Rites of Passage.* London: Routledge and Kegan Paul.

Gibbons, M. (2004) 'Globalization, innovation and socially robust knowledge', in King, R. (ed.) *The University in the Global Age.* Basingstoke: Palgrave, pp. 96–115.

Giddens, A. (1979) *Central Problems in Social Theory: Action, Structure and Contradiction in Social Analysis.* London: Macmillan.

Giddens, A. (1991) *Modernity and Self-identity.* Cambridge: Polity.

Giddens, A. (1994) 'Living in a post-traditional society', in Beck, U., Giddens, A. and Lash, S. *Reflexive Modernization.* Cambridge: Polity.

Glover, D. and Mardle G. (eds) (1995) *The Management of Mentoring.* London: Kogan Page.

Goffman, E. (1959) *The Presentation of Self in Everyday Life.* Harmondsworth: Penguin.

Goffman, E. (1968) *Stigma.* Harmondsworth: Penguin.

Goffman, E. (1971) *Relations in Public.* Harmondsworth: Penguin.

Gouldner, A. (1957–8) 'Cosmopolitan and locals: towards an analysis of latent social roles', *Administration Science Quarterly*, 2: 281–306.

Grayling, A. (2004) *The Mystery of Things.* London: Phoenix.

Green, A. (1997) *Education, Globalization and the Nation State.* Basingstoke: Macmillan.

Grusky, O. and Miller, G. (eds) (1970) *The Sociology of Organizations.* New York: Free Press.

Habermas, J. (1981) *The Theory of Communicative Action*, Vol. 1. Cambridge: Polity.

Habermas, J. (1987) *The Theory of Communicative Action*, Vol. 2. Cambridge: Polity.

Habermas, J. (2001) *The Postnational Constellation* (trans. M. Pensky). Cambridge: Polity.

Hanifan, L. (1916) 'The rural school community center', *Annals of the American Academy of Political and Social Science*, 67: 130–8.

Hargreaves, P. and Jarvis, P. (2000) *The Human Resource Development Handbook* (revised edition). London: Kogan Page.

Hayek, F. (1944) *The Road to Serfdom*. London: ARK Paperbacks, published in 1986.

Held, D., McGrew, A., Goldblatt, D. and Perraton, J. (1999) *Global Transformations*. Cambridge: Polity.

Herman, L. and Mandell, A. (2004) *From Teaching to Mentoring*. London: Routledge-Falmer.

Hewison, J., Dowswell, T. and Millar, B. (2000) 'Changing patterns in training provision in the National Health Service: an overview', in Coffield, F. (ed.) *Differing Visions of a Learning Society*, Vol.1. Bristol: Policy Press, pp. 167–97.

Holloway, J. (2002a) *Change the World without Taking Power: The Meaning of Revolution Today*. London: Pluto.

Holloway, J. (2002b) 'Twelve theses on changing the world without taking power', *The Commoner* (May) www.commoner.org.uk/04holloway2.pdf

Houle, C. (1961) *The Inquiring Mind*. Madison: University of Wisconsin Press.

Hoyle, E. and Megarry, J. (eds) (1980) *Professional Development of Teachers – World Yearbook of Education*. London: Kogan Page.

Hughes, C. and Tight, M. (1998) 'The myth of the learning society', in Ranson, S. (ed.) *Inside the Learning Society*. London: Cassell, pp. 178–88.

Hull, M. (2002) *The Hidden Philosophy of Hannah Arendt*. London: RoutledgeCurzon.

Husén, T. (1974) *The Learning Society*. London: Methuen.

Hutchins, R. (1968) *The Learning Society*. Harmondsworth: Penguin.

Illich, I. (1971) *Deschooling Society*. Harmondsworth: Penguin.

Illich, I. and Verne, E. (1976) *Imprisoned in a Global Classroom*. London: Writers and Readers.

Jarvis, P. (1977) 'Protestant ministers: job satisfaction and role strain in the bureaucratic organisation of the Church'. Unpublished PhD thesis, University of Aston.

Jarvis, P. (1983) *Professional Education*. London: Croom Helm.

Jarvis, P. (1985) *The Sociology of Adult and Continuing Education*. London: Croom Helm.

Jarvis, P. (1987) *Adult Learning in the Social Context*. London: Croom Helm.

Jarvis, P. (1992) *Paradoxes of Learning*. San Francisco, CA: Jossey-Bass.

Jarvis, P. (1997) *Ethics and the Education of Adults in Late Modern Society*. Leicester: NIACE.

Jarvis, P. (1999) *The Practitioner Researcher*. San Francisco, CA: Jossey-Bass.

Jarvis, P. (2001a) *Universities and Corporate Universities*. London: Kogan Page.

Jarvis, P. (2001b) *Learning in Later Life*. London: Kogan Page.

Jarvis, P. (2004) *Adult Education and Lifelong Learning: Theory and Practice* (third edition). London: RoutledgeFalmer.

Jarvis, P. (2005a) 'Learning and earning in the knowledge society: some ethical considerations', in Strain, R. and Robinson, S. (eds) *The Teaching and Practice of Professional Ethics*. Leicester: Troubador.

Jarvis, P. (2005b) 'Transforming Asian education through open and distance learning

– through thinking', in *Proceedings of Transforming Asian Education through Open and Distance Learning*. Hong Kong: Hong Kong Open University.

Jarvis, P. (2005c) 'Infinite dreams, infinite growth, infinite learning: the challenges of globalisation in finite world', *Lifelong Learning in Europe*, 10(3): 148–55.

Jarvis, P. (2006) *Towards a Comprehensive Theory of Human Learning*. London: Routledge.

Jarvis, P. and Chadwick, A. (eds) (1991) *Training Adult Educators in Western Europe*. London: Routledge.

Jarvis, P. and Gibson, S. (1997) *The Teacher Practitioner and Mentor in Nursing, Midwifery, Health Visiting and the Social Services* (second edition). Cheltenham: Stanley Thornes.

Jarvis, P. with Griffin, C. (2003) *Adult and Continuing Education: Major Themes in Education* (5 vols). London: Routledge.

Jarvis, P. and Parker, S. (eds) (2005) *Human Learning: A Holistic Perspective*. London: Routledge.

Jaurlaritza, E. and Vasco, G. (n.d.) *The Basque Country: A Learning Region White Paper on Lifelong Learning*. San Sebastian: Donostia.

Jenkins, R. (2004) *Social Identity* (second edition). London: Routledge.

Johnstone, J. and Rivera, R. (1965) *Volunteers for Learning*. Chicago, IL: Aldine.

Joint Action for the Future of Distance Education: Innovation and Collaboration (2003) Shanghai: Shanghai Television University.

Joll, J. (1977) *Gramsci*. Glasgow: Fontana.

Katz, R. and Associates (1999) *Dancing with the Devil*. San Francisco, CA: Jossey-Bass.

Keddie, N. (1980) 'Adult education: an ideology of individualism', in Thompson, J. (ed.) *Adult Education for a Change*. London: Hutchinson.

Kerr, C., Dunlop, J., Harbison, F. and Myers, C. (1973) *Industrialism and Industrial Man* (second edition). Harmondsworth: Penguin.

Kett, J. (1994) *The Pursuit of Knowledge Under Difficulties*. Stanford, CA: Stanford University Press.

King, R. (ed.) (2004) *The University in the Global Age*. Basingstoke: Palgrave.

Klein, D. and Prusack, L. (1994) 'Characterizing intellectual capital (working paper). Boston, MA: Ernst and Young Center for Business Innovation.

Kok, W. (2004) *Facing the Challenge*. Brussels: European Commission.

Kolb, D. (1984) *Experiential Learning*. Englewood Cliffs, NJ: Prentice-Hall.

Korten, D. C. (1995) *When Corporations Rule the World*. London: Earthscan.

Kumar, K. (1978) *Prophecy and Progress*. Harmondsworth: Penguin.

Kumar, K. (1987) *Utopia and Anti-Utopia in Modern Times*. Oxford: Blackwell.

Kumar, K. (1991) *Utopianism*. Milton Keynes: Open University Press.

Kumar, K. and Bann, S. (eds) (1993) *Utopias and the Millennium*. London: Reaktion Books.

Lacey, A. (1989) *Bergson*. London: Routledge.

Laksamba, C. (2005) 'Policies and practices of lifelong learning in Nepal'. Unpublished PhD thesis, University of Surrey, Dept of Political, International and Policy Studies.

LaValle, I. and Blake, M. (2001) *National Adult Learning Survey 2001*. London: Department for Education and Skills.

Lave, J. and Wenger, E. (1991) *Situated Learning*. Cambridge: Cambridge University Press.

Learning for Life: Learning Through Life (2000) Hong Kong: Education Commission.

Learning for Life: White Paper on Adult Education (2000) Dublin: Stationery Office.

Lee, W.O. (1996) 'The cultural context for Chinese learners: conceptions of learning in the Confucian tradition', in Watkins, D. and Biggs, J. (eds) *The Chinese Learner*. Hong Kong: CERC and Victoria: ACER.

Lengrand, P. (1975) *An Introduction to Lifelong Education*. London: Croom Helm.

Lester-Smith, W. (1966) *Education – An Introductory Survey*. Harmondsworth: Penguin.

Levinas, E. (1991 [1969]) *Totality and Infinity*. Dordrecht: Kluwer.

Levinson, D. and Levinson, J. (1996) *The Seasons of a Woman's Life*. New York: Ballentine.

Levinson, D., Darrow, C., Klein, E., Levinson, M. and McKee, B. (1978) *The Seasons of a Man's Life*. New York: Knopf.

Levitas, R. (1990) *The Concept of Utopia*. New York: Philip Allan.

Levitas, R. (1992) 'Review of "Utopia" by K. Kumar', *Sociology*, 26(2): 355–6.

Lifton, R. Jay (1961) *Thought Reform and the Psychology of Totalism*. Harmondsworth: Penguin.

Lippitt, R. and White, R. (1958) 'An experimental study of leadership and group life', in Maccoby, E., Newcomb, T. and Hartley, E. (eds) *Readings in Social Psychology*. New York: Holt.

Livingstone, D. (2002) 'Lifelong learning in the knowledge society: a North American perspective', in Edwards *et al.* (eds) *Making Knowledge Work: Supporting Lifelong Learning*, Vol. 3. London: RoutledgeFalmer.

Longworth, N. (1999) *Making Lifelong Learning Work: Learning Cities for a Learning Century*. London: Kogan Page.

Longworth, N. (2006) *Learning Cities, Learning Regions, Learning Communities*. London: Routledge.

Longworth, N. and Davies, K. (1996) *Lifelong Learning*. London: Kogan Page.

Luckmann, T. (1967) *Invisible Religion*. London: Macmillan.

Lukes, S. (2005) *Power: A Radical View*. Basingstoke: Palgrave.

Lyon, D. (2001) *Surveillance Society*. Buckingham: Open University Press.

Lyotard, J.-F. (1984) *The Postmodern Condition: A Report on Knowledge*. Manchester: Manchester University Press.

McGill, I. and Beaty, L. (1992) *Action Learning* (second edition). London: Kogan Page.

McGivney, V. (2006) *Adult Learning at a Glance*. Leicester: NIACE.

McIntosh, N. (1979) 'To make continuing education a reality', *Oxford Review of Education*, 5 (2), republished by NIACE, Leicester.

McKinlay, A. (2000) 'The bearable lightness of control: organisational reflexivity and the politics of knowledge management', in Prichard *et al.* (eds) *Managing Knowledge* London: Macmillan, pp. 107–21.

McLaren, P. (2005) *Capitalists and Conquerors: A Critical Pedagogy against Empire*. Lanham, MD: Rowman and Littlefield.

McNiff, J (1992) *Action Research: Principles and Practice*. London: Routledge. (Originally published in 1988 by Macmillan.)

Mannheim, K. (1936) *Ideology and Utopia*. London: Routledge and Kegan Paul.

Marshall, T. H. (1950) *Citizenship and Social Class and Other Essays*. Cambridge: Cambridge University Press.

Marsick, V. (ed) (1987) *Learning in the Workplace*. London: Croom Helm.

Marsick, V. and Watkins, K. (1990) *Informal and Incidental Learning in the Workplace*. London: Routledge.

Martin, B. (1981) *A Sociology of Contemporary Cultural Change*. Oxford: Blackwell.

Mayo, P. (2004) *Liberating Praxis*. Westport, CT: Praeger.

Megginson, D. and Clutterbuck, D. (1995) *Mentoring in Action*. London: Kogan Page.

Meister, L. (1998) *Corporate Universities* (second edition 2000). New York: McGraw-Hill.

Merriam, S. and Clark, C. (1991) *Lifelines: Patterns of Work, Love and Learning in Adulthood*. San Francisco, CA: Jossey CA-Bass.

Michels, R. (1966) *Political Parties*. New York: Free Press.

Ministry of Education (1999) *Education, Training and Research in an Information Society: A National Strategy for 2000–2004*. Helsinki: Ministry of Education.

Monbiot, G. (2000) *The Captive State*. London: Macmillan.

Murray, M. with Owen, M. (1991) *Beyond the Myths and Magic of Mentoring*. San Francisco, CA: Jossey-Bass.

Nadler, L. and Wiggs, G. (1986) *Managing Human Resource Development*. San Francisco, CA: Jossey-Bass.

Nozick, R. (1974) *Anarchy, State and Utopia*. Oxford: Blackwell.

Oakeshott, M. (1933) *Experience and its Modes*. Cambridge: Cambridge University Press

O'Neill, J. (1993) 'McTopia: eating time', in Kumar, K. and Bann, S. (eds) *Utopias and the Millennium*. London: Reaktion Books.

Organisation for Economic Cooperation and Development (1973) *Recurrent Education: A Strategy for Lifelong Learning*. Paris: OECD.

Organisation for Economic Cooperation and Development (1996) *Lifelong Learning for All*. Paris: OECD.

Organisation for Economic Cooperation and Development (2001) *Cities and Regions in the New Learning Economy*. Paris: OECD.

O'Sullivan, E. (1999) *Transformative Learning*. London: Zed Books.

Parker, P. (2005) 'The biology of learning', in Jarvis, P. and Parker, S. (eds) *Human Learning: A Holistic Perspective*. London: RoutledgeFalmer, pp. 16–31.

Parsons, T. (1951) *The Social System*. London: Routledge and Kegan Paul.

Pedlar, M., Burgoyne, J. and Boydell, T. (1997) *The Learning Company* (second edition). London: McGraw-Hill. First published in 1991.

Peters, R. (1966) *Ethics and Education*. London: Unwin.

Peters, R. (ed.) (1967) *The Concept of Education*. London: Routledge and Kegan Paul.

Poster, M. (ed.) (1988) *Jean Baudrillard: Selected Writings*. Cambridge: Polity.

Preston, J. and Hammond, C. (2002) *The Wider Benefits of Further Education: Practitioner Views*. University of London: Centre for Research on the Wider Benefits of Learning, Report No. 1.

Prichard, C., Hull, R., Chumer, M. and Willmott, H. (eds) (2000) *Managing Knowledge: Critical Investigations of Work and Learning*. London: Macmillan.

Putnam, R. (2000) *Bowling Alone*. New York: Simon and Schuster.

Ranson, S. (1994) *Towards the Learning Society*. London: Cassell.

Ranson, S. (ed) (1998) *Inside the Learning Society*. London: Cassell.

Revans, R. (1980) *Action Learning*. London: Blond and Briggs.

Reich, R. (1991) *The Work of Nations*. London: Simon and Schuster.

Reisman, D. (1950) *The Lonely Crowd: A Study of Changing American Culture*. New Haven, CT: Yale University Press.

Rifkin, J. (1995) *The End of Work*. New York: Tarcher/Putnam.

Ritzer, G. (1993) *The McDonaldization of Society*. Thousand Oaks, CA: Pine Forge.

Ritzer, G. (1998) *The McDonaldization Thesis*. London: Sage.

Robertson, R. (1995) 'Glocalization: time–space and homogeneity–heterogeneity', in Fatherstone *et al.* (eds) *Global Modernities*. London: Sage.

Robinson, D. and Robinson, J. (1989) *Training for Impact*. San Francisco, CA: Jossey-Bass.

Robinson, W. (1996) *Promoting Polyarchy: Globalization, U.S. Intervention and Hegemony*. Cambridge: Cambridge University Press.

Rumble, G. and Harry, K. (eds) (1982) *The Distance Teaching Universities*. London: Croom Helm.

Sargant, N. (1991) *Learning and Leisure*. Leicester: NIACE.

Sargant, A. and Aldridge, F. (2002) *Adult Learning and Social Division* (2 vols). Leicester: NIACE.

Sargant, N., Field, J., Francis, H., Schuler, T. and Tuckett, A. (1997) *The Learning Divide*. Leicester: NIACE.

Scheler, M. (1980 [1926]) *Problems of a Sociology of Knowledge*. London: Routledge and Kegan Paul.

Schiller, H. (1981) *Who Knows: Information in the Age of the Fortune 500*. Norwood, NJ: Ablex.

Schön, D. (1971) *Beyond the Stable State*. Harmondsworth: Penguin.

Schön, D. (1983) *The Reflective Practitioner*. New York: Basic Books.

Schön, D. (1987) *Educating the Reflective Practitioner*. San Francisco CA: Jossey-Bass.

Schuller, T., Baron, S. and Field, J. (2000) 'Social capital: a review and critique', in Baron, S., Field, J. and Schuller, T. (eds) *Social Capital*. Oxford: Oxford University Press.

Schuller, T., Brassett-Grundy, A., Green, A., Hammond, C. and Preston, J. (2002) *Learning, Continuity and Change in Adult Life*. University of London: Centre for Research on the Wider Benefits of Learning, Report No. 3.

Schutz, A. and Luckmann, T. (1974) *The Structures of the Lifeworld*. London: Heinemann.

Schutz, T. (1961) *Investment in Human Capital: The Rise of Education and Research*. Basingstoke: Macmillan. Reprinted in Jarvis, P. with Griffin, C. (eds) *Adult and Continuing Education*, Vol. 5. London Routledge.

Senge, P. (1990) *The Fifth Discipline*. New York: Doubleday.

Shepherd, J. (2006) 'Wealthy sultans of spin-offs cash-in on their ideas', *Times Higher Education Supplement*, 20 January, pp. 8–9.

Sherry, S. and Dubin, S. (eds) (1990) *Maintaining Professional Competence*. San Francisco, CA: Jossey-Bass.

Sklair, L. (1991) *Sociology of the Global System*. Hemel Hempstead: Harvester Wheatsheaf.

Slaughter, S. and Leslie, L. (1997) *Academic Capitalism*. Baltimore, MD: Johns Hopkins University Press.

Smiles, S. (1859) *Self-Help*. London: John Murray. Reprinted and published by Murray in 1958.

Smith, A. L. (Chair) (1919) 'Adult Education Committee Final Report', reprinted in *The 1919 Report*. Nottingham: Dept. of Adult Education, University of Nottingham.

Smith, J. and Spurling, J. (1999) *Lifelong Learning: Riding the Tiger*. London: Cassell.

Social Trends 2006, No. 36. Office of National Statistics. Basingstoke: Palgrave Macmillan.

Society for College and University Planning (SCUP) (2005) *Trends in Higher Education* www.scup.org (downloaded Jan. 2006).

Stehr, N. (1994) *Knowledge Societies*. London: Sage.

Stewart, T. (1997) *Intellectual Capital*. New York: Doubleday.

Storan, J. (2000) 'AP(E)L: from margins to mainstream', in Baile, S. and O'Hagan, C. *APEL and Lifelong Learning*. Belfast: University of Ulster.

Strauss, A. (ed.) (1964) *George Herbert Mead on Social Psychology*. Chicago, IL: University of Chicago Press.

Taylor, W. (1980) 'Professional development or personal development', in Hoyle, E. and Megarry, J. (eds) *Professional Development of Teachers*. London: Kogan Page, pp. 327–39.

Thompson, E. P. (1977) *William Morris: Romantic Revolutionary*. London: Merlin Press.

Thompson, P., Warhurst, C. and Callaghan, G. (2000) 'Human capital or capitalising on humanity? Knowledge, skills and competencies in interactive service work', in Prichard *et al.* (eds) *Managing Knowledge*. London: Macmillan, pp. 122–40.

Toennies, F. (1957) *Community and Society*. New York: Harper Row. First published in German in 1877.

Tough, A. (1979) *The Adult's Learning Projects* (second edition). Toronto: Ontario Institute for Studies in Education.

Tuckett, A. (2005) 'Enough is enough', *Adults Learning*, 17 (1): 6–7.

Tuckett, A. and Aldridge, F. (2006) 'Green shoots?', *Adults Learning*, 17 (9): 14–15.

Tuomi, I. (1999) *Corporate Knowledge*. Helsinki: Metaxis.

Turner, B. (1990) 'Outline of a theory of citizenship', *Sociology* 24 (2): 189–217.

Turner, R. (1962) 'Role taking: process versus conformity', in Rose, A. (ed) *Human Behaviour and Social Processes*. London: Routledge and Kegan Paul.

Turner, V. (1969) *The Ritual Process*. London: Routledge and Kegan Paul.

UNESCO (1990) *World Declaration on Education for All*. Paris: UNESCO. http://unesco.org/education/efa/ed_for_all/background/jomtiem_declaration.shtml

UNESCO (2000a) *NGO Declaration on Education for All*. Paris: UNESCO. http://unesco.org/education/efa/wef_2000/cov_ngo_declaration.shtml

UNESCO (2000b) *Education for All: Meeting our Collective Commitments – Expanded Commentary on the Dakar Framework for Action*. Paris: UNESCO.

UNESCO (2003) *Unesco's Basic Texts on the Information Society*. Paris: UNESCO.

UNESCO (2005) *Towards Knowledge Societies*. Paris: UNESCO.

UNESCO Institute for Statistics (2005) *Education Trends in Perspective* http://www.uis.unesco.org/ev.php?ID==6293_201&ID2==DO_TOPIC (downloaded Jan. 2006).

UNESCO (2006) *Education for All: Global Monitoring Report*. Paris: UNESCO.

U3A News (2005/6) No. 73: 8. London: Third Age Trust.

van der Zee (1991) 'The learning society', *International Journal of Lifelong Learning*, 10 (3): 210–30.

Venables, P. (Chair) (1976) *Report of the Committee on Continuing Education*. Milton Keynes: Open University Press.

Vollmer, H. and Mills, D. (eds) (1966) *Professionalization*. Englewood Cliffs, NJ: Prentice-Hall.

Walker, I. and Yu Zhu (2003) 'Education, earnings and productivity: recent UK evidence', *Labour Market Trends*, 111 (3): 145–52.

Wallenstein, I. (1974) *The Modern World System*, New York: Academic Press.

Walshok, M. (1995) *Knowledge without Boundaries*. San Francisco, CA: Jossey-Bass.

Watkins, K. and Marsick, V. (1993) *Sculpting the Learning Organization*. San Francisco, CA: Jossey-Bass.

Weber, M. (1930) *The Protestant Ethic and the Spirit of Capitalism*. London: Unwin.

Weber, M. (1947) *The Theory of Social and Economic Organization*. New York: Free Press.

Weber, M. (1948) 'Class, status, power', in Gerth, H. and Wright Mill, C. (eds) *From Max Weber*. London: Routledge and Kegan Paul.

Webster, F. (2002) *Theories of the Information Society*. London: Routledge.

Weede, E. (1990) 'Rent seeking or dependency as explanations of why poor people stay poor', in Albrow, M. and King, E. (eds) *Globalization, Knowledge and Society*. London: Sage.

Wenger, E. (1998) *Communities of Practice*. Cambridge: Cambridge University Press.

Williams, M. (2001) *Problems of Knowledge*. Oxford: Oxford University Press.

Williamson, B. (1998) *Lifeworlds and Learning*. Leicester: NIACE.

Willis, S. and Dubin, S. (eds) (1990) *Maintaining Professional Competence*. San Francisco, CA: Jossey-Bass.

Wilson, B. (1967) *Patterns of Sectarianism*. London: Heinemann.

Wilson, J. (1972) 'Indoctrination and rationality', in Snook, I. (ed.) *Concepts of Indoctrination*. London: Routledge and Kegan Paul.

Wrong, D. (1963) 'The over-socialized conception of man in modern sociology', *American Sociological Review*, 26: 183–93.

Yakhlef, A. and Salzer-Morling, M. (2000) 'Intellectual capital: managing by numbers', in Prichard *et al.* (eds) *Managing Knowledge*. London: Macmillan, pp. 20–36.

Yarnit, M. (ed.) (1998) *Learning Towns, Learning Cities*. London: Network for Learning Communities.

Yeaxlee, B. (1929) *Lifelong Education*. London: Cassell.

Young, M. (1998) *The Curriculum of the Future*. London: Falmer.

Index